Arran

Travels, Treasures and Tales

The Author

Ian McMurdo was born the son of a coalminer and raised in New Cumnock, a small Ayrshire village which will always have a very special place in his heart.

As a glassy-eyed, would-be footballer who readily concedes that his ambitions far outweighed his talents, he eventually found his niche in young adult life as an aspiring Chemistry teacher, before climbing all the way up the greasy pole of management to the heady heights of Director of Education.

Now retired, Ian lives with his wife Nan and their two dogs in the village of Kildonan on the southernmost tip of the island of Arran. It is their favourite place on earth. He remains a well-known educational commentator and occasional journalist.

Other books by Ian McMurdo:

A Life Worth Living

Dogmanese for Daydreamers

The Juniors – the Story of Cumnock Juniors Football Club

Knockshinnoch -The Greatest Mines Rescue in History

Arran

Travels, Treasures and Tales

Ian McMurdo

CARN PUBLISHING

First Published in Great Britain, 2019.
Reprinted 2020

ISBN – 978 1 911043 08 9

Published by Carn Publishing Ltd.,
Lochnoran House,
Auchinleck, Ayrshire, KA18 3JW.

www.carnpublishing.com

Printed by Bell & Bain Ltd,
Glasgow, G46 7UQ.

Contents

Acknowledgements

I am grateful to a great many individuals and organisations for their advice, support and patience during my research for this book. If I have accidentally omitted anyone's name from the list below, then I sincerely apologise and give my assurance that this was due to a rapidly-deteriorating memory rather than any intended slight on my part.

In particular, I would like to thank Sheila Gilmore for her ongoing support throughout the writing of this book. Sheila's knowledge and advice were indispensable to me, but her enthusiasm and passion for her beloved Arran were truly inspirational.

Many thanks to all of you.

Rev Angus Adamson (Minister, Church of Scotland); Aileen Aitcheson; Fraser Aitcheson; Jim Anderson (Director of Vessels, Caledonian Maritime Assets Ltd); Neil Arthur; Davie Ballantyne; Duncan Bannatyne; Alastair Bilsland; Jim Blakey; Robbie Brown ; John Bruce; Colin Cameron; David Cannon (Public Affairs Manager, David MacBrayne Ltd); Graham Chappel (Arran Graphics); Elspeth Cheshire; Russell Cheshire; Charlotte Clough (Arran Vets); Finlay Cook; Ian Cook; Jan Crawford ; Robbie Crawford (Kinloch Hotel); Davie Crossley; Charlie Currie; Liz Dale; Alastair Dobson (Director & former Chairman, VisitArran); Martin Dorchester (former Chief Executive, David MacBrayne Ltd and former Managing Director, CalMac Ferries Ltd); Lady Jean Fforde; Sheila Gilmore (Managing Director, VisitArran); Stewart Gough; Dr Alastair Grassie; Dr Libby Grassie; Marc Head; Janis Heaney; Ian Henderson; June Henderson; Alastair Hendry; Albert Holmes (Eas Mor Ecology); Ali Hume ; Alan Johnston; Linda Johnston (Auchrannie Resort Hotel and Spa); Johnny Kelso; Willie Kelso; Stewart Lambie; Jim Lees; Kenny Leishman; Gillian Langley; Ani Lhamo (Samye Ling Monastery);); Jack McConnell (former First Minister of Scotland, now Lord McConnell of Glenscorrodale); Davie McKinnon; Christine McLeod; Iain MacMillan; Sandra McMillan; Denise Mann; Ronnie Mann; Iris Mansfield; Stewart Maxwell (General Manager, National Trust for Scotland); Chris Mills (National Trust for Scotland); Ramsay Muirhead (Head of Engineering, Caledonian Maritime Assets Ltd; Kirsten Nicholson (Kirsten Nicholson Photography); Archie Nicol; Avril Paton; Edna Picken; Phyllis Picken; Ann Pringle; Andrew Russell (Arran Aromatics); Duncan Russell (Arran Aromatics); Janet Russell (Arran Aromatics); Kate Russell; John Sillars; Ravey Sillars; George Stewart; Mamie Stewart; Anne Tattersfield (Isle of Arran Distillery); Gerard Tattersfield (Isle of Arran

Distillery); Hugh Walker (National Trust for Scotland); Faye Waterlow (Isle of Arran Distillery); John White; Max Worthington; Alastair Yates; Fiona Yates.

Disclaimer

This book contains many stories about life on the island of Arran. All are founded on real events. Every individual quoted was interviewed personally by the author. A few have preferred to remain anonymous and their names have been changed or omitted in accordance with their wishes.

All information presented was accurate at the time of writing, but some details may have changed in the period leading up to publication.

The author accepts no responsibility for the safety or well-being of anyone who might choose to tackle any of the walks or activities which he describes in this book.

Introduction

Like most people, I have always wanted to live the dream. And for me, living the dream could only ever mean one thing. Living on an island.

There was just one little problem with fulfilling that dream. An essential prerequisite for living on an island is competence in that most precious of practical skills, 'DIY'. In short, to survive and thrive on an island, you really must have the ability to 'Do It Yourself'. Put another way, you must be able to make things and sort things and exchange those things with your neighbour, confident in the knowledge that the things you have made and sorted and exchanged are good and reliable and safe.

That, then, was always going to be my Achilles' heel, because try as I surely have on more occasions than I care to recall, I can neither make nor sort anything at all, let alone exchange it with my neighbour. If I even come near my neighbour carrying anything that looks remotely self-assembled, he will instinctively draw his blinds, bolt his doors and pretend he has gone away on holiday. This probably explains why he steadfastly refuses to lend me his chainsaw, something which he assures me he'd sooner share with an escaped mass-murderer. No, the sad fact of the matter is that on a purely practical level, I have one skill and one alone; an innate ability to break things and render them lethal. For me, there has only ever been one true definition of DIY - 'Destroy It Yourself'.

Therefore, against this background, quite how I have contrived to make an island my home for the past decade remains something of a mystery to me. Personally, I put it all down to good fortune, good friends and an overbearing spouse who won't even tell me where she hides the key for the garden shed. What I will say, though, is that living on an island has been the most wonderfully uplifting period of my life.

Other than for one very hazy recollection as a mere three-year-old toddler, my first completely memorable visit to Arran was on the seventh of August 1971, this as a 22-year-old university student. It was a Saturday, and in those days I never went anywhere on a Saturday. Saturdays were for playing football and golf, but never for going anywhere or doing anything that didn't involve booting a big ball or battering a smaller one with a stick. Saturdays were completely sacrosanct, and nothing short of clinical surgery could possibly have prised me away from my precious sport on a Saturday.

Well, clinical surgery and Nan.

For the record, Nan was the girlfriend who had just taken leave of her senses by pledging to become my fiancée, thereby introducing a whole new concept into my hitherto jack-the-lad lifestyle. It was called 'responsibility'. Things were about to change, she had assured me, and I had better get bloody-well used to it. In typically smug response I had just smiled at her politely, before muttering two mutinous little words under my breath. 'Aye, right.'

Imagine the shock to my system, then, when I found myself one Saturday not on a big muddy field amidst the collective immaturity of my fellow student mates, but in a clapped-out red Austin A40 van with Nan at the wheel, on account of the rather unforgettable announcement she had made to me a couple of days earlier. The essence of it was that we would be doing something 'quite different' at the weekend, and that any protests would be futile. That, she had added with a determined look in her eye, was that. The times they were a-changing, and I had already found myself on the first rung of the get-bloody-well-used-to-it ladder of responsibility.

And 'quite different' that particular weekend most certainly turned out to be. By mid-morning on the Saturday, there we both were, standing on the deck of a huge ferry boat called the *MV Glen Sannox*, and sailing over the Firth of Clyde towards a mysterious little island situated some twelve miles off the Ayrshire coast, with not a single football or golf ball in sight.

I had tried my best to be in a foul mood that day, but the whole experience was catching me flat-footed, the mystique of the approaching island taking my breath away. The moment we arrived at the bustling port on the other side of the ocean, I began to detect a very strange vibe. There was a real atmosphere to this little island, something very different, something very strange. It seemed electrified with energy. The port was called Brodick, the island, Arran.

The whole place sparkled in the morning sunshine, as those standing waiting on the pier waved excitedly to their loved ones and friends disembarking from the big boat. Never before had I seen so many happy-looking people in the one place at the one time. Nor indeed had I ever clapped eyes on so many carefree individuals dressed in such a diverse range of outrageous clobber. Wispy-haired old granddads in knee-length khaki shorts and multi-coloured V-neck golf sweaters. Pleasant-faced grannies sporting blue-rinse hairdos and clip-clopping around in matching flip-flops. Mums and dads with buttocks squeezed asphyxiatingly into shorts that once fitted them, pushing Silver Cross Carlton prams and Carnival pushchairs. Hordes of ecstatic kids darting all over the place in their flared denims and pleated skirts, squeezing GI Joe and Barbie dolls as if their very lives depended on them. Long-haired hippies clad in Jesus sandals, washed-out jeans and psychedelic T-shirts, puffing away on cigarettes of dubious content. And, of course, more waggy-tailed mutts than you could ever hope to find in an inner-city dog pound.

The funny thing, though, was that every last one of them appeared to be sporting a smile as wide as the Firth of Clyde itself. It really was a scene of genuine mirth. From the very second my feet hit Arran's *terra firma*, I had clocked that this little island must be a very special place indeed. Little did I realise at that moment the impact it would go on to have on the rest of our own lives.

In the event, Nan and I enjoyed a truly wonderful weekend on Arran. We climbed Goat Fell, the island's and southern Scotland's loftiest mountain. We spent hours horse-riding in the glorious meadows of Glen Cloy. We walked for miles along a couple of the island's innumerable sandy beaches, and up through the magnificent Glen Rosa. We sped across Brodick Bay on a family friend's speedboat, and I watched in admiration as Nan zipped over the waves on a pair of water skis. We wined and dined in umpteen pubs and restaurants, and spent countless hours roamin'-in-the-gloamin' along Brodick's stately promenade. In essence, we had the time of our lives.

When, on our way back home, we stood hand-in-hand on the deck of the mighty *Glen Sannox* watching the vessel's V-shaped wake whisk us away from this idyllic little island as it receded agonisingly into the distance, I felt a lump form in my throat. I had already been hopelessly smitten by the magic of Arran. One visit was all it took, and I knew there and then that the island's magnetism would pull us back again very soon. Or at least, so I thought.

Alas, the pressures and responsibilities of newly married life, fledgling teaching careers and financial constraint would conspire to prevent us from returning to Arran for three long years more, by which time Nan would be crippled by Multiple Sclerosis, that dreadful degenerative neurological disease which delights in tearing apart the lives of so many healthy young adults.

For Nan and me, fate had conspired to ensure that there would be no more horse-riding together, no more water-skiing and no more magical hand-in-hand strolls through the heather or along the sand. However, there was one thing that the dreaded MS could never rip mercilessly away from us. And that was Arran itself, the tiny little island which would soon become our favourite place on earth, our private bolt-hole, our personal sanctuary.

Many years later, when Nan and I found ourselves approaching retirement after two whole working lives had passed in the blink of an eye, we began to harbour this romantic notion of settling down someday soon to somewhere very pleasant. Two distinct possibilities were emerging from the pack. One was Lee County in Florida on the south-east of the United States of America, where the sun shines all day long. The other was the island of Arran off the west coast of Scotland, where the sun doesn't shine all day long. When decision day finally beckoned, we both sat down and weighed up the pros-and-cons of each move. A sort of 'options appraisal', if you like.

So, what was it to be then, we pondered painstakingly? 'The Sunshine State' or 'Scotland in Miniature'? Wall-to-wall sunshine or four-seasons-in-one-day? Miami Beach or Machrie Moor? Lake Okeechobee or Loch Garbad? Boca Raton or Brodick Bay? Alligators, crocodiles, manatee and mosquitos or seals, otters, jellyfish and midges? 'Have a nice day' or 'how's it hingin'?'

Arran it was, then, no contest. A no-brainer, as the youth of today might say. Sure, the temperatures in Brodick in the height of summer might struggle to reach those of Fort Myers Beach in the depth of winter. However, Arran was Arran and that was that, decision made. No more hanging around airports for hours on end waiting for something called 'wheelchair assistance' – a gross misnomer if ever there was one – to take us to our latest seriously-delayed flight. No more claustrophobic aeroplanes with seats so tight that an anorexic stick-insect would have great difficulty keeping its arse from protruding out into the aisle. No, from now onwards, for airports read ferry terminals, and for aircraft, 'ro-ro' ferries. And as everyone who lives on the island of Arran already knows, at least ferries are never subject to delay or cancellation. And pigs fly.

When my long-suffering publisher asked me if I would be interested in writing this book, I fairly leapt at the chance. However, given everything that Arran has meant to my family and to me personally ever since that auspicious day almost fifty years ago, you might appreciate why stepping back to take a considerably more objective look at the island was a very strange experience indeed. Poacher-turned-gamekeeper, if you like.

In introducing this book, I feel that I must make one very important point from the outset, and that is this. The book was never intended to be a comprehensive study of the island of Arran, never at any time. I'll leave that to the historians, geographers and other aficionadas who are far better qualified to do that than me. Instead, this is a book about 'our Arran', the Arran that my own family and I have come to love and cherish, etched indelibly in our memories and inspired by the words of some of our wonderful island friends.

So, for those of you who love Arran, I hope you will feel that I have done the island justice. And for those of you who have never visited, I hope you will jump on that big boat very soon.

One word of warning, though. If, on your travels, you happen to encounter an ageing hippy carrying a chainsaw, do keep your distance.

Over The Sea To Arran

Rockin' the Boat

There is one other essential prerequisite for living on an island, basic competence in DIY apart, and that is possessing the ability to swim. After all, islands tend to be surrounded by water. At least in my experience, anyway.

Sadly, swimming is yet another of the ever-expanding list of practical life-skills which seems to have passed me by. And by that, I don't mean I can't swim very well. I mean I can't swim at all, not a single stroke. Personally, I put it all down to a near-drowning experience in the Lugar Water on the afternoon of my eleventh birthday. There again, perhaps I'm just a big aquaphobic wimp, who knows? Whatever the root cause, it would be no exaggeration to say that if by some unfortunate twist of fate, I happened to be dumped by an ill-intentioned helicopter pilot onto a barren piece of rock in the ocean separated from a well-stocked supermarket by only a few feet of deep water, I would die of starvation. Honestly.

That, then, was the background against which I decided to retire with my wife to Arran. An island, no less. Indeed, one compact enough to ensure that I would seldom find myself further away from the mighty ocean than a mere couple of hundred yards at most. Mercifully, though, my galloping aquaphobia has never quite extended to sailing on boats (as long as the boats are big enough, that is). For some reason, big boats somehow succeed in convincing my sorely-pressed psyche to accept that while I may well be surrounded on all sides by deep water, I'll be absolutely fine as long as my eyeballs don't have to suffer the trauma of actually witnessing its physical manifestation. Alas, tiny little boats fail miserably to offer that same reassurance, as you will soon discover if you read on.

Sunday 16 July 2017 was a very strange day indeed. It was the first time I had ever boarded the Ardrossan-to-Brodick ferry armed only with a notebook and a pen, instead of six suitcases, ten holdalls, half the contents of Tesco's wine aisle and two behaviourally-challenged Labrador Retrievers. My strategy that day was to wander around the vessel observing and recording the dynamics on the boat for the purposes of writing this book, as opposed to performing the customary ritual of just sitting on my ample posterior for the entire duration of the journey, stuffing my face with coffee and biscuits. To find myself sailing over the Firth of Clyde with my senses switched from autopilot to manual really was a whole new experience.

The boat was mobbed, full to the gunnels. It was a July 'changeover' day after all, one of the three busy weekend days when the summer holidaymakers tend to head for their hotels, B & Bs and self-catering establishments on Arran, or return home from them. As the long snaking queue of foot passengers exited the ferry terminal and marched up the raised gangway onto the deck of the MV Caledonian Isles ferry, a seemingly never-ending line of cars, lorries, camper-vans and bicycles slid from the loading bay down the big ramp and onto the ship's vast vehicle deck, from which their occupants then climbed the stairs to join the others above as they made their way to the on-board facility of their choice.

As the queue for food tailed out of the cafeteria and into the muster area near the ship's main doors, the large-and-rotund sat at their tables delving into their 'full Scottish' breakfasts with commendable gusto, while the wiry-and-dainty delicately nibbled away at their healthy-option salads. In the ship's bar area, the pints of ale and glasses of wine were being sipped contentedly, while in the far corner a slightly more boisterous 'hen party' was getting well-and-truly stuck into heaven-knows how many bottles of chilled Prosecco, doubtless in preparation for the pub-crawl which awaited them when their unsteady feet hit the streets of Brodick.

Next door, the laid-back-and-chilled-out brigade dozed away the entire crossing in the comfort of their recliner seats, while next again in the pet area, a whole canine choir ranging from the bass-baritone of the German Shepherd to the grating-tenor of the West Highland Terrier entertained and annoyed the ship's clientele in roughly equal measure, entertainment just pipping annoyance at the post. Meanwhile, up on the top deck, the kids on the leeward side of the ship threw crusts at the swooping seagulls, while those on the windward giggled gleefully as their well-intentioned projectiles came flying back towards them.

For someone whose frequency of crossing makes him take such things so completely for granted that he now hardly notices the excitement and joy that this journey evokes for so many tourists to Arran, the experience took me right back to the wonderful day in 1971 when I first visited the island together with Nan. That magical journey had passed in a heartbeat, and this one sure didn't seem to take much longer.

Suddenly, the giant ship's PA system sprang into action, as a cultured voice began drifting from the speakers. It was the clarion call that everyone aboard the 'Caley Isles' had been waiting for.

'Your attention please! The vessel is now arriving in port!'

The excitement began to build as the holidaymakers realised they were now approaching their island destination. 'We're in Arran!' a couple of youngsters shrieked gleefully to their parents. Sure, the smooth sailing may only have taken a modest 55 minutes, but in what had seemed like an instant, the good old 'Caley Isles' had somehow managed to teleport its seven-hundred-plus passengers to a mystical 'foreign' land. Abroad, by any other name.

The announcement sparked a real flurry of activity. Upstairs on the extensive two-tier viewing deck, windswept holidaymakers marvelled at the splendours of Brodick Bay as the giant ship glided across the surf towards the waving crowds on the pier, while their children continued to chuck half-eaten sandwiches towards the brazen gulls.

Downstairs in the restaurants and bars, the froth adorning innumerable cups of Cappuccino and pints of Arran Blonde were being licked from contented, smiling faces. Toddlers' cake-splattered lips got scrubbed clean, and enterprising adolescents found themselves being hauled away from the gaming machines. Leads and leashes were looped over panting dogs' necks, as canine lips salivated at the last remaining crumbs being picked from a bag of cheese-and-onion crisps, dripping their final drops of anticipation onto the tiled floor. Meanwhile, drivers fumbled frantically for car keys, as their passengers limbered up to deliver the wise navigational advice that would be laughably superfluous once they hit the single coastal road that circumnavigates the entire island of Arran.

The continuing loudhailer announcement proceeded to crank up the excitement yet another notch.

'Would all drivers please now make their way to the car deck and occupy their vehicles.'

Mayhem ensued as those on the main deck sprang to their feet in gleeful anticipation, whilst those above gulping the incomparably fresh sea air began leaping down the treacherously steep stairs two at a time. Everyone, it seemed, was now euphoric beyond description.

Everyone, that was, except the dungarees-clad farmer sitting quietly in the corner of the cafeteria, sipping his last mouthful of tea. His name was George, and George had been off-island for almost twelve hours by now, or in his own parlance, 'Away ower tae Scotland for the day'. You see, to the born-and-bred islanders, Arran is Arran, and Scotland is ... well ... somewhere other than Arran. As indeed is everywhere else for that matter.

'Bloody tourists!' George remarked to me under his breath, mildly irritated by the spiralling excitement, whilst cleverly disguising his heart-felt appreciation that those same hyperactive incomers are actually the veritable lifeblood of an island so completely dependent on tourism.

Queues began forming at the big metal doors, as eager foot passengers prepared to await the magical moment when the ferry staff would set about hauling them open to display the ramped gangway that would finally allow everyone to set foot on God's own island. Meanwhile down below, the car deck was already swarming with bewildered maws, paws and bairns as they bumped variously into each other in frantic search of their assorted vehicles, while half-a-dozen car alarms blared and flashed on account of the mighty 'Caley Isles' rolling gently from port-to-starboard-to-port as it made its final preparations to berth at Brodick pier.

This was only one of today's continuous Ardrossan-to-Brodick sailings, and the island of Arran smiled warmly in the midday sunshine as it prepared to greet yet more visitors. Meanwhile its 56-mile-long coastal road groaned at the daunting prospect of yet another one-hundred-plus vehicles rolling off the ship's metal ramp onto the pier's concrete link-span.

As eagle-eyed holidaymakers began driving off the ferry beaming from ear-to-ear, umpteen lanes of stationary vehicles sat facing in the opposite direction, the sorry eyes of their depressed occupants staring out at the 'Caley Isles', as the big ferry now beckoned them away from this magical little island and back towards the dreary offices and associated drudgery which would await them on Monday morning.

One thing was for sure, though, and that was this. They would be back. Okay, it might be another whole year, but they would be back, and for one very good reason. This little island possesses a magnetism like no other place on earth. A magnetism that is irresistible, mystical, incomparable.

A magnetism that is strangely spiritual.

As I walked down the gangway towards the car park where Nan and the 'twa dugs' would be waiting to pick me up, I marvelled once more at the towering Goat Fell as it looked down in magisterial splendour, radiating its subliminal message to the island's latest visitors.

'Welcome to our enchanted little island. Welcome to Arran!'

A Life on the Ocean Waves

Hardly surprisingly, the history of Arran is inextricably linked with the mighty ocean. Today, the island is connected to the Scottish mainland by two vehicle-and-passenger ferries, both operated by CalMac Ferries Ltd, vital island services about which I hope you will allow me to give you a brief potted history. Very brief, in fact, so you will try to stay awake, won't you?

Caledonian MacBrayne started life away back in 1851 as a 'steamer company', one which in its various shapes and forms over the intervening years has continued to provide lifeline services to and from Scotland's numerous islands and peninsular communities, many of which are geographically very remote. Having required to reinvent its operational raison d'etre several times during the blistering period spanning both World Wars, it was in 1948 that the company finally found itself being hauled under the auspices of the Scottish Transport Group (STG), this as a consequence of an all-encompassing programme of nationalisation by the country's new Labour government, led by Prime Minister Clement Atlee. Soon afterwards, Caledonian MacBrayne Ltd was formed to operate the shipping services, with MacBrayne Haulage handling heavier lorry and freight vehicles, and David MacBrayne directing a range of more minor but still commercially vital seafaring operations.

It wasn't until 1990 that the company and its component parts were finally able to throw off the shackles of the STG, at which point they transferred to the ownership of the Secretary of State for Scotland (the then 'Scottish Office' of our Westminster government), and subsequently after devolution to the Scottish Executive, which in 2006 decided that under European law, ferry services required to be put out to competitive tender. However, since many of the ships and the ports to which they sailed were already owned by Caledonian MacBrayne Ltd, the parent company was deemed to be in a position of advantage over its competitors when the tendering process kicked in. The decision was taken to rename the company as Caledonian Maritime Assets Ltd (CMAL), and thereby retain the various marine vessels and ports under public ownership, but also to create a new company, CalMac Ferries Ltd (CFL), to operate the ferry services. Both CMAL and CFL are now subsidiaries of David MacBrayne Ltd, which itself remains under the ownership of Scottish Ministers in the devolved Scottish Government. In 2007, CalMac was awarded the contract for the Clyde and Hebrides services, and even after subsequent retendering processes, the same company still operates those lifeline sailings today.

Are you still with me? Excellent!

The long and short of it is that Arran's ferry services are now run by CalMac. Thus, for the avoidance of causing further bewilderment to any readers who might otherwise be choking on unnecessary acronyms, the ferry company name to which I will refer throughout the remainder of this book is 'CalMac'. Pedantic nit-pickers, take careful note. Nit-picking pedants, likewise.

At the time of writing, the island was being served by two ferries, the now-ageing Caledonian Isles (aka the 'Caley Isles') which operates on the route from Ardrossan on the Ayrshire coast to Brodick on Arran's mid-east, and the spanking-new Catriona which sails between Claonaig on the Kintyre peninsula and Lochranza on the island's northerly tip. An additional ferry supplements the Ardrossan-to-Brodick route during the increasingly busy summer months of the peak tourist season, while a regular local service sails between the island's east-coast village of Lamlash and the adjacent Holy Island. It would therefore be no exaggeration to say that Arran's ferry services are the island's veritable umbilical cord.

'Weel-kent' Arran man, Robbie Brown, is now long-retired from his heady post of CalMac's Regional Manager for the Clyde Area. As a past Chairman of Brodick Improvements Committee and Director of VisitBute as well, the vastly-experienced Robbie still remembers the early and more humble days with fond amusement.

'To say that things were a bit more relaxed in those days would be putting it mildly. On my very first day at work, the Pier Master met me at the terminal and decided to introduce me to the ship's Purser. I'll never forget his first words to me. "Welcome aboard, son. You'll just be havin' a wee dram, then!" It was only eight o'clock in the morning, and I had just had my breakfast!

'After a while, I was promoted to Clerk-in-Charge, a position which seemingly propelled me from relative obscurity to having the honour of sitting in the bar of the old Glen Sannox one day with a well-known senior seaman, who was on his third double-gin-and-tonic. As we were sailing into Brodick Bay and the routine passenger announcement was informing drivers that they should now return to the vehicle deck, I immediately followed suit and stood up to make my own way back to my car, at which point he looked a bit surprised and said, "Sit down son, you've still got plenty of time". When I asked him what he meant, he just smiled, took another big slug of gin and said, "because it's me that's taking her in!"

'The relationship between crew and passengers was a lot less formal in those days too. I remember a couple of exchanges in particular. There was one crew member who had an unfortunate facial disfigurement. One day, he got into an argument with a passenger, who eventually lost the head and called him a "two-faced b-----d". So, the crewman replied, "listen pal, if I had twae faces, dae ye think I'd be walkin' aboot wae this wan on?"

'The other incident took place one day when the Clansman had been diverted from Ardrossan to Gourock, because of stormy weather conditions. This infuriated an elderly lady passenger, who immediately took her frustration out on the very first person in authority she could find, a notoriously bad-tempered crewman. So, she yapped and yapped at him until his famous short fuse eventually blew, then he turned to her and said, "Haw missus, away an' bile yer heid!" The lady was flabbergasted, and quite rightly too, so she marched straight up to the Purser's office and reported the incident. The Purser then informed the skipper, who immediately instructed the crewman to seek out the lady in question and offer his sincere apologies. So off he went searching around the ship's deck, the Purser at his shoulder as a witness, until he found her sitting in the cafeteria, still seething. "Are you the wuman that I telt tae go an' bile yer heid?" he enquired. The old lady hit back in indignation, "Yes, indeed I am!" So, the crewman replied, "Well, ye've no' tae bother!"'

Travelling even further back in time to the mid-nineteenth century, Arran's smaller north-western villages of Lochranza and Pirnmill were actually served by 'steamers' before the more populous villages on its east-coast, and it was only when Ardrossan harbour was built that a regular service began to sail to the stone jetties in Brodick and Lamlash, and subsequently further south to Whiting Bay. The twentieth century witnessed a continuum of advances and improvements in passenger ferries, all set against the backdrop of incessant in-fighting between the various railway companies which owned them and the violence and destruction of World Wars I and II.

It wasn't until the early 1970s that 'roll-on, roll-off' vessels were introduced commercially on the Arran route, or 'ro-ro ferries' as they are now more commonly known. Their welcome introduction immediately signalled good riddance to the earlier hoist-loading ships' lack of vehicle capacity and subsequent delays in port, heralding the era of more modern passenger ferries capable of taking significantly greater numbers of vehicles which could be driven straight onto their lower decks on arrival and straight off again at destination. With the port of Ardrossan by then exclusively available to serve the Brodick run, thereby cutting fifteen minutes off the earlier sailing route a few miles further up the Ayrshire coast to Fairlie, the revised timetable could be extended at a stroke from four to five return sailings each day (albeit reduced proportionately on Sundays and during the winter season).

The first ro-ro ferry to serve the Ardrossan-Brodick route was the Caledonia, which began its life as the Swedish-built Stena Baltica and had to suffer the indignity of being radically overhauled in dry-dock in the port of Greenock, in order to comply with Britain's much stricter maritime safety standards. However, the introduction of the Caledonia, even with its significantly-reduced turn-around time of 25 minutes, did not enjoy universal acclaim by the good people of Arran, principally because it had replaced the dearly-loved Glen Sannox, which sailed at two-knots faster and accommodated 1,100 passengers compared with the Caledonia's mere 650.

On a personal note, the one thing I will always remember about the wonderful old Glen Sannox was its hugely atmospheric public bar, which in those crazy student days was deemed to be the most important facility on board (the ship's engine included). While my rapidly-dwindling memory may not serve me nearly as reliably nowadays, I seem to recall that the bar was downstairs, roughly circular or oval in shape, and either wholly or partially devoid of windows to the outside world, all of which contributed significantly to its cosy, intimate ambiance. Several pints of lager helped too, of course, as Nan and umpteen other carefree hippies sat on the floor strumming their acoustic guitars and belting out the haunting melodies of Crosby, Stills & Nash and The Incredible String Band. Happy days.

By the mid-seventies, Britain's 'foreign package holiday' trend had become very popular, resulting in Arran's well-established pattern of holidaymakers who traditionally took a self-catering property for a full month being deconstructed somewhat, letting times finding themselves getting chopped to fortnightly or even weekly duration. Paradoxically, this departure from the previous norm gradually led to a situation in which the conventional mad rush of visitors at the beginning and end of each month subsided, but only to be replaced by more consistently busy sailings every weekend, particularly on the Saturday, Arran's main 'changeover day'. As a consequence, the Caledonia and the island of Mull-based Clansman exchanged routes in 1976, the latter and larger ferry having some 25% more passenger capacity and capable of carrying almost 50% more vehicles. However, with both vessels experiencing serious manoeuvrability problems getting in and out of Ardrossan harbour in stormy conditions, it was becoming clear that the Arran route really needed a custom-built, fit-for-purpose ferry.

And thus it was in December of 1983 that the Clyde-built MV Isle of Arran ro-ro ferry was launched from Port Glasgow at a construction cost of £5.5 million. Very significantly for Nan, this was also the first ferry on the Arran route to be equipped with an in-built passenger lift, hence providing her with the opportunity to move upstairs for a coffee, a buttered scone and a view of the mighty ocean, rather than being left stuck in her car on an eerily-vacant vehicle deck beside our first dog, Cindy, listening to the ship's huge engines relentlessly thumping away. The 'Invalid Lift' they called it in those days, but patronising terminology notwithstanding, at least there was now an on-board facility available to enable disabled passengers to enjoy the sailing. For the life of me, I cannot remember the price of a passenger ticket on the Isle of Arran back then, but I will never forget the one we had to purchase for dear old Cindy.

'One Dog or Bicycle, 20p.'

Capacity problems on Arran's second ferry route, the Claonaig-Lochranza sailing, were addressed in 1987 by the introduction of the Loch Ranza, only for the vessel subsequently to be replaced a mere five years later by the still larger Loch Tarbert. Then in 1989, tears flowed freely when the beloved Glen Sannox was finally withdrawn altogether from her old Western Isles haunts to be refitted as a luxury cruise-ship and sent on her way to pastures new in the Middle East where, very sadly, her remains lie beached and prostrate today.

However, Arran's own islanders were finally able to rejoice in May of 1993, when the Princess Royal launched the huge, custom-built MV Caledonian Isles to service the Ardrossan-Brodick route. With an enormous capacity for passengers and cars, the latter courtesy of a mechanically-controlled and flexible-use 'mezzanine' deck, the mighty 'Caley Isles' was the biggest vessel in the entire CalMac fleet, indeed the largest Clyde steamer in history.

At the time of writing, the 'Caley Isles' is still operating on the Arran run after some 25 years of loyal service, although about to be replaced and demoted to relief status by the arrival of a brand-new vessel of even greater capacity, one equipped with the most modern navigational and technological equipment imaginable. Her name? Well, the islanders are a sentimental lot, so perhaps not surprisingly one name won the consultation exercise by a landslide. Yes, you've guessed it, the MV Glen Sannox.

The 330 feet (102.4-metre) 'ro-pax' ferry is one of two innovative dual-fuel vessels being built by owner CMAL at the Ferguson Marine Engineering shipyard in Port Glasgow. The combined contract value for both vessels is a whopping £97 million, which CMAL claim will secure hundreds of jobs and provide a much-needed boost for commercial shipbuilding on the Clyde. The brand-new Glen Sannox was launched on 21 November 2017, amid a blaze of publicity, although she still remains in dry-dock for further essential modifications, much to the islanders' frustration.

CMAL's Director of Vessels, Jim Anderson, spoke enthusiastically about the many benefits which people sailing to and from the island of Arran will enjoy when the Glen Sannox finally hits the waves.

'The introduction of the new ferry along with the redevelopment of the ferry terminal at Brodick will allow the people of Arran and the many tourists who visit to enjoy world-class, modern and safe ferry travel for many years to come. Marking a first for both Scotland and the United Kingdom, the new Glen Sannox is capable of operating on either diesel oil or liquefied natural gas (LNG), offering the environmental benefits of reducing harmful emissions. The design of the ship provides enhanced levels of manoeuvrability and redundancy of propulsion systems.

'The vessel will carry more passengers and vehicles than previous ferries which have served the island, with room for 16 HGVs and 127 cars. It will have accommodation for 1,000 passengers, with superior facilities for comfort and accessibility, including four passenger lifts with access to all decks, and accessible toilets on decks 5 and 6. It will have a forward observation lounge with full-height windows, a quiet lounge, dining area, games area, shop, aft viewing lounge, family area, children's area and external seating on decks 6 and 7.'

So, according to the boffins, it's onwards and upwards for the new state-of-the-art Arran ferry. Quite how she will cope with getting in and out of the tricky Ardrossan harbour in a force-nine gale we shall have to wait and see, but excitement abounds as we all look forward to her long-awaited arrival.

Couple this with the recent introduction of Road Equivalent Tariff (RET), and it's easy to see why the prospect of sailing to Arran is becoming increasingly attractive these days. RET is a Scottish Government policy which CalMac requires to apply, and it operates on a distance-based formula to bring some consistency to how the government body, Transport Scotland, sets the nation's ferry fares. It has unquestionably been a major contributory factor in a recent and sustained upsurge in ferry traffic. This is notably so on the Arran route, where vehicle bookings have increased dramatically, resulting in many island businesses and services experiencing very significant hikes in 'footfall' and turnover. Indeed, in 2017, the number of visitors to Arran topped the 400,000 mark for the very first time, an incredible achievement for such a small island and a testament to the sterling efforts and dedication of everyone involved in Arran's burgeoning tourist industry.

As for the Brodick ferry terminal itself, most of the old pier, the terminal building and the associated infrastructure was constructed away back in the 1970s, and at over 40 years of age it was reaching the end of its useful lifespan. In addition, capacity was becoming a real issue, because with increasing vehicle and passenger traffic travelling to the island it was clear that bigger ferries were needed, ferries far larger than the old terminal was originally designed to accommodate.

CMAL's Head of Civil Engineering, Ramsay Muirhead, was very upbeat about the new pier facility.

'The extensive redevelopment project, which began in 2016 and came to fruition in 2018, was a £30 million investment by the harbour's owner, CMAL, with support from a range of national and local partner agencies. The project has completely transformed the terminal. The new facilities include a longer and deeper pier to accommodate larger vessel sizes, with a second side of the pier available to allow other vessels into port while still maintaining the island's ferry services. The much bigger new terminal building is now better equipped to cater for the passenger and staff numbers using the port. The inclusion of an "airport style" gangway also enhances safety and comfort for passengers boarding and disembarking from vessels. Finally, there is additional car-parking space and improved car-marshalling capacity, and for the first time, drop-off/pick-up and taxi areas, which sit next to the new bus stances. Also, and very importantly, the terminal has been designed to accommodate both current and future passenger numbers, and so to allow for further expansion, if necessary, over the 50-year lifespan for which it has been designed.'

So, it's all systems go for the island of Arran as it embraces much cheaper ferry fares and attracts more and more visitors each year, while welcoming the brand-new ferry into the brand-new ferry terminal.

As far as my nearest-and-dearest is concerned, it's a case of some you win and some you lose. As for the new terminal, she thinks it's much too big and imposing for a nice wee place like Brodick, and she much preferred the old one, limitations and all. But come on, not just one, but four accessible passenger lifts on the new ferry! And not even one of them to be called the 'Invalid Lift'.

And so, at last, Nan assures me, she'll be spending the entire duration of her sailings across the Firth of Clyde, not stuck in the gloomy depths of the car deck with the 'dog-or-bike' as in the old days, but playing a rather novel game of vertical hide-and-seek with her three grandchildren.

And, no doubt, pursued by a stern-faced CalMac officer brandishing his health and safety manual and shouting, 'Haw missus, away an' bile yer heid'.

'Scotland in Miniature'

Now, I did say in my introduction that this was never intended to be a book for the so-called anoraks, trainspotters and other terribly serious souls of that ilk. At least I'm being honest.

If it's geographical, historical or even statistical minutiae that float your boat, then there are plenty of weighty tomes bending the shelves of bookshops scattered all across the island of Arran. However, this is not, and was never intended to be one such. So just in case you're thinking about leafing through these pages in eager search of the whys-and-wherefores of Arran villages' ancient etymology, or every last detail about the island's mesolithic and neolithic pre-history, or indeed what your Great-Uncle Willie might traditionally have eaten for breakfast in his Glen Shurig croft away back in the nineteen-thirties, then you are about to be mightily disappointed.

I will, however, endeavour to offer a bit of basic information about the island, which I hope will be sufficient to provide an intelligible context while still being brief enough to prevent eyelids from drooping in galloping tedium. Right, here goes.

Arran, official designation 'Isle of Arran', is the seventh-largest island in Scotland, but at 167 square miles (432 square kilometres), the largest in the Firth of Clyde. It is located between the Ayrshire coast and the Mull of Kintyre, from each of which the spectacular sight of the island's 'Sleeping Warrior' can easily be viewed on a clear day. The Warrior is a range of 'Corbetts' - mountains at heights ranging between 2,500 to 3,000 feet – which collectively and uncannily portray the outline of a famous old soldier lying peacefully on his back. The loftiest of Arran's peaks is the famous Goat Fell, which at 2,866 feet also makes it the highest mountain in southern Scotland. The Warrior's other main features are three breathtakingly scenic Corbetts towards the north-east of the island called Caisteal Abhail, Cir Mhor and Beinn Tarsuinn. Indeed, the name 'Arran' itself is most probably an ancient Brittonic/Brythonic derivation meaning 'high place', which is consistent with the fact that the island is much loftier than all other surrounding land masses on either side of the adjacent mainland.

Like the country of Scotland to which it belongs, Arran is divided into highland and lowland areas, both separated by the Highland Boundary Fault, which as many an eager geologist will delight in telling you, runs in a north-easterly to south-westerly direction across the entire country of Scotland. The island's 'south-end' is much less mountainous than its 'north-end', laying the foundation for a fascinating contrast in terms of scenery, ambiance and even climate. It is for this reason, and a good many others too, that Arran is often portrayed as 'Scotland in Miniature', the island's many spectacular and contrasting features resonating closely with those of the country as a whole.

For many years now, Arran has been recognised and celebrated as something of a geologists' paradise. This is because of the island's completely unique rock formations, the study of which apparently takes us all the way back to the origin of Planet Earth itself. That was some 4.6 billion years ago, or the beginning of the Precambrian Era as our salivating geologist chums tend to refer to it. In other words, and without any exaggeration, the study of rocks on the island of Arran has actually proved to be enormously important to the boffins in understanding the very origin of our planet itself. Imagine that.

The main discovery occurred in 1787, when the renowned geologist, James Hutton, identified a particular geological anomaly near Lochranza on the north of the island, a phenomenon which would later be named 'Hutton's Unconformity'. This provided him with all the evidence he needed to support his 'plutonist theories of uniformitarianism' (try saying that after a couple of 'nippy sweeties'), and prompted geologists world-wide radically to reconsider their hitherto perceived collective wisdom about the age of the earth, and to agree that it really was much, much older than they had previously thought. 4.6 billion years old, in fact. Had I known about Arran's celebrated role in my fourth-year Geography class, I might have paid less attention to the drop-dead-gorgeous Miss Templeton herself, and much more to what she was actually scribbling on the blackboard.

Arran has been inhabited more or less continuously since the Early Neolithic Period (4000 – 2500 BC), as evidenced by the quite striking concentration of prehistoric remains which have been uncovered, including numerous Neolithic cairns and standing stones. Typically rectangular or trapezoidal in shape, those prehistoric man-made rock creations adorn numerous ancient underground structures which once played host to public display in their forecourts whilst providing eternal interment for the deceased in their earth-covered chambers. Many examples can be found on the island, for instance on its east coast in Monamore Glen outside Lamlash, and at the site of the 'Giants' Graves' high above Whiting Bay. The ruins of two Iron Age forts can still be seen at Torr a' Chaisteal Dun just south of the small hamlet of Sliddery on the west coast, and on the north side of the spectacular Glenashdale Falls, also near Whiting Bay.

Perhaps most famously of all, though, Machrie's six spectacular 'stone circles' are to be seen to be believed, and attract countless visitors each year. Stonehenge, move over.

However, it wasn't until the sixth century that Arran was eventually colonised by Goidelic (Gaelic-speaking) people from Ireland, who immediately called the island Eilean Arainn, and set about converting it into a sort of religious sanctuary. Likewise, all other hitherto Brythonic place-names on Arran were replaced by Gaelic equivalents. This remarkably peaceful way of life was then somewhat usurped during the Viking Age (793 – 1066), when our rather determined Scandinavian ancestors decided to grab Arran all for themselves, rename it either Herrey or Hersey, and render it to the ill-gotten gains of the Norwegian Crown.

Thankfully, Arran reverted to the Kingdom of Scotland in the thirteenth century. Indeed, it is believed that Robert the Bruce, no less, took shelter for a period of time in the impressively cavernous King's Cave on Arran's west coast in the very early part of the fourteenth century, thereafter returning to the island in 1326. Then in 1503, James, 2nd Lord Hamilton, was appointed as Earl of Arran. The local economy at that time was based on the 'run-rig' system of farming, which involved narrow strips of ploughed and cultivated land being allocated to each tenant by lot and rotation, in order to provide everyone with a fair share of the best and the worst of the land. As such, it was a system which worked well, and one which was seen by the tenants themselves to be entirely fair and equitable. Arran's population peaked at around 6,500 in those days, and was largely sustained by the basic crops of barley, oats and potatoes.

Sadly, however, things changed dramatically in the nineteenth century when Alexander, 10th Duke of Hamilton, embarked on his infamous programme of 'clearances', which would have an utterly devastating effect on the island's. population. In one fell swoop, land that had historically been rented out to as many as 30 families at a time was converted into a single farm, with the dubious carrot of alternative farmland being promised to each male adult who agreed to uproot his family from their island home and emigrate to far-off Canada. Needless to say, the land of milk and honey that was to await them on the other side of the Atlantic turned out to be anything but, as the 86 islanders who boarded the vessel Caledonia in April 1829 found out to their dreadful cost. On disembarking at the Canadian port of Quebec after a gruelling two-month sail across the pond, they would soon discover that the total area of farmland available to the entirety of the Arran ex-pat families would amount to a miserable 100 acres, and much of it of highly questionable arability.

And thus, the whole character of the island of Arran changed in a relative instant, particularly for those previously connected to the farming industry, and by the early part of the twentieth century the era of sheep-and-cattle-farming had become well established. Much less labour intensive and physically punishing than ploughing, propagating and harvesting crops, this new order heralded richer pickings for the landowners and fewer jobs for the considerably poorer 'Jock Tamsons' of the island.

Happily, in more modern times, the island's population and economy have recovered, largely due to the expansion of the tourism industry which these days is positively booming. And while the vast perennial invasion of holidaymakers, which traditionally descended on Arran each summer throughout the first half of the twentieth century, took a major hit when the fashionable foreign package holiday fad exploded in the 1960s, the island's tourist numbers are again exceptionally high today. However, it's not just the quantitative dimension of Arran's tourist trade which is pleasing to all concerned, it's the huge improvement which visitors now see in the quality of the experience on offer.

Sheila Gilmore, Executive Director of the island's 'umbrella' tourist body, VisitArran, is in no doubt about Arran's enviable profile and immense potential as a leading holiday destination.

'Sure, Arran has changed a great deal over the years, but it hasn't simply changed, it has evolved, because the islanders are very resilient. The tourist trade is huge now, hence our mantra, "tourism is everyone's business". It's much more than a mantra, though, it's our way of life here on the island. There's a lot less bed space now than there used to be, but the quality of the holiday experience has improved massively. Tourists are no longer satisfied with getting what they have at home, they now want even more than they have at home, and it's up to us to deliver it. So yes, Arran is very much an island on the up, but we must never be complacent. We must keep improving the holidaymaker's experience, but we must also ensure that we maintain our island way of life.'

In terms of political governance, from as far back as the seventeenth century Arran was traditionally part of the County of Bute, along with the islands of Great Cumbrae, Little Cumbrae, and Bute itself where the council's Rothesay headquarters were based. Then after many years of fierce political debate, Scotland's council areas were eventually redefined by the Local Government (Scotland) Act 1973, with elections taking place in June of the following year. The 1973 act effectively created nine 'regional' and three 'island' local authority areas, each supplemented by a matrix of 'second-tier district councils'. The regional councils were charged with responsibility for the 'big' services like education, social work and economic development, while the district councils would manage the smaller-scale operational aspects such as planning, housing and refuse collection. The largest, by far, of the former was the colossal Strathclyde Regional Council with a land mass of 3,336,550 acres (1,350,283 hectares) and a population of 2,286,800 (roughly half the population of the whole country), with the smallest being Orkney Council at 241,122 acres (97,581 hectares) and only 19,600 people.

To the consternation of the good folks of Arran and many other quaint little islands located just off the south-western coast of Scotland, they found themselves not in an island authority as they would dearly have wished, but lumped into the mighty Glasgow-based Strathclyde Region, which was so huge in scale that it would famously boast 'the largest education authority in Western Europe'. Therefore, in essence, Arran's little Corrie Primary School with its tiny handful of pupils would find itself under the same strategic governance as the city's vast Holyrood Secondary School with its near-2,000 pupil roll. The second-tier authority to which Arran was allocated was Cunninghame District Council, based in the Ayrshire coastal town of Irvine. To say that not everyone on the island was pleased with the overall outcome of local government reorganisation would be a rather diplomatic way to put it.

Then, after more than two decades of operation, the country's two-tier system was finally abolished by the Local Government etc. (Scotland) Act 1994, which led to the creation of a total of 32 'unitary authorities', each with responsibility for all of the services previously carried out by the antecedent regions and districts. Arran became then, and still remains an integral part of North Ayrshire Council, many would argue the veritable jewel in its crown. The council has its headquarters in Cunninghame House in Irvine to deliver the strategic dimension of its business, and a local 'one-stop-shop' office in the village of Lamlash on the island's mid-east coast, which deals with local and operational matters at first hand.

Former North Ayrshire councillor John Bruce, who was raised in the Scottish central belt's 'new town' of East Kilbride, but who has lived in the village of Corrie since 1985 and represented Arran on the council for five years, much of his term as a cabinet member, has no doubt about the island's capacity to keep moving onwards and upwards, reinventing itself wherever and whenever the need or opportunity arises. Nor does he doubt the islanders' determination and tenacity to do whatever requires to be done to take Arran to the next level.

'We are now a new twenty-first century Arran within a new twenty-first century Scotland, and the quality of our brand is higher than ever. And, believe me, the islanders are a resilient lot. They fight ferociously for their rights and defend their communities to the end, so Arran will always be in the vanguard of progress. You can be sure of that.'

So, there you have it. Eons, eras, periods, epochs and ages may come and go, as indeed may county, island, regional, district and unitary councils, but one thing is for sure.

'Scotland in Miniature' will still be leading the way.

2

The Metropolis

The 'Wee Town' of Brodick

All of this does, of course, take us back to where we left off earlier, which if you remember, is the ferry. And which if you've really been paying attention, has now arrived in port.

The port of Brodick, no less, the same port into which the Vikings once sailed their mighty longships over one thousand years ago, manically swishing their assorted weapons of war above their heads and screaming Scandinavian oaths of pillage, rape and destruction towards the terrified, peace-loving islanders trembling on the shore. 'Breda Vick', the Norsemen called the little seaside settlement, literal translation 'broad bay', a place-name which would stick for a good few centuries before eventually appearing in the official Scottish records of 1456 as 'Brodick'.

The original village of Brodick was actually located on the north side of the crescent-shaped bay, in an area still known today as Cladach. There for many years, the old quay and its burn estuaries played host to hordes of approaching seafaring vessels, carrying with them their multitudinous cargoes of foot passengers, farm and domestic animals, all sorts of necessary provisions and eventually even the islanders' mail. Visitors to Arran would often stay in the Old Inn at Cladach, which contemporary tourists will more readily recognise these days as 'The Wineport', a modern bar/bistro which operates as a welcome watering hole for those who have just scaled the magnificent Goat Fell.

Nowadays, Brodick's main population centre sweeps all around the south side of the bay, into which one's entrance by ferry these days tends to be rather less dramatic than that of our Norse predecessors, something you might find reassuring. The Brodick of today may well present to visitors as a geographically homogenous, refreshingly modern and invariably busy-and-bustling seaport. However, many local residents still prefer to regard the twenty-first century village as an enduring amalgam of its traditionally-named older districts, viz., Strathwhillan, Corriegills, Springbank, Upper and Lower Mayish, Invercloy, Glen Cloy, Mossend, Rosaburn, Glen Shurig, Glen Rosa and the aforementioned Cladach.

As we drive off the boat onto the long concrete link-span, a huge new ferry terminal greets us. Such is the building's imposing presence, that it might immediately suggest to first-time visitors and astonished returners alike, that by some tragic progress-driven twist of fate, Arran has somehow been completely transmogrified from the once-quaint little island of yesteryear into some futuristic twenty-first century holiday resort. How wrong could they be?

Yes, Brodick Pier has certainly undergone countless refurbishments over the years since its inception in 1872, rendering it nowadays a grand ultra-modern facility. However, the very moment we leave the terminal building behind and turn the corner, there towering above us like an enormous guardian angel stands the mighty Goat Fell, instantly reminding us that the 'old Arran' still rules supreme.

An approaching T-junction demands that we now make a pressing navigational decision, namely, whether to tackle our circumnavigation of the island in a clockwise or anti-clockwise direction. So, for no particular reason, let's agree on the latter trajectory, and make a right turn.

A drive, or better still a stroll along Brodick's wide and stately promenade is a veritable delight in aesthetic beauty and a bracing exercise in self-renewal. Although merely second to the neighbouring village of Lamlash in terms of population, the town is still regarded as the island's main hub, principally because of the vital importance of its ferry terminal which connects Arran to the mainland. With permanent residents numbering just over the 600-mark, Brodick hosts a wide array of residential properties, a fair proportion of which operate as holiday homes, bed-and-breakfast establishments and letting premises.

Among its wide variety of buildings, Brodick boasts its spanking-new £30 million ferry terminal, a tourist information centre, an optician practice, a local newspaper office, a dental practice, an electronics centre, two supermarkets, a hardware store, two estate agencies, a pharmacy, the island's main post office, a property rental and maintenance office, a 'crazy-golf' course, a fire station, the island's mountain rescue centre, a brewery, an outdoor clothing centre, a chocolate factory, a bookstore, a health centre, two churches, a leisure complex, a veterinary centre, a nursing home, a primary school, a heritage centre, several clothes and gift shops, a graphics centre, two banks, a bakery, a florist, two hairdressers' shops, a bicycle hire outlet, a transport haulage depot, several building construction yards, a charity shop, a modern sports pavilion and outdoor sporting facilities, an outdoor bowling green, an 18-hole golf course, a village hall, a public library, and a fuel filling station. Throw in umpteen hotels, restaurants, pubs, fish 'n' chip shops and cafeterias of all shapes and sizes, and you might just begin to appreciate the enormous strategic importance of Brodick to the infrastructure and economy of the whole island.

Heading along the promenade, the splendour of Brodick Bay will delight, with its sweeping two-mile-long shoreline in the foreground, almost the full length of which provides home to a wide assortment of grand old residences, modern bungalows and various commercial premises. Meanwhile in the background, the whole vista is being guarded jealously by the majestic Brodick Castle, whose turrets rise imperiously above the sprawling pine forests, with the imposing Goat Fell as a spectacular backdrop.

For those of you in my own creaky age-group who might find yourselves returning to the island for the very first time since the halcyon days of the 'sixties and 'seventies, one thing you will immediately notice is how much Brodick's famed hostelries have changed. Gone are many of the old hotels which once graced the three-quarter-mile stretch through the village centre. Much-loved names like St Denys, Ennismor, Kingsley, Gwyder Lodge, Heathfield, St Elmo and Altanna have disappeared from the radar. And, alas, gone with them too are the post-Woodstock haunts of my own hippy youth, together with the scampi-and-chips-in-a-basket lunches and Younger's Tartan Ale beverages in such memorable eateries as Duncan's Bar. Now, in their stead, sit various modern-day shops, boutiques, noshing joints and watering holes which may well tickle today's more discerning tastes and palates, but which still fall considerably short of sweeping away this fussy old romantic's pangs of deep nostalgia.

Now, don't get me wrong. I fully understand and accept the need for all of us to embrace the process of change in this rapidly-developing world of ours. And believe me, the island of Arran is undoubtedly a shining example of a forward-looking community which will always strive to be leading the way. It is also a community which has willingly embraced the spirit of openness within its strong work ethic and rich culture, and where you will always be met with a warm smile and a courteous welcome. However – and this is the crucial point – it is one where the pragmatics of community sustainability will always outrank the semantics of political correctness. Where am I going with this? Well, just take a look around the rest of the nation's 'PC landscape' if you will, and you'll soon see exactly where I'm going.

For example, did you know that Tunbridge Wells Council has ditched the frequently-used buzz-word 'brainstorming' from its professional vocabulary? Well, yes it has ... and for fear of offending epileptics, would you believe? So, no more brainstorming sessions in Tunbridge Wells, I'm afraid. From now on it'll be 'thought showers'. They must have been up all night thinking that one up.

Then there's our good old Houses of Parliament, and the renowned Strangers' Restaurant in particular, which has seemingly banned from its menu the name of the nation's favourite seven-centuries-old suet-and-raisin pudding, 'Spotted Dick', citing 'complaints about inappropriate terminology'. Its new name? Yes, you've guessed it ... 'Spotted Richard'. And please remember, those who complained are not merely passing through for pudding, they're actually running our country. Or as TV presenter Piers Morgan put it, 'what a bunch of Richard-heads'.

However, the dubious gem which really made my chin hit the floor a few months back was that of the Hertfordshire recruitment agency which was informed by a local Jobcentre Plus outlet that it would have to dump the terms 'reliable' and 'hard-working' from its list of essential criteria for job applications ... because they might be 'offensive to unreliable people'. No kidding.

So never mind the PC brigade, just come instead to the island of Arran where you will meet our reliable and hard-working people, and with whom you can have a brainstorming session over a big plate of spotted-dick-and-chips. And where they still call a spade a bloody shovel.

It was during the blisteringly 'permissive' years of the 'sixties and 'seventies that quite a few lasting changes came to Brodick. That was when many of the old trees, hedges and tiny front gardens of old were ripped away to widen the promenade and render the village with its more modern-day character. And while almost all the buildings which once housed the old shops and other commercial premises still stand proudly today, most of their names and functions have undergone the inevitable makeover. However, one which still stands aloof is Brodick's main Post Office, with its twin post-boxes labelled 'Local' and 'Other Places'. Another reminder of the islanders' deeply-held conviction that Arran is Arran, and everywhere else is simply ... well ... somewhere other than Arran.

Driving on past Auchrannie Road and Brodick Primary School, the old blacksmith's shop and a row of dwelling houses situated at Rosaburn on the north side of the village have been preserved and converted into the impressive Arran Heritage Museum. Comprising an authentic nineteenth-century cottage, original 'smiddy', stable block, computerised archive/genealogy centre and tearoom, the recently renovated museum is now a highly authentic cultural centre which attracts many visitors each year and provides a window into the fascinating history of Arran. For the inquisitive visitor, it is well worth a visit. For the aforementioned 'anoraks', it is an absolute must.

Anyway, so much for my own words of questionable wisdom, but what do the local movers-and-shakers think of the latest stage in Breda Vick's fascinating journey?

Calling a Spade a Shovel

The good folks of Arran are nothing if not polite. Courteous and affable to a fault, they invariably epitomise the very essence of an open and welcoming community. However, be warned, they are no shrinking violets either. Ask an islander a straight question and you'll get a straight answer.

Let me give you a good example. The same day we moved into our new home in Kildonan, Nan had a palm tree delivered for me to plant in our front garden. Now to be honest, this isn't nearly as exotic as it sounds, since Arran is positively littered with the things, but it was still very nice of her, don't you think?

So, along comes our good friend and neighbour with his 'sit-on' lawnmower, to help us get our fledgling lawn into shape. He prefers to remain anonymous, so let's call him Fraser. As I stand there admiring my new and decidedly oversized botanical specimen, the conversation goes something like this.

'Hiya, Fraser. Do you like my new palm tree? Nan got it for me as a house-warming present!'

'Aye, it's a cracker right enough.'

'Do you like palm trees, Fraser?'

'Aye, they're braw big things, an' I quite like them. No' very much, mind you.'

'Why, what's wrong with them?'

'Nothin' really, nothin' at a'. Except these big leaves they've got. Fronds they ca' them, an' when the wind blaws they get scattered a' ower the grass an' bugger up the blades on my lawnmower. Bloody nuisances, that's whit palm trees are.'

Then comes the *coup de grace*.

'Tell you whit I'll dae, Ian. I could bring my chainsaw along an' cut the bloody thing doon for you. An' I'll no' even charge you for it!'

I call it 'Arran diplomacy'. Anyway, let's head back to Brodick for another dose.

These days, 'the metropolis' is self-evidently no longer the humble little port hamlet of yore. Thankfully, it has lost none of its quaint charm, but it is now a bustling, thoroughly modern village which has readily embraced the social, economic and high-tech developments of the twenty-first century. Indeed, local farmer John White would contend that it is no longer a 'village' at all.

John, who was raised on the island's south-end in High Kildonan, but who has since run Brodick's High Glencloy farm for the past sixty-odd years, has seen more than a few changes over the years, as my questions to him eventually revealed. Only after he had made mincemeat of my first two, that was.

What age are you now, John, I asked him?

'76 years auld, an' in the words o' my Heilan' cousin, I look every day o' it.'

So, what brought you from Kildonan to Brodick, then, John?

'I think it was the bus, but it micht have been a lorry.'

At last he got serious.

'Brodick isn't so much a village any more, it's much more like a wee town now. The small shops like Curries, Alexanders and Coopers have been replaced by the big supermarkets, which I suppose is sad in a way, but it's not all bad since the choice and variety are better. In the old days, the tourists were foot passengers, their trunks sent on ahead. Then came the car ferries and everything changed. Nowadays, recession or not, the tourists have much more disposable income, and it's not unusual to see three cars parked outside a holiday let. Farming has also changed dramatically. Back then, all the farms were working farms, and they were everything to the island. Today, it's almost impossible for the farmers. Their overheads are still the same, but milk is cheaper than water. Even the climate has changed. It's warmer and wetter now, and spring comes earlier, all of which affects the crops. We hardly ever get a frost here, while my wee pal in Lanarkshire always seems to be moaning about not being able to get his car door open for ice. The island's temperature was always a degree or two above the mainland's, but it's even hotter now.'

Likewise, born-and-bred Brodick man John Sillars has observed the ever-changing dynamics over the years. A long-serving councillor and highly-respected local resident, John is very proud of the development of Arran as a holiday island.

'Tourism has always been vital to the island's economy, its lifeblood if you like. In the old days, householders would do anything to free up accommodation for visitors. They would build wooden chalets to move into, while the holidaymakers took over their own homes. They would sleep in bunk beds. Some farmers even cleaned up their barns and moved their families out so that the tourists could live in their own farmhouses, and the rents were very cheap. The holiday season ran from the Easter weekend through to September, peaking in July and August, but there was absolutely no tourism from October to March. The pattern was of well-heeled mainland families taking a house for the full month, the mother and children coming over for the whole four weeks, and the working father joining them for his Glasgow, Kilmarnock or Paisley "Fair" fortnight. The same families came to the same villages and the same houses, year after year. The men played golf, and the kids built sandcastles on the beach at Brodick Bay and paddled in the sea, while the mothers supervised them from their rented beach huts … except the one at the far side of the beach, of course, which was owned by the Duke and Duchess of Montrose!

'The whole thing changed in the 1960s with the introduction of foreign package holidays. Four weeks on Arran became two, and then one, which was often a second holiday for the richer families who had spent their main holiday abroad. The less well-off families would bring their tents and camp up Glen Rosa or over at Springbank. Nowadays, though, the island is very much on the up. We are now a proper all-year-round holiday destination, and the dramatic reduction in ferry prices through *RET* has given us another terrific boost. However, the most important thing that has happened to the island in recent times is the tremendous success which the late Iain Johnston has made of the Auchrannie Hotel. The Auchrannie is now a first-class resort hotel which caters for all ages and all tastes in all sorts of weather. Many other hotels on the island have adapted well to the changing holiday pattern too. All in all, Arran now has a much higher status as a holiday island and delivers a much better quality product, with such great attractions as Arran Aromatics, A Taste of Arran and Arran Distillery now leading the way, alongside many others.'

Back then to Sheila Gilmore, who in addition to her key ambassadorial role for Arran, just so happens to be the daughter of the late and sadly-missed icon that was Fisher Gilmore, a local hotelier of legend. Sheila too has witnessed many a change over the years in the island's profile and fortunes, and she was happy to offer her own viewpoint from the personal perspective of an island-reared girl who has lived through the best and worst of times.

'Brodick was a great place for a child to grow up. We were brought up in the "cottage" at the Ormidale Hotel. It was really just my dad Fisher, my mum Betty and me. I had a big bother Tommy, and a big sister Ann, but they were both away at boarding school and I didn't really know them as a child. In fact, mum and dad told me that I used to call both of them "Tommyann" when they came home!

'It was a very happy childhood, but to be honest, a bit wild. My friends and I were well cared-for, but taught to look after ourselves. Mum would drop me off in the morning with maybe a tomato sandwich, and sometimes if I was lucky, sixpence for a bag of chips at Middy's (Middleton's) chip-van and told to be home for tea. We could tell the time by the boats going in and out.

'If Fisher Gilmore was the public face of the Ormidale Hotel, then my mum, Mrs G as she was known by the staff, was the grafter. She cooked all the breakfasts, lunches and dinners, and then worked in the bar after that. Any time a hotel guest or bar customer ever left the tiniest scrap of food, she took it as an insult and dispatched the mortified staff to find out what was wrong! And she had very definite ideas about the food we served. No chips, only boiled potatoes and vegetables. When Spaghetti Bolognese was served, the spaghetti was broken up into tiny pieces and mixed into the sauce, to be served alongside potatoes and veg, whether the diners wanted it that way or not. Curry was the same, served with rice, potatoes and vegetables!

'As an island community, we are determined to move with the times, but we're also committed to maintaining the values, culture and lifestyle which have been shaped and passed down through the generations. And believe me, Arran is very well placed to take things to the next level. The pros of cheaper ferry fares brought about by the introduction of RET vastly outweigh the cons, and we can expect even greater numbers of tourists coming to Arran, but we also have to sustain those vitally important features which define island life. People pulling together and supporting each other, the things which promote genuine joint working, such as school playgroups and community events, where everyone just rolls up their sleeves and gets stuck in. It's this which characterises island life and makes Arran such a great place to live.'

Local businessman Alastair Dobson, Director and former Chairman of VisitArran, has a similarly upbeat take on the island's direction of travel.

'There are a lot of businesses on Arran, many theoretically in competition with each other, but we all share a common purpose, because we're all "Jock Tamson's bairns". It must never be about self-promotion, it's about promoting the island as a top-quality tourist destination, and as a great place to live and work. Tourism is everything to Arran. We want our tourists to come to the island, to relax and mix with the locals, and to keep coming back. Our aim is to ensure that they don't really feel like tourists at all, but that they've actually "bought time in our community". We operate on the principle of synergy, groups of people pulling together and taking the island to the next level. It's just what we do.'

Alastair's family background is rather unique, involving as it does a grandfather who worked as a farm labourer in Ireland's County Donegal and who once walked all the way to Belfast to get the ferry over to Scotland; a grandmother who was a lady-in-waiting for the aristocracy; and a father born in Lanarkshire's Bellshill who went on to rear Hereford cattle in Argentina. The latter, well-known and much-revered retired businessman Russell Dobson, was always on the front foot and ahead of the game, as son Alastair readily conceded.

'My dad has always been a risk-taker, that's for sure. He was brought up in West Knowe farm in Brodick, looking after about seventy dairy cattle and growing potatoes, because back then milk production and the island's famous "tatties" were central to its way of life and economy. Then one hot summer's day when he was toiling away in the fields, he stopped to take a breather and wipe the sweat from his brow. As he looked down over Brodick Bay, he spotted a couple of speedboats zipping over the waves, pulling water-skiers behind them. And that was when the penny dropped. "I've got this all wrong!" he said to himself. The very next day, he hired a farmhand to look after the tattie fields, bought his own speedboat, started trailing the water-skiers all over the bay and made himself a small fortune!'

Sadly, things were about to take a turn for the worse, as far as the island's once-burgeoning dairy farming industry was concerned. However, Russell Dobson was again on that famous front foot, immediately stepping in to take another huge risk and deliver a bit of welcome leadership to the dairy farmers, as Alastair recalled.

'Even as recently as the late 1970s, there were over fifty dairy farms on Arran, compared with just two today. The whole thing changed in 1977 with the Brucellosis outbreak, which led to pasteurisation of milk becoming European law. After various discussions with the Scottish Milk Marketing Board and the island's dairy farmers, my dad eventually took the plunge and decided to set up his own pasteurisation plant down near Brodick pier. In those days the access road was called "Coup Road", because that was where the landfill site was. He quickly realised that he couldn't have a high-tech food safety operation on something called Coup Road, so he got it re-named "Market Road" and established a new company, Arran Dairies. Then in 1979, he did a deal with a mainland-based refrigeration operator and formed the Arran Frozen Food Company. My dad would never stand still. He could always spot an opportunity and stay ahead of the game.'

Meanwhile son Alastair, having decided to spread his own wings and head to the mainland for a time working on various farms, trying his luck in sales and studying agriculture at Ayrshire's Auchencruive College, met his future wife at a rugby match of all places, and eventually returned once more to set up home on the island of his childhood. It was a move which delighted Russell, and soon father-and-son were running the family business together. By 1999, Alastair had become a chip off the old block, as clearly demonstrated by an audacious new business venture.

'I had found myself in the very fortunate position of having not just one good mentor, but three. My dad will always be my role model, but the late Iain Russell and Iain Johnston were also tremendously inspirational to me, and their contribution to Arran is immeasurable. One thing I learned from all of them was that if you want to achieve something, you've got to stick your neck out and take a risk. So, one day I decided to march straight into Nardini's famous ice-cream parlour in Largs, and ask Mr Nardini himself if he would teach me how to make ice-cream! I was sure that his first reaction would be to tell me to go and get lost, but I explained to him that this would be about one thing and one thing only, my new product, Arran Dairy Ice Cream. Not a competitor to his own mainland business, but a niche product for the island of Arran. I don't know how I managed it, but I got taught how to make ice-cream by none other than Nardini's of Largs!'

These days, Alastair is an ambassador for A Taste Of Arran, a bold corporate initiative established to promote food and drink made locally on an island which has become renowned for excellent quality in both. The range of local fare is remarkably wide and varied, but what makes it so uniquely impressive is the islanders' commitment to using as many locally-produced and natural ingredients as possible. For example, the milk used in the manufacture of Arran's famed cheeses and ice-cream is uplifted daily from the two island farms which still produce it. Alastair is very proud of the initiative.

'Our award-winning products are handmade by people who care passionately about food and the wonderful environment in which they're fortunate enough to live and work. Each product captures the essence of Arran, and every bite gives a taste of island life. The "Arran Brand" is becoming increasingly well recognised and synonymous with excellence, and our products are regularly sighted on the menus of some of the country's leading restaurants. We can also spread our net very widely now, and we regularly supply mixed temperature deliveries all over the UK and internationally, using our established network of distribution partners.'

So, there you go then. If you're looking for a unique all-action holiday destination by day, but one with so much to eat and drink in the evening that your gastric juices will be dancing a merry jig, the island of Arran is certainly the place for you.

The choice available is enormous. From leg-of-lamb, to Arran haggis, to Arran black pudding. Freshly-baked bread, to traditional oatcakes, to cranberry-flavoured biscuits. Arran Dunlop, to Arran blue, to crushed stem-ginger cheese. Baby beets, to elephant garlic, to mizuna/oakleaf/nasturtium leaves. Arran mustard, to pear-and-plum chutney, to ruby-grapefruit marmalade. Creamy caramel fudge, to rich dark chocolate, to Mrs Tilley's tablet ice-cream. And of course, you can then finish the whole thing off with a couple of James' chocolates, a bottle of Arran Blonde beer and a wee dram of either Arran Gin or the Devil's Punch Bowl, the latter being only one of Arran's many famed single-malt whiskies.

However, after that little feast you'll be needing a good night's sleep, followed the next morning by a bracing hike along the seashore. Which takes us nicely to 'Fisherman's Walk'.

'Fisherman's Walk' ... and Flying Projectiles

As a busy 'hub' town, one of Brodick's great paradoxes is its capacity to provide a totally rural waymarked trail parallel to, but amazingly separate from its sprawling main drag.

'Fisherman's Walk' is by no means one of Arran's most exacting, but it presents an extremely pleasant way to spend a peaceful, relaxing couple of hours on the doorstep of the island's second most populous centre. The walk is only one of the many and varied sections of the famed 'Arran Coastal Way', the wonderfully scenic but at times very taxing 68 mile (109 kilometre) long route around the island's stunning coastline, so very popular with ramblers.

Accessed from the large car park adjacent to the 'Wee Co-op' building at Cladach Beach in the centre of Brodick, the walk begins along the lawn between the children's playpark and the beach, the latter having been restored after many years of the terrible coastal erosion which until very recently had blighted its former glories of a once-magnificent sandy bay populated by a long row of multi-coloured beach-huts. The 180-degree views over Brodick Bay are superb, from straight in front the majestic castle on the hillside with the mighty Goat Fell as its protective backcloth, to straight behind the gentle slopes of Clauchlands Hill and the ancient hill fort of Dun Fionn.

A two-minute stroll leads to a footbridge over the estuary of the Glencloy Water (known locally as the Cloy Burn), where a recently-constructed raised wooden walkway over the salt-marshes will take you to a small concrete bridge and along a narrow path towards the fifteenth green of Brodick Golf Course. At this point, any dogs should be put on the lead to protect the well-manicured fairways and greens, and considerable care taken to avoid being inadvertently anaesthetised by stray golf balls flying at enormous velocity from the disorientated club-faces of eager but hopelessly uncoordinated amateur hopefuls.

Trust me, a bad golfer with a great deal of enthusiasm can be a lethal mix. In fact, there's a big metal sign on a public right-of-way about 100 yards in front of Brodick's seventh tee, which is decorated by so many deep indentations that you'd think it had been riddled by a hail of bullets from the barrel of an AK-47 automatic assault rifle. Had any one of those misdirected projectiles actually missed the sign while some innocent elderly couple just happened to be striding past hand-in-hand, one of them would be looking in the bushes for the other's dentures.

Anyway, death by misadventure from stray missiles notwithstanding, you will soon arrive at a long footbridge which takes you across the estuary of the Glenrosa Water (more affectionately known as the Rosa Burn) as it widens its banks in preparation for liaising with the Firth of Clyde. I laugh out loud every time I cross that bridge, at the recurring mental imagery of the spring morning when my then fourteen-year-old son hauled off his socks and shoes to wade through the ice-cold waters of the Rosa in pursuit of 'lost' golf balls that had failed to reach their target on the opposite bank. His final tally that day was a very commendable eighteen, jubilation swiftly turning to anguish when he suddenly slipped, protruding eyeballs enveloped in disbelief as his backside hit the water, while his treasured golf balls burst out of the plastic poke and splattered back into the burn like pellets from a detonated shotgun cartridge.

Once across the bridge, a footpath veers off sharply right to divert pedestrians from straying onto the golf course straight ahead. While this path does skirt the remainder of the course right to its extremity at the wonderfully picturesque eleventh tee, a slight detour up through the gorse bushes will take you onto the secluded golden sands of Strabane Beach. From there, you can continue your walk along to the end of the golf course, while if you have timed things properly, watching the CalMac ferry glide into port, turning the calm waters of the bay into a surge of cascading waves, and if you're very lucky, marvelling at the heads of a couple of inquisitive seals bobbing up from the depths of the ocean to cast their suspicious gaze in your own direction.

Another wooden bridge then takes you over the Cnocan Burn, which itself will have flowed all the way from just beneath the shoulder of Goat Fell down to the bay, bringing you out at the modern timber-built Arran Mountain Rescue Centre. At this juncture, it's dogs on the lead again and over the main road to The Wineport bar/restaurant, then up several flights of concrete steps into the sprawling forests and exotic gardens of Brodick Castle and Country Park (to which we shall return shortly and in considerably more detail). Following the footpath to the left, a gentle stroll of about half-a-mile will bring you out onto a narrow tarmac road, which is the main vehicular route through the park. Straight across on the other side of this road you will see a sign heralding the route to the summit of Goat Fell, but we shall leave that more demanding challenge to another day. Instead for now, a left-turn will lead you down through the castle grounds, and past the tall hedgerows and farm-fields populated by Highland cattle and other assorted bovine beasts.

About a mile or so further on, you will re-join the island's main circular road, the A841, from which a right-turn followed by a sharp left at the bend will take you to the Arran Heritage Centre at Rosaburn on the outskirts of Brodick, where you can decide either to spend a leisurely and very informative hour or two followed by a cup of tea, or plod on ahead into the town centre and back to your car.

Just past the Heritage Centre, a delightful detour will take you to your left down a narrow lane and across a stone-built footbridge over the Glenrosa Water, then back to your point of departure via the same golf course. It is from this little bridge that the customary raft of ducks will doubtless be paddling contentedly beneath your feet, awaiting your administration of the bird-feed that can be collected at an 'honesty box' for the princely sum of 50p a handful. Not recommended, I must advise, if you happen to be accompanied by two hyperactive Labrador Retrievers, as I found out to my own humiliated cost one summer's afternoon at the height of the tourist season. As soon as the stale breadcrumbs hit the crystal-clear streams of the Rosa that day, so too did the outstretched limbs of my water-loving mutts. Never before have I heard so many screams of horror from innocent holidaymakers, nor indeed witnessed such a flurry of bird feathers fluttering skywards. Never before, and certainly never again.

In summary, 'Fisherman's Walk' is a very pleasant way to recharge the batteries while your wife hits the shops or your husband downs a pint in the wonderful Brodick Bar, a mere fifty yards away from the rural splendour of this enchanting coastal sojourn. And so refreshing will you find this idyllic little jaunt, that by your journey's end there will not be one single gender stereotype in sight.

A Wee Libation … or Heavenly Salvation?

For some strange reason, the geographical proximity of Brodick's Ormidale Hotel and St Bride's Church always manages to remind me of a scene from the 2007 film, *The Simpsons Movie*, a masterpiece of cinematic animation, albeit one blessed with a title screaming out for a well-placed apostrophe.

By way of explanation for those of you who have yet to be converted to *The Simpsons'* cause and as such have surely led a rather sheltered life, the movie scene in question revolves around an enormous alien spaceship which descends from the skies above to hover menacingly over the adjacent pub and church in the all-American town of Springfield. Blind panic ensues. Suddenly, the boozers rush en masse out of the front door of the pub and bolt into the church in search of salvation, whilst simultaneously the church's entire congregation flees from the sacred premises to invade the pub in desperate pursuit of strong drink.

Now I'm not implying that any such confused cross-fertilisation of belief systems has ever troubled the near-neighbours on Brodick's Knowe Road, not for a single moment. However, any time I'm around that particular neck of the woods, the same recurring mental image always manages to burst forth to assault my senses in all its cartoon glory.

The Ormidale is one of Brodick's last-remaining hostelries-of-old, tucked away amongst the exotic shrubbery of its own expansive grounds, behind what used to be the first three holes of Brodick Golf Course, where now stands the impressive Ormidale Pavilion and its modern all-weather playing fields. How vividly I remember marching each morning onto the first tee of the old course and gulping in apprehension at the big sign that warned the amateur hopefuls like myself, 'It is easier to replace the turf, than to re-turf the place', before blootering yet another wayward drive straight into the magnificent hydrangeas in Mrs Mary Bannatyne's front garden, to howls of laughter from my so-called mates. Not, though, on a Sunday morning, high-noon being the first permitted tee-off time, the well-established witching hour when the staunch kirk-goers were finally let loose to tear off their Sunday best and dive into their Slazenger trousers and Pringle sweaters.

The Ormidale sits almost straight across Knowe Road from the Church of Scotland, both fine old buildings constructed from genuine Arran red-sandstone. 'The Dale', as the dear old hotel is much better known locally, housed the one pub which above all others defined island life for me during the long-haired, psychedelia-infused phase of my formative years. In those days, there were three well-established student meccas. First there was Stonehenge, then there was Glastonbury … and then there was the famous 'glass-house' of the Dale, a truly iconic joint if ever there was one.

Owned by the late and inimitable Fisher Gilmore, 'Fisher's Bar' was something else, it really was. From its incredible kaleidoscopically-tiled gents' toilet, to the glass-paned, plant-lined old hothouse where the long-haired hippies of the day would strum their acoustic guitars until their fingers bled, and blast youthful spittle through their harmonicas for hours on end whilst lubricating parched lips with gallons of ale, the old place was one of a kind, as indeed was its much-loved owner.

The tales of Fisher's antics are legend. Like the one of the bemused English tourist handing him an old 'ten-bob note' in exchange for four pints of beer, and Fisher refusing to accept it, his explanation being that 'ten-bob notes are no' legal tender here on Arran, son'. Alas, the poor chap found himself with little alternative but to return to his table and rather sheepishly ask his wife for a one-pound note instead, which he then handed to Fisher, who just muttered 'thanks', rang the transaction through the till and handed him a ten-bob note in his change.

Indeed, it was the same Fisher who rather mischievously marched one evening into the local golf clubhouse for a well-earned pint, accompanied as always by his loyal canine companion, in the full realisation of the dubious welcome that the man-and-dog combo would receive from the bar steward. 'Come on now Fisher, you know the rules. No dogs allowed in the clubhouse!' The pair of them then duly departed without demur, only for the great man to return a few minutes later … riding his donkey, Moses, into the club bar. As astonished onlookers sat open-mouthed with beer dripping down their chins, it was left to Fisher to explain his actions. 'Well, maybe there's a rule that says there's nae dugs allowed in this place, but there's nothin' that says nae dunkeys!'

To this very day, the Dale continues to be a real magnet for locals and visitors alike, particularly those who are fond of a good meal, a decent pint and a wee bit of 'craic'. One local worthy, who preferred to remain anonymous, recalled the time that a local doctor of Irish descent demonstrated an amazing piece of resourcefulness in Fisher's bar.

'He just sat there on a bar stool, ordering a double-gin-and-tonic every ten minutes or so. Each time the barmaid came over to serve him, he just lifted his glass and shouted, "on account"! This went on for a good hour or so, before Fisher eventually appeared on the scene and asked him what he meant by "on account", to which the well-oiled doctor lifted his glass again and shouted, "on account of the fact that oi've got no feckin' money!"'

Perhaps it was a local preacher that the poor inebriated doc really needed, rather than another dram. A preacher like Rev Angus Adamson, for example.

Arran born-and-bred and immensely proud of it too, Angus is Church of Scotland minister for the parishes of Brodick, Corrie, Lochranza, Pirnmill and Shiskine, which is a fair chunk of the whole island when you think about it. A down-to-earth, modern-thinking man-of-the-cloth who, in addition to his core religious duties has always willingly immersed himself in all aspects of the island's social, cultural and domestic fabric, Angus freely admits that he's had some decidedly hard-line predecessors to follow.

'The island's churches have always enjoyed robust attendances, and our own congregation here in Brodick still turns out in very healthy numbers. However, old habits die hard on Arran, and I've had to follow in the footsteps of a few fairly hard acts, that's for sure. I'll give you a good example. One stormy night many years back, the roof blew off the local golf clubhouse down there, and the members got themselves organised in no time. By the Monday evening, it had been fully repaired and everything was back to business as usual. The following Sunday, the formidable local minister fairly tore into them in his sermon, lambasting them mercilessly. "I wonder if you lot would've been so quick to respond, if instead of the golf clubhouse roof it was the kirk roof that had got blown off!"

'In the old days, Arran was deeply divided in terms of choice of church, with the east coast being Church of Scotland and the west coast mainly Free Church, and there were lots of ministers servicing the various parishes. The west was predominantly "Irish Gaelic"-speaking, and that whole side of the island was traditionally "dry". Later, when the west-coast hostelries were given their bar licences, the only people who could get a drink on the Sabbath Day were "bona fide travellers" who had made the trip from other villages.

'I always thought that the division between the churches was perfectly illustrated by the story of an old Brodick worthy, Jimmy Davidson, walking all alone one "Communion Sunday" from his Glen Rosa home, down through the village in the direction of the Free Church over at Strathwhillan, and passing the hordes of pedestrians, buses and brakes heading in the completely opposite direction towards the Church of Scotland building here. A local resident happened to make an innocent remark to old Jimmy about the impressive loyalty of the huge throng winging its way towards the latter, to which he just smiled politely and replied, "Yes indeed. Such as they are! Such as they are!"

'Arran is only thirty-five miles off the Irish coast, so it's hardly surprising that "Arran Gaelic", the language formerly spoken by the islanders, was derived from "Irish Gaelic", which was quite different in style and dialect to "Western Isles Gaelic", so much so that when people started arriving here from the Hebrides, the two different factions often couldn't understand each other. Furthermore, there were no Roman Catholics on Arran until very recently, simply because there was nowhere to take mass, and it wasn't until 1982 that Brodick got its first chapel, after which a few Catholic families then began to arrive.

'The island had another traditional old hard-line minister, who in the early 'sixties campaigned strongly to oppose the opening of the Ormidale bar, then famously won the *Evening Times'* "Spot-the-Ball" competition a couple of weeks later! Meanwhile down in Kilmory, Rev McLeod Wright had a horse called Paderewski which seemed to harbour its own particular social prejudices, because it would only ever turn left in the direction of Kildonan, but downright refused ever to turn right towards Sliddery!'

One recurring theme which I picked up during my interviews with the many great local characters who feature in this book is the island's unwritten demarcation system – light-hearted on the surface, but occasionally more deeply-held – which has traditionally seen Arran's population split into two very distinct categories, 'islanders' and 'incomers'. As far as I understand matters – my convenient get-out-of-jail card - an 'islander' is someone who was actually born on Arran (quite possibly even extending to the moment of conception as well, although I thought it best not to stray too far into the physiology of the process), whereas an 'incomer' is any person who was born anywhere else on Planet Earth (although quite where that leaves someone who was conceived on the island, but who then entered this world somewhere other than Arran, I haven't the foggiest idea). Moreover, 'islanders' are called just that, 'islanders'. On the other hand, 'incomers' can also be referred to by any one of three further terms, viz, 'interloupers', 'blaw-ins', or 'single-tickets', depending on the describer's mood and the position of the describee on the social popularity/unpopularity spectrum.

But had I got this definition right or not, I questioned myself? So, I thought, if in doubt, ask a minister (as you do). Thankfully, Angus Adamson managed to put the whole thing into crystal-clear perspective for me.

'First of all, let's be absolutely clear about one thing. Arran people are never clannish. They never have been, and they never will be. We have a tremendous community spirit and self-support culture all across the island, and Arran people are among the most welcoming and sociable you will ever have the good fortune to meet. As for the great 'islanders versus incomers' debate, well the late Ian Davidson from Glen Rosa encapsulated it perfectly. "We're a family of incomers," he once told me with the utmost sincerity, "because we've only been on the island since 1680."

'I'll give you another very similar example. One day in the public bar of the Lagg Hotel down in the island's south-end, a real working man's pub if ever there was one, an increasingly acrimonious argument between two local farmers almost came to blows when one of them shouted at the other, "You lot are nothin' but a bunch o' bloody interloupers anyway!". Apparently, the accuser's reasoning was that the accused's family had only come over to Arran in the late-1720s!

'Mind you, it's not just about islanders and incomers, it can get even more parochial than that at times. For example, there was the Brodick man who insisted all through his adulthood that his expectant mother had chosen for him to be delivered in Glasgow's Queen Mother Hospital maternity unit rather than in our own Arran Memorial Hospital, "so that I would never have to live all my life with the stigma of having been born in Lamlash!"'

'Seriously, though, Arran people are very, very proud of their history and heritage. Through many centuries of great change and goodness-knows how many local government reorganisations, Arran people will simply *not* identify themselves with the county of Ayrshire. They will always much more readily associate themselves with Argyll and Bute. It's only the Brodick folks who are facing the mainland, and they are therefore more-or-less self-sufficient because that's where the boats come in. However, ask them where Corriecravie is, and half of them couldn't tell you!'

Another thing I have noticed personally since first coming to Arran with Nan all those years ago, is just how polite and articulate the great majority of the island's population happens to be when it comes to conversation. Having spent the entirety of my own working life in the education service and in areas ranging from huge poverty-stricken inner-city schemes to assorted leafy suburbs, the quality of diction on Arran has always been something which struck me as particularly noteworthy. From plumbers to policemen, joiners to janitors and dinner ladies to doctors, the vast bulk of islanders tend to have very highly-developed verbal communication skills. I have often wondered why, so again who better to ask than 'the minister'?

'Arran children have always enjoyed a good education, and local teachers have always worked hard to develop and promote their linguistic skills. However, over the last few generations, Arran families increasingly encouraged their children to "speak proper English", and at the expense of the traditional Arran Gaelic, because speaking English was seen to be central to those children "getting on in the world". And the proof of the pudding is in the eating, because Arran children do get on in the world. Arran children make good use of their well-grounded formal and informal education, they speak well, they develop into fine adults, they travel well, and they enjoy considerable success, some remaining or returning to the island, others following rewarding careers on the UK mainland, and quite a significant number abroad.'

So, in summary, if you're ever visiting the 'wee town' of Brodick, you'd be well-advised to check out the dynamics on Knowe Road. There you will find those strange bedfellows, libation and salvation, living straight across the road from each other, and in perfect harmony.

All of which you might find very reassuring, particularly if you ever happen to encounter any weird-looking cartoon characters alighting from a giant spaceship in the skies above Ormidale Park.

It's A Vet's Life

I don't know about you, but my own adolescent years were not exactly blessed with clarity of thought about direction of travel through life.

There are, of course, several very good reasons for our post-pubescent trials and tribulations, the most glaring of which I will happily body-swerve. Perhaps most importantly, though, adolescence signals that the time has finally come for us to make our first major decisions, such as which line of study to choose and which career trajectory our young lives should follow, and all of this at an age when the most significant decision we have taken thus far has been choosing whether to put HP or Tomato Sauce on our chips.

In our house, there was no perceived requirement for existential self-determination on my part, merely an unchallengeable assumption that I'd be 'going to the uni', whatever that meant, and whether I wanted to or not. Now don't get me wrong, I'm not blaming my parents for wishing me to demonstrate a wee bit of ambition, in fact I'm now very grateful to them that they did. The point I'm making here is that having to make decisions of such enormity whilst still squeezing plooks is plainly ridiculous.

In the event, I eventually wore my mother down, because at the end of fourth year at school and rather than committing to a fifth, I got her to agree that I could take the whole eight-week summer holiday period to 'reflect on my future', suitably confirming my status as an arrogant, jumped-up little git. Convincing my father was a different story. He had been a coalminer ever since leaving school as a mere fourteen-year-old, and he had nearly lost his life in a catastrophic mining disaster. He was a man of few words, but believe me, he had the wonderful gift of making every one of them count.

'You can do anythin' you like,' he eyeballed me the next afternoon, upon hearing of my laughably-pretentious self-reflection strategy. 'But you're no' goin' doon the pit!'

That part was fine, because I had no earthly intention of ever going down a searing-hot, dust-infested coal mine anyway. However, it was what he said next that made me catch my breath.

'And see while you're reflectin'? Well, you can get a bloody job like the rest o' us, an' help to pay for your keep!'

I hadn't seen that one coming, no siree. And worse was to follow, because at half-past-six the following Monday morning, there I was pedalling in the pouring rain on an old clapped-out bike along the back-roads of deepest Ayrshire, and wishing that I'd kept my big mouth shut. My old man had just got me a job as a labourer at the local brickworks some five miles away from my childhood home, and situated in a moorland location so utterly bleak and desolate that it would have made the middle of nowhere look like a tropical paradise. If the Russians had detonated a fifteen-megaton thermonuclear bomb directly overhead, it would have caused about a tenner's worth of damage.

There in that hellhole, for twelve hours each day and two whole months of what turned out to be a glorious summer when all my school pals were out playing football and chasing girls, my job was to shovel broken bricks into an old metal wheelbarrow and dump them into the 'crusher', easily the most violent industrial contraption ever assembled by mankind (thermonuclear bombs notwithstanding). Honestly, if some poor guy had accidentally stumbled into that thing, his next of kin would have been collecting his remains in a jam-jar.

Needless to say, when late-August finally beckoned like an angel of liberation, I was back at my school desk as fast as my brand-new plimsols could carry me, having learned a rather unforgettable lesson. Life does *not* owe you a living.

Island vet, Charlotte Clough, on the other hand, had no such difficulty in deciding which particular career path she would follow. Ever since she was a young child, Charlotte wanted to be a vet, and come hell or high water, a vet she was always going to be.

'I was brought up in a small farming community in South Derbyshire, and from a very early age I was always fascinated by animals and birds of every possible description. Since as far back as I can remember, I always wanted to be a vet, and no other career could ever have come close. The problem was that I got no encouragement at school, none at all. Time after time I was told that I could never be a vet, and for one simple reason. A vet's job was a man's job, and I was a girl!

'Anyway, I never let those attitudes bother me. In fact, if anything, I think they only succeeded in making me even more determined to pursue my dream. So, I just stuck in at school, passed my exams and went to the University of

London's Royal Veterinary College. It was with great relief that I qualified after five years of study and penury, and I was then able to start looking for a paid job in practice.

'There were always going to be plenty of opportunities in veterinary practice, from the smallest pets to large farm animals. However, following the introduction of new European legislation in 1984 setting up milk quotas, and the dreadful spectacle of farmers having to cull vast numbers of cattle, I was unable to get a start in a dairy practice that I had hoped for.'

'I got myself a job in a mainly small animal practice in Manchester, before moving onto other practices in Bournemouth, Reading and Farnborough. I also studied for an extra qualification in Dermatology, which I was awarded in 1993. I then worked part-time in practice while my children were young, and also operated on a self-employed basis seeing Dermatology referrals.'

One year that Charlotte will never forget was 2001, the year of the outbreak of Foot and Mouth Disease (FMD), an 'Epizootic' which quickly developed into a national crisis. It was a crisis so serious that it ultimately led to the slaughter of over six million cattle, sheep and pigs, threatened the livelihoods of farmers the length and breadth of the country, cost the United Kingdom's economy over £8 billion, and even resulted in a delay to the nation's planned general election.

'We ran a small farm at the time, and we were very worried that Foot and Mouth might spread to Hampshire. The Ministry of Agriculture, Fisheries and Food (MAFF) was desperate to enlist as many vets as possible to help out, and I was keen to volunteer, so I contacted the Gloucester office to offer assistance. There I met up with my old boss, who although retired by then had also signed up to help. We were given lists of farms to visit, where there was either a suspicion of the disease or where it was in close proximity to an infected farm, and our job was to inspect the entire livestock on the farm. It was a very onerous job, but critically important.

'By that stage, MAFF's directive was "slaughter on suspicion", which put huge pressure on vets. Our protocol was to call the London office and report any suspicious symptoms, which on one occasion I did personally only to discover that I was speaking to one of my old and much-loved university lecturers! He immediately sent out a full-time official to the farm to assess the situation, which was a very worrying time for everyone concerned. In the event, a "standstill" was placed on the farm, greatly restricting movement in and out, but no FMD was found and no cull was ordered, which was a huge relief for the farmer and myself. It turned out that the suspicious symptoms in this case had been caused by the sheep eating turnips growing in stony ground, and not ulcers in the mouth caused by the FMD virus.

'The Foot and Mouth crisis lasted nearly a year before the restrictions were eventually lifted, but it was an incredibly difficult time for the farming industry. I was proud of the very small part that I had played in helping to control the outbreak, though I didn't agree with all the methods used. That same year after finishing in Gloucester, I moved to a position in the very busy custom-built Barn Animal Veterinary Hospital in Britain's fastest-growing town, Basingstoke, where I worked until 2015, combining my veterinary duties with running a small family farm where we had Dexter cattle and sheep.

'Although my career had gone as well as I could have hoped, veterinary practice had already changed dramatically compared with when I graduated, and I felt I was getting into a bit of a rut. I had holidayed on the west of Scotland many times before, and I loved the lifestyle there. I really needed something different, a change from inner-city specialisms to the much wider variety of a rural vet practice. I was a fully-qualified "General Practitioner" after all, which meant that I was qualified to treat all species across the full spectrum, from generalist to my own specialist field, which is "small animal Dermatology".

'Then about three years ago, I saw the Arran vet practice advertised, and was immediately interested, despite some nerves. I understood that it represented a huge challenge, but it was one that I really needed. I was moving from state-of-the-art veterinary hospital premises in a large urban environment to what was effectively three old portacabins in a rural island community, and from the Basingstoke practice which catered exclusively for small animals of which 45% were dogs, 42% cats and an increasing number of pet rabbits, to one with 75% small animals and 10% horses, the other 15% being farm animals. Not only that, but 75% of Arran's small animals are dogs, with many fewer cats and hardly any rabbits, so I realised that I would soon be losing all my rabbit skills!

'I took over the Arran practice in April 2015, and I've never looked back. Yes, the changes in my working environment and daily routine have been massive, but thankfully I've been very warmly received by the island's community. At one time, the islanders really feared that they might not have a vet at all, so I can understand why I've been welcomed with open arms!

'Arran is a very special place, the people are terrific and things have worked out very well. And when I'm not working, I love to spend my time walking and birdwatching, accompanied as always by my Border Collie, Ted. I mean, where else in the world could you find more beautiful places to walk your dog than on Arran?

'The practice itself had been long-established on Arran, with well-respected local vet Malcolm Wheeler retiring after many years of caring for the island's animal population. The plan was always to develop new and more modern veterinary premises, and to take on another vet as my assistant. We now have our new premises, and not only one additional vet but two who job-share, so I'm very pleased with the way the practice has progressed.'

'The "Arran Vets" practice moved to our newly-acquired and fully-refurbished premises in September 2017, a modern, fit-for-purpose facility which is ideally situated in Knowe Road in the centre of Brodick, and well-placed to cater for the needs of Arran's animals and birds for many years to come. We are a very mixed veterinary practice committed to providing a caring, personal and up-to-date service for "all creatures great and small", in other words for all pets, horses, farm animals and birds across the island. We also work closely with The Glasgow Veterinary School to provide specialist referral services whenever required.

'Most importantly of all, we have a great team here at Arran Vets. We're very well supported by Shona Hume and Gemma Ferguson. Shona has been working in the practice for 34 years now. She also works locally as a dental nurse, which has been known to cause a bit of confusion for people bringing their pets to the surgery after having had their teeth attended to earlier in the day! Gemma was brought up on the island, and despite having a young family to look after, she still finds time to work as a volunteer with the local Coastguard Service.'

Clearly, Charlotte Clough has brought with her to Arran a huge wealth and range of experience. I asked her for a quick top-of-the-head assessment of what she has already come to recognise as the main issues for pets in an island environment.

'On Arran, I would say that there are three principal dangers to pets. The most obvious is that presented by the island's resident poisonous snake, the adder. However, the others are much less obvious ... jellyfish and cold water!

'There are quite a few tales of animals – and, of course, of their owners too – being bitten by adders, simply because they have been too nosey and inquisitive, when they should just have left them alone. And, believe me, an adder bite can be very serious if not treated quickly. Arran's glens, moors and heather are the perfect natural habitat for adders, and they are occasionally sighted by walkers, particularly during spells of dry, sunny weather when they love to bask in the sunshine. However, the message is always the same. Leave them alone, and they will leave you alone. And never let your dog sniff at an adder!

'However, most people are less well aware of the other two main dangers. Take jellyfish, for example. Sometimes, Arran's beaches can be covered in them, particularly at low tide, and they can cause terrible distress to dogs in particular

... coughing, vomiting, shaking uncontrollably ... it really isn't a pleasant sight. The problem is that the condition can often be very difficult for us to diagnose, because owners don't always notice their dogs sniffing at the jellyfish. So, it's always best to keep your dog on the lead, or at least under very firm control, when there are jellyfish on the beach.

'And then, of course, there's the cold water of the Firth of Clyde. Quite often, people, particularly tourists, don't always realise how very cold our local waters can be, even during the summer months. We had one incident a couple of years back when a three-year-old Labrador bitch was swimming in the sea at Whiting Bay, and her heart stopped suddenly from the shock of the cold water. The dog had "died" and was floating listlessly on the surface with her head under the water. Amazingly, a local paraglider just happened to be passing at the time, so she grabbed the dog by the scruff of the neck and hauled her out onto the shore. She was then taken to our surgery, but on arrival the situation looked very bleak. The dog was stone-cold, she was barely breathing, her eyes were lifeless, and we were getting absolutely no response at all. I could detect nothing other than a very faint pulse. Her lady owner was very distressed indeed and kept pleading with me to save her. I told her that I would try my very best, but that I held out little hope. So, I started administering intravenous fluids for shock and to warm the dog up, turning and changing her position continuously, but for a very long time nothing was happening.

'As a last resort, I then called my own dog, Ted, through to the consulting room and he started sniffing at the Labrador. Suddenly, she woke up! However, since she had suffered a catastrophic shock and hadn't breathed for such a long time, I still had my doubts if she would ever pull through. After a few minutes, I carried out a full medical check-up, including looking for signs of brain damage, but the dog was absolutely fine. She eventually made a full recovery, enjoyed the rest of her holiday on Arran and went back home to live a perfectly normal life!

'Mind you, it's not all about dogs on Arran. One day I treated a pure-bred Eriskay pony over on Holy Island. I got a phone call from one of the Buddhist nuns. She was calling because one of the beautiful wild ponies had foaled and was having great difficulty feeding its foal. Thanks to the kindness of Russell and Elspeth Cheshire who deliver supplies to Holy Island, we were able to put the little foal into their "rib" ferry and sail it back over to Arran. Carolyn and Tracey Warwick, two local kind-hearted horse owners, willingly looked after it in their stable for a few days. Unfortunately, all our efforts turned out to be in vain, and the poor thing died as he had not had enough colostrum at birth. That was a very sad day for all of us.'

So, what does Charlotte think of 'a vet's life' on Arran, compared to her experience in Basingstoke's vast super-duper, state-of-the-art veterinary hospital?

'It really is a great life as an island vet. It's very hard work, but tremendously interesting and very rewarding. However, veterinary work on an island presents many huge challenges as well. Even with three vets now, we have no cover or back-up available, something which is simply taken for granted on the mainland. We also face many financial challenges. For example, we have to keep stocks of anti-venom available, which costs about £300-a-shot and only lasts between six and twelve months.

'People really care for each other on Arran, you know, and they really care for their animals too. If I'm called out to a farm to check on a sick horse, I can almost guarantee that there will be three other horse-owners there already by the time I arrive, giving support to the owner.'

One stormy afternoon in January 2018, Charlotte gave me a 'guided tour' of the Arran Vets' brand-new premises on Knowe Road. She is clearly very proud of the new facility, and no wonder. At risk of continuing to beat the same old drum, the first thing I noticed was its suitability for disabled visitors. From the level car-park and up a very gentle ramp through a door easily wide enough to accommodate a wheelchair, a generously-sized disabled toilet lies to your left. A good start, I thought.

Straight ahead, a very comfortable reception area awaits with ample seating and space to provide a relaxing ambiance for pet and pet-owner, as the former doubtless sits trembling in apprehension of the unknown on the comforting knee of the latter. (That is, if you're anything like me and mine. My sadly-departed chocolate-brown Labrador, Meg, used to get so nervous at the vet's surgery that she would routinely spit the staff's kind offer of a dog biscuit straight back at them, and once famously had to be dragged out from underneath the waiting room bench by two vets, two vet assistants and myself, by which time to complete my humiliation she had peed the floor.)

From the reception area, equipped with receptionist's desk and workstation, and an adjacent secure medicine store, a corridor leads through to a number of separate rooms. The main consulting room is well-furnished, bright and airy, and provides a private environment for the vet to examine and treat your pet whilst having a completely confidential discussion with you. Across the way, there are two separate 'accommodation' rooms, one for dogs and the other for cats, each housing comfortable secure units, and in one of which that afternoon someone's beloved Collie was lying totally spaced-out and completely at peace with the world, still heavily anaesthetised and recuperating from his operation.

A door across the same corridor leads out onto a large enclosed grassed garden area, where the surgery's assorted inmates can relieve themselves as required, a facility which in my own experience is not always available at veterinary surgeries. Then there's the X-ray room, complete with its lead-lined doors and windows, where routine medical 'imaging' can be carried out under the strictest and safest of controls. And, of course, there's the operating theatre itself, again superbly well-equipped and bright-and-breezy, where the practice's routine and emergency operations are carried out.

Factor in a small kitchen area for the staff and a large adjoining flat where the job-sharing vets presently reside, and the Arran Vets' building really is the modern, all-singing-and-dancing, fit-for-purpose facility that the good folks of Arran and their multitudinous animals need and deserve.

So, there we have it. For the Derbyshire girl who was once told that she could never become a vet simply because a vet's job was a man's job, Charlotte Clough is now living the life she always coveted. For Charlotte, it really is 'a vet's life'. And not only that, but a vet's life on an idyllic island, and working with the people and their assorted zoological companions whom she has grown to admire and cherish.

City Life ... or Island Life?

Before we leave the 'wee town' of Brodick behind us, please indulge me while I regale you with a little tale.

It is one which does, I believe, completely capture the enormous chasm between those two great polar opposites, city life and island life. The central characters are a now-retired couple from the north-end of the village. They prefer not to be named, so we'll just call them Tommy and Betty Morrison (although in real life, he actually looks more of a Tommy than she does a Betty, but let's not get bogged down with semantics).

First, a wee bit of background. The Morrisons originally hail from the city of Edinburgh, in which they worked their fingers to the bone for some forty-odd years, Tommy as a senior manager for a national telecoms company and Betty as a school teacher (and that should blow their cover immediately). Well acquainted with the stresses and strains of responsible jobs and the frantic pace of city life, one thing above all kept them going. Holidays on Arran.

In the late 'nineties, the couple finally took the plunge and bought their own holiday home in Brodick, which has been their private bolthole ever since. To say that Arran is in the Morrisons' blood would be putting it mildly. Arran courses through their veins like a tsunami.

Anyway, to their tale. One morning a few years back, Tommy and Betty were striding energetically along the promenade in Brodick at what they themselves readily concede was 'city pace', when they noticed two old codgers sitting on a park bench, puffing away on their pipes and giving them the once-over.

'Look at that couple ower there', one of the elderly gents remarked to the other, probably a bit louder than he had intended. 'Baith rushin' aboot, an' naewhere tae go!'

It was a droll throwaway comment which made Tommy and Betty laugh out loud. It was also one which would soon make them seriously rethink their ridiculous pace of life. Soon, though, but certainly not right at that moment, and for one very good reason. They simply had to get back to their car in the next few minutes in order to catch the 11.05 am CalMac ferry to the mainland, because Tommy could not afford to miss his 3.00 pm appointment with his cardiologist in Edinburgh Royal Infirmary. The old geezers' subliminal message would wait, but the MV Caledonian Isles would not.

In the event, the Morrisons just managed to make the ferry with seconds to spare, and Tommy would soon find himself sitting in the city hospital waiting room in remarkably good time. He had been complaining of 'palpitations' recently (no doubt brought about by the stress of being a rabid Heart of Midlothian supporter), and he wanted everything checked out just to be on the safe side. Happily, the consultation went well, and Tommy was suitably reassured. He made his way back to the car with a real spring in his step and a joyous song in his heart.

So far, so good, I'm sure you'll agree. However, do read on, because the story is now about to take a rather sinister turn, involving as it will more disparate characters than one might expect to find in a particularly convoluted John Le Carre spy movie. Here goes.

As Tommy was driving home along Edinburgh's notoriously busy city bypass, with not a care in the world and singing like the proverbial linnet ('Hearts, Hearts, Glorious Hearts', just for the record), he suddenly became aware that his car engine had started to labour somewhat. Soon the labour became a splutter, and the splutter an asphyxiated gasp. He decided that there was only one thing for it, signalled left and headed in the general direction of the hard shoulder. There was no hard shoulder.

A few seconds later, his engine completely gave up the ghost. Stuck there in the left-hand lane of the manic motorway with half of Auld Reekie's assorted vehicular contraptions whizzing past him and honking their horns in disgust, Tommy switched on his hazard lights and looked at his fuel gauge. The pointer was welded to the 'empty' mark. Keep calm, he counselled himself, and shoved his hand into his inside jacket pocket where he always kept his mobile phone.

Well, almost always. No mobile phone. Two short words and an exclamation mark formed on his parched lips. They would have rhymed perfectly with 'duck's drake'.

Still managing to retain his self-discipline, Tommy got out of his car to umpteen more exasperated honks and made his way on foot to an 'SOS box' which he had spotted a couple of hundred yards up the motorway in a lay-by. By the time he had half-walked and half-sprinted his way there, his old ticker was doing the hokey-cokey and his palpitations were once again in fine fettle. Tommy opened the emergency telephone box. His eyeballs fell out. No bloody telephone.

Just at that, an articulated lorry pulled into another lay-by a few hundred yards further down the bypass. As Tommy puffed and panted his way towards the lorry, its driver (let's call him Character No. 1) switched off the engine and began to arrange his sandwiches and a flask of tea on the dashboard.

'Hi mate,' Tommy panted through heavily-laboured breath, eyes in pleading desperation. 'I don't suppose you've got any spare diesel, have you? I've run out. That's my car stranded up there.'

'Sorry pal,' the driver replied as cheerily as if he had just backed eight draws on his football coupon. 'I've got nane, nane at a'. An' dae ye ken the funny thing? I normally carry a can' o' diesel just in case I run oot masel', but I left the can in the yard this mornin'. Is that no' just like the thing? I could gie you a cup o' tea, if you like?'

Tommy bit his lip and continued. 'No, it's okay mate. You wouldn't happen to have a mobile phone, would you?'

This time, his wish was granted. Glory be, he thought, and immediately phoned the long-suffering Betty (Character No. 2), to explain his predicament. Betty's scarcely-concealed mirth at the driver's offer of a cup of tea *in lieu* of a can of diesel did not exactly help to lift her husband's mood. Suitably chastised, Betty then offered to phone Tommy's cousin, Andy (Character No. 3), who worked as a mechanic in the garage just up the road from their own home in Edinburgh's plush south-west. Betty duly phoned the garage, only to discover from the garage secretary, Lesley (Character No. 4), that the aforementioned Andy was actually on holiday. On hearing of Tommy's unfortunate situation, the garage owner, Ronnie (Character No. 5), came to the phone, only to explain that since Andy was on holiday and his mechanic, Tam (Character No. 6), was presently out with the pick-up truck rescuing a broken-down van, there was really nothing he could do at the moment. Given the perilous nature of the situation, namely Tommy's car being stuck on the inside lane of one of the busiest motorways in the country, Ronnie advised Betty to call the Automobile Association (AA) immediately.

Betty agreed and made the call. The helpful, articulate chap who answered the AA telephone and called himself Amir (Character No. 7) took down all the relevant details, and asked Betty if Tommy's car was parked 'in a position which might cause an accident'. Betty replied in the affirmative, and the wheels of the mighty AA immediately burst into furious action. Someone will be there with your husband in a flash, she was assured. Please God, let it be a flash and not a smash, she prayed silently.

Meanwhile back on the city bypass, Tommy returned the mobile phone to the lorry driver with a sincere 'many thanks', followed by a further exasperated 'no thanks' to the latter's latest offer of a cup of char. He then shuffled his way back towards his prostrate car, to the now familiar cacophony of vehicular horns blaring at him, simply assuming that the beleaguered Betty had done the business and that cousin Andy would already be winging his way towards him with a can of diesel. What the hell am I doing here anyway, Tommy cursed himself? I should be sitting with my feet up in my back garden in Brodick!

When the big 'artic' then pulled away with its driver munching on his last-remaining sandwich, Tommy's still-palpitating heart sank for the merest instant, only to be kick-started again by the glorious sight of said mechanic, Tam, waving towards him from the westbound carriageway of the motorway, driving in the opposite direction. Thank the lord, Tommy muttered to himself with a huge sigh, assuming that cousin Andy had dispatched Tam to his rescue, but little knowing that Tam would be doing no such thing, since he was actually speeding towards the broken-down van. The plot thickens.

Some twenty minutes later, and still no sign of Andy, nor indeed of his can of diesel. By this time the mobile-phone-deprived Tommy, effing and blinding like the proverbial trooper, had found himself totally unable to contact Betty to find out what the hell was going on, on account of the SOS telephone being non-existent and the lorry driver having absconded with his own. Then, completely out of the blue and to Tommy's indescribable relief, who should pull up beside him but cousin Andy himself.

'Am I glad to see you, Andy!' he exclaimed. 'How's it goin', big man? And by the way, where's your diesel can?'

'Diesel can? Whit are ye talkin' aboot, Tommy?' Andy replied in the familiar east-coast lilt, deeply perplexed. 'I'm on holiday this week, an' I was just headin' hame along the bypass when I saw your motor. Whit's happened, like?'

The two bemused cousins then began to exchange stories, before heading off in Andy's car towards the nearest fuel station, from which Tommy phoned Betty to inform her of the still-disastrous state of play. Betty immediately telephoned the AA once more, and informed a young lady called Abby (Character No. 8) who answered her call this time that Tommy now had sufficient fuel supplies to get home and no longer needed assistance, only to be told in no uncertain terms that an AA van was on its way and could not now be cancelled, and that he must await its arrival. Alas, by this stage, the two unenlightened relatives had returned to Tommy's stricken vehicle, armed with a ten-litre can of diesel.

No sooner had Andy begun the tricky procedure of pouring the diesel down the parched throat of the fuel tank than a police car pulled up with its blue lights flashing and siren blaring. Out leapt two white-helmeted traffic-cops (Characters No. 9 & 10) with facial expressions which could have curdled milk.

'And just what the hell do you pair think you're doing?' the older of the two policemen demanded.

'Whit does it look like?' replied an irritated Andy. 'Fillin' up ma pal's tank, that's whit!'

'You'll be doing no such thing!' rasped the officer. 'Stop right now!'

There then followed an increasingly acrimonious spat between the two cousins and the two officers, which escalated to the point where one of the latter threatened to book Tommy for abandoning his vehicle 'while in a dangerous position' and impound the thing, at which point he completely lost the rag, palpitations and all.

Finally, it was left to six-foot-two Andy to defuse the situation by making a statement of even more profound menace.

'Now listen here tae me, you twa'!' he snapped at the police officers. 'This man's just been tae the cardiologist wae a heart condition, so if you dinnae calm yoursel's doon, it'll no' just be a bloody car ye'll be disposin' o', it'll be a deid body an' a'!'

And that was when the penny dropped. The next thing Tommy knew, the arm of the younger police officer's high-vis jacket had been wrapped lovingly around his shoulder, and words of hastily-contrived reassurance were being whispered into his ear.

'So, can we a' go bloody hame, noo?' Andy enquired, shaking his head in exasperation.

The two officers-of-the-law then clearly decided that discretion was the better part of valour and replied in the affirmative, before bidding the two cousins good-day and speeding off into the distance with their blue lights still flashing. Peace at last, thought Tommy, who by this time was in serious need of his favourite armchair, a cup of tea and a big hug from Betty. What a day, he cursed, what a bloody day. At least it's all over now.

And that was when the AA van turned up.

Out stepped another two uniformed officers (Characters No. 11 & 12), sporting the obligatorily officious facial expressions.

'So whit ... whit the hell are you twa' daein' here, noo?' Andy gasped, incredulous. 'Ma pal's got his diesel, we've just got rid o' the polis, he's deid on his feet an' just wants tae go hame, and noo you twa' chancers turn up oot o' the blue!'

'It was actually the gentleman's wife who phoned us, sir,' came the smarmy, po-faced reply. 'We always respond to emergency call-outs. We're the AA, you know.'

'Aye, you might be the AA, but you're aboot hauf-a-day late, man!' Andy exclaimed, the veins on his muscular neck sticking out like power lines on a factory wall. 'So bugger aff!'

And to their great credit, off they buggered.

Meanwhile back in the capital's suburbs, Betty got a phone call from her friend Carol (Character No. 13), whose son Jason (Character No.14) had been travelling along the city bypass in a school minibus and was worried about 'Uncle Tommy' whose car appeared to have broken down. Carol had immediately informed her husband Gregor (Character No. 15), who made his way at once to the scene of the incident. Having then cruised up and down the bypass several times, Gregor had failed to locate Tommy's stricken vehicle and decided just to drive straight back to his house. The very moment Gregor arrived at the front door, in walked Tommy and cousin Andy too.

In Betty's own words, 'I honestly wouldn't have been surprised in the slightest if the cardiologist had turned up as well'.

Exactly twenty-four hours later, Tommy and Betty Morrison found themselves once more inhaling the glorious sea air of Arran's Brodick Bay, as they walked hand-in-hand along the tranquil promenade, only this time at a snail's pace.

'That's mair like it,' opined a pipe-smoking elder citizen, as he sat chilling out on a park bench.

'Aye,' his old pal added, 'because you're a long time deid.'

And that, dear reader, is the difference between city life and island life.

Spoilt for Choice

Clearly, what the Morrisons really needed, after their day from hell in Auld Reekie, was a good bracing walk. And one thing's for sure. They would have been spoilt for choice in the 'wee town' of Brodick.

One of the most popular walks on Arran starts at the entrance to the internationally-famed Auchrannie Hotel, to which we shall return shortly. The great thing about this particular walk is that it lends itself to umpteen different routes of varying distance, duration and scenery, and being roughly circular in layout, to various starting and finishing points according to preference.

I normally set off from the Auchrannie itself, which can be accessed by turning left along the road of the same name just around the bend to the north of the clubhouse at Brodick golf course. A few hundred yards along, and rather than veering to the right up to the hotel, a rough track leads straight on past the wooden lodges located beside the gentle streams of the Glencloy Water. The track soon narrows through a small copse and alongside some farm fields, until you reach the ruins of an old thatched-roof cottage, where a charming lady called Sheila Kerr once operated her horse-riding stable. Many a wonderful memory I have of my own two young children perched proudly atop Sheila's horses, helmets on their heads and feet in the stirrups, beaming the biggest, widest smiles that a parent could ever wish to see. Happy days.

A rough grassy path skirts the burn up to a wooden stile at the far end of the top field, where a signpost points the way towards Cnoc na Dail some three miles further on, a Bronze Age stone circle which in ancient times also served as a meeting place for local crofters. First, though, a winding and gently undulating path takes you to a wooden footbridge over the Glencloy Water in Gleann Dubh, this being a popular picnic area for recreational ramblers, and the scene of yet another of my own bumbling *faux pas*.

This one occurred many years ago on a beautiful summer's morning, my companion on that occasion being Katy, our beloved Golden Retriever. Weighed down by the quite unnecessary bulk of the *Sunday Times*, a few homemade cheese sandwiches and a flask of piping-hot tea, all of which I had hauled up Glen Cloy from our rented cottage in the village centre, I dumped the whole lot down on a wooden table before retiring to the woods for a quick pee. Needless to say, by the time I had washed my hands in the burn and returned to the picnic area absolutely famished, my cheese sandwiches were 'in the dog' as they say, as indeed were the cling-film and paper pokes which had once provided them with shelter. As I sat there sipping at my tea and munching ravenously on one of Katy's dog biscuits, my nostrils twitching in deep annoyance, she simply smacked her lips and stared at me in innocent defiance. Her familiar facial expression conveyed the same three-word message that she had once deployed after devouring an entire catering-size 'Pavlova' pudding intended for a children's birthday party. 'It wisnae me'.

Once over the footbridge, an hour will take you all the way up the gentle slope of the Forestry Commission track to the top of the hill, from which you will be able to wallow in the most magnificent views across Brodick Bay, with the stately Brodick Castle and the imperious Goat Fell dominating the background. A further ten-minute walk will lead you to the car park at the summit of the main A841 Brodick-to-Lamlash road at Cnoc na Dail, where another picnic site sits in wait to give rest to your weary legs.

It is from this spot that you then have to decide whether to cross the road and tackle a further strenuous hike up the energy-sapping slopes of Clauchlands Hill, or instead choose the easier option and head downhill through 'Fairy Glen' back into Brodick.

The latter is a much gentler walk, and takes you parallel to the main road for the first half-mile, before cutting inwards through the forests and onto another wooden footbridge, this over the Strathwhillan Burn. The path climbs steeply towards the outskirts of Brodick at Springbank, then continues down through a couple of gates and back into the 'wee town' itself at the Glenartney Hotel, just above the Post Office.

The former is a much tougher climb, but it is well worth the effort for the spectacular views over both Brodick Bay and Lamlash Bay. Crossing the road from the car park at Cnoc na Dail, another Forestry Commission track will lead you through a metal gate, where the route splits in two.

The one to the left will take you around the north side of the slopes, and about a mile further on, up a very steep and gruelling incline towards Clauchlands Hill. The one to the right skirts around the south side of the hill, and although a much shorter route, will cause you to miss out on the best of the views. My preference is to start along this track to the right, but after about 100 yards or so, to then cut up left onto the narrow path which climbs steeply through the pine forest, and out onto the open slopes and clearly-formed footpath of the heather-clad hillside, where a stiff scramble up and over a succession of peaks and plateaus will eventually lead to a cairn at the summit of Clauchlands Hill.

From this spot, you will gaze in wonder at the sight before you. On one side, down to your left, stretches the entire length of the sweeping, crescent-shaped Brodick Bay, which will doubtless be peppered with an array of small seafaring vessels, and with a bit of luck possibly even the CalMac ferry too, its pointed bow sailing strongly in or out of port, its V-shaped wake trailing loyally behind. On the other, the view will be even more jaw-dropping, as Lamlash Bay lies resplendently beneath your feet, dotted with its customary armada of fishing boats and yachts, with the mystical Holy Island lying just offshore as a dramatic centrepiece, so intriguingly close that you'll feel you can actually reach out and touch it.

On an island with so many magnificent views, the panoramic vista from the cairn on the summit of Clauchlands Hill is surely one of Arran's very best, and you really should take time to enjoy it.

With the most taxing part of the walk now behind you, the path continues downhill in a gentle snaking fashion, until you reach a wooden signpost which indicates left to Brodick and right to Lamlash. First, though, you would be well-advised to tackle the small hillock straight ahead. This is the site of the ancient hill fort, Dun Fionn. A narrow path leads uphill to the 'trig point' on its summit, from which the panorama over the Firth of Clyde is truly superb. However, when you see the sheer drop over the cliffs on its north side, you will immediately understand why Dun Fionn used to be a rather good vantage point for a fort once under threat of siege from unruly neighbours.

Clearly, if your adventure started at the Auchrannie Hotel, you will choose the route back to Brodick, where a good two-mile walk will take you steeply down the hillside and onto a rough vehicular track past a number of rural cottages, then over a road-bridge on a U-turn to the charming little hamlet of Corriegills. A narrow tarmac road then leads back down to the island's main circular drag, where a final right turn will take you past the ferry terminal into Brodick and back to your point of departure.

There is, however, an alternative route from the foot of Dun Fionn, which is to head in a southerly direction towards Lamlash, where another narrow path leads down to a metal gate which opens out into a grazing field, at the far end of which trickles a small burn. A wooden stile then takes you into a second field, where another at the bottom leads you onto the track past Clauchlands farm, one of the only two remaining milk-producing farms on Arran. Following this track for half-a-mile or so then brings you to another wooden stile on your left, from which a much narrower path will take you over a small burn and down past Prospect Hill cottages onto the tarmac road which leads to the impressive Arran

Outdoor Centre and onwards to the car park at Clauchlands Point, opposite the tiny Hamilton Isle, itself dwarfed by the adjacent Holy Island.

It was this section of the wonderful Brodick-to-Lamlash walk which heralded one of the saddest days of my life, on what should have been one of the most uplifting. That was the day when I walked my six-year-old chocolate-brown Labrador, Meg, and her one-year-old jet-black soulmate, Tanna, from the Auchrannie all the way to Clauchlands Point, where Nan was waiting in her car to pick us up. About half-way through our three-hour walk, I had begun to notice that Meg was becoming unusually tired, and by the time we had reached the aforementioned cairn – the remotest point on our whole journey - she was panting with exhaustion. When I eventually got her back to the car after several enforced pit-stops, she was absolutely out on her feet. The very next day, my beloved Meg was diagnosed with Lymphoma. She died in my arms one beautiful sunny morning some three weeks later, in what should have been the prime of her young life. Nan and I were heartbroken. Tanna, still only a puppy, was devastated.

However, despite the great sadness of that particular day, the Clauchlands Hill walk is still one of my most cherished favourites on an island which is blessed with so many. So just choose a nice day, load up your camera and go for it.

However, if you happen to be a dog owner, do remember to lock up your cheese sandwiches.

'Johnston's Folly!'

Many of the people I interviewed were completely agreed on one of the principal reasons for the enormous improvement in the quality of Arran as a holiday destination in recent years.

Nestling in sixty-acres of rural splendour in the heart of Brodick's majestic Glen Cloy, the vast Auchrannie Resort is an internationally renowned, multi-award-winning business which is now absolutely central to the life and economy of the island of Arran. It is a massive hotel and leisure complex with an astonishing 500-bed capacity, which when you think about it makes it theoretically capable of accommodating more than ten percent of the island's entire population. Comprising two four-star hotels, 85 four-star bedrooms, 30 five-star self-catering lodges, two leisure clubs, three distinctly branded restaurants, a destination spa, a children's play-barn and the Arran Outdoor Adventure Company, the Auchrannie is Scotland's one-and-only island resort hotel. And without a doubt, it is right up there with the other 'big boys' of the tourist industry.

However, it is the Auchrannie 'story' itself which I find particularly fascinating. Long-term joint-owner and current Managing Director, Linda Johnston, took me through the whole journey over a cup of coffee one afternoon in the hotel's Brambles Restaurant.

'We started from very humble beginnings back in 1987, as a small family-run hotel with only twelve bedrooms,' Linda reflected. 'Now I have to pinch myself every time I remember that we've become a huge international all-year-round resort complex, accommodating over 40,000 guests every year and employing 160 full-time staff, with a turnover of £7.3 million. It has been some journey, that's for sure.'

The co-founders of the modern Auchrannie project were Linda and her husband, Iain Johnston, who sadly passed away in 2015, aged 82. Glasgow born-and-bred, Iain's childhood holidays were spent with his family on Arran, and like so many other holidaymakers he instantly fell in love with the island, eventually leaving his professional vocations in banking and customs and excise to settle where his heart lay. Once on the island as a permanent resident, he bought a grocer's shop in Blackwaterfoot, before spending a spell as a tourist officer and trying his luck in another couple of small business ventures, including setting up the Book and Card Centre in Brodick with his brother Forbes and sister-in-law Eileen, a stationery shop which still flourishes to this day. It was back then that Iain and Linda met.

'I was actually a trained PE teacher working in a number of primary schools in Ayrshire, when I was offered a job as the sole female PE teacher on Arran,' Linda explained. 'It was a completely different challenge, allowing me to teach children of secondary school age in Arran High School while still retaining a reduced peripatetic role across the island's seven primary schools, so I jumped at the chance. That was when I met Iain, and we later got married.

'Believe it or not, the Auchrannie project was simply to do with our conviction that the island really needed a facility with a swimming pool and leisure facilities. You see, Iain had been trying to whip up support by arguing his case in the local newspaper, the *Arran Banner*, and he had ruffled a few local feathers. He actually referred to the project at the time as "Johnston's Folly"! Then in 1987, the Auchrannie came up for sale. It was a sixteen-bedroom guest house with some very basic wooden "ranchettes". Iain asked his friend, Ronnie Mann, himself the owner of the island's Whiting Bay Hotel and the adjacent Nags pub/bistro, to come and have a look at the buildings.'

Ronnie's reaction was instantaneous. 'I was gobsmacked! The potential was immediately apparent. A ten-acre site with room for 98 "ranchettes", and a wonderful traditional sandstone building. It really was an opportunity too good to miss.'

It didn't take long for the two friends to agree that the Auchrannie project looked like a really solid investment, so Iain took the plunge and went for it. However, his determination to achieve the coveted 'four-star' rating meant that a considerable amount of work would be required to provide the requisite en-suite bathrooms, restaurant and bar facilities.

Ronnie remembers burning the midnight oil with the Johnstons, to get the project up and running.

'It was a frantic time. In the period between October 1987 and the formal entry date of March 1988, we pored over the plans in Iain and Linda's home in Whiting Bay. I well remember warning them just how much time and effort would be required to achieve their goal. Sixteen-hours-a-day and seven-days-a-week might do it, I told them, but it didn't put them off because they were on a mission. By the time of entry, I had sold both the Whiting Bay Hotel and Nags, and Iain and Linda invited me to join their team. Since my own team from Whiting Bay was still available, we were confident that we could open the Auchrannie in June, with key staff who had already worked well together. I vividly remember Kate Hill, our proposed head receptionist, being so committed that she actually got involved in the demolition works herself, boiler suit, manicured nails and all. Within hours, the walls were coming down and her nails were in tatters!'

Kate vividly recalls those crazy days.

'I remember as clear as day the "bloody marvellous" Alan Johnston, now sadly no longer with us. Both of us were standing there with our masks on, ripping out the plasterboard, when he turned to me and told me that I was easily the most glamorous building apprentice he'd ever worked with! Happy memories of happy days and a wonderful man.'

'It was a ridiculously fierce schedule,' Ronnie laughed. 'In fact, on the very day that the new hotel was due to open, everyone was still vacuuming the new carpets and dusting the furniture when our first two guests arrived at the door. Completely unfazed, they just put their cases down, rolled up their sleeves and set about helping us to lift the furniture into place, including the chairs in their own room. That summer, we enjoyed an amazing occupancy and the guest feedback was superb, which gave Iain and Linda the confidence they needed to press ahead with their expansion plans.'

Another big task which had to be undertaken right away was the relocation of the ranchettes, and while many guests often spoke about the wonderful holidays they enjoyed in the thirty feet (ten metres) long by ten feet (three metres) wide wooden units, there was never any question about them becoming part of the new business venture, as Ronnie recalled with some amusement.

'When the ranchettes were all sitting there together, the whole thing looked like a prisoner-of-war camp! So, we decided to relocate them to the far end of the ten-acre site and redeploy them as local letting units and staff accommodation. The big problem was that they had been built "in situ", and they were an absolute nightmare to shift. We tried dragging them, winching them up and lifting them, but all we ended up with was a massacred site and a bunch of seriously damaged ranchettes. We eventually had to hire a large digger and have a trailer manufactured locally to shift the things, then ended up selling some of them off and scrapping the rest.'

Linda would be the first to admit that things didn't always go quite according to plan in the early days.

'I had very little hospitality experience, but of course I was keen to learn and help out. One evening, I was trying to assist our Restaurant Manager, Aileen Aitcheson, and I was clearing a large table that had been placed in an awkward location. I had managed to stack up a big pile of plates, cutlery and some leftover potatoes, and I was feeling rather pleased with myself. Suddenly, my foot got entangled with an empty metal wine stand, but with both hands full of plates I could do nothing about it. So, I just kept smiling and walked out of the restaurant dragging the wine stand behind me, leaving a long trail of potatoes rolling off the plates and onto the floor, which Aileen just picked up ever so discreetly as I went. She was so professional that I'm sure none of the guests even noticed!'

'On another occasion, Kenny, our supervisor in Brambles Restaurant, who was a man of diminutive stature and very distinctive gait, was coming out from behind the bar grasping a wet wiping-up cloth by the corner. As his foot went down the step, it landed on a stray chip that had been dropped, and he fairly "skited" across the floor. Instinctively, his arm shot up in the air, and the wet cloth wrapped itself around the face of a rather tall guest who was standing at the bar at the time. As Kenny, who was a good foot shorter than the guest, apologised profusely while trying to dab the tall chap's face dry with a towel, he just stood there glowering, unable to see the funny side. Unlike the rest of us, that was, who by then had disappeared into the kitchen in fits!'

I asked Linda about the family's philosophy and vision for the project.

'To be perfectly honest, we didn't have a philosophy as such. All we wanted was to provide the island with swimming and leisure facilities, and neither of us had the slightest inkling that it would ever mushroom into an operation of this scale. What Iain and I did do, though, was to establish a set of principles. It was never about making a fast buck, never at any time. We just wanted people to have a happy experience, and we wanted them to come back. Did we want the hotel to make a profit? Of course we did, but our driving force was customer satisfaction, and it still is today.'

It goes without saying that running an operation of this magnitude and scale is not without its challenges, as Linda readily acknowledges.

'Yes, over the years we've had just about every imaginable crisis and emergency situation thrown at us. And not surprisingly, most of those have occurred in the depths of winter, particularly around the festive season when the hotel is always packed full. We used to put up marquees in our grounds at Christmas and New Year, only for them to be flooded or blown away, so bitter experience has taught us to hold our festive celebrations indoors from now on! On one occasion, the Glencloy Water burst its banks in a flood when a footbridge upstream was swept away and blocked the burn. The result was several lodges and cars under water. Thankfully, local outdoor clothing retailer, Bilslands, came to the rescue and provided us with a supply of wellies, so that we could get our guests out of the flooded lodges.

'On Hogmanay evening of 2004, the St Elmo Hotel building, which is where we accommodated our staff, went on fire. Since all the staff were working that night, nobody knew anything about the unfolding drama until they were told later that their accommodation and their belongings had gone up in flames. And that was when the famed Arran community spirit kicked in yet again, with other neighbouring hotels, guest houses and even some of our own staff opening their doors to give them a bed, and Bilslands once more coming to the rescue by providing emergency clothing for those who were caught short. The incident would be known ever after as "St Elmo's Fire!"

'We even had a burst water main in Brodick one Christmas, which meant that we didn't have sufficient water pressure to flush the toilets, but local shop, Homestyles, immediately answered the call by supplying us with dustbins which the Fire Brigade filled up with water, so that our guests could flush their loos. Meanwhile, I spent most of my time up a ladder looking into the water tanks, so that we could tell our guests in turn when they could have a shower. We called it our "water tank monitoring system", but basically it was me and my ladder!

'And, of course, there are the dreaded power cuts, which for some strange reason have also tended to be most common in the festive period. The worst was during the big Boxing Day storm of 1999. We were hosting a "Titanic" theme night, but around 8.00 pm the lights suddenly went out. Our guests thought that this was a stroke of genius, adding extra authenticity to the evening, before they eventually realised that it was the real thing. However, the team just carried on regardless, stoking up the coal fires, handing out candles to guests and cooking sixty meals using only the gas hobs. Trees blew down all over the place, one of which buried our cocktail manager's car, while another blocked the hotel entrance, with the result that local guests going home by taxi had to be helped over the tree's trunk and through its branches to get to their taxis. We didn't get power back until the following morning, but our staff were terrific, and our guests had a great time and were still talking about it many years later.

'By far the biggest infrastructure failure to hit Arran occurred much more recently in late-March of 2013. It will forever be known as "Snowmageddon", with a catastrophic snowfall knocking out the power supply to all Arran homes and businesses for a whole week. Since we had our own generator at the Spa Resort, we were quickly selected as the "emergency control centre" for all the various services providing emergency help to the island's population. We did, of course, have to cancel all our bookings for the week, but we managed to keep the Spa up-and-running to service the needs of the local community and to provide a secure base for the emergency services. It was a vitally important job that had to be done, and everybody worked superbly well together to make sure that it got done properly.'

While Linda's staff have always answered the call even in the most trying of circumstances, there have been a few real characters among them down through the years.

'Each year we close the hotel for one night only, so that our staff can let their hair down at our annual staff party. One evening many years ago, a couple of staff managed to gain access to the swimming pool, and decided to have a wee dip in their underwear. After their little jaunt, they very responsibly locked up the pool and re-joined the party. The next morning, one of them remembered that she had left her wet underwear in the changing rooms, and while it was her best matching set, she was still horrified at the thought of her colleagues finding it. So, she searched and searched, but to no avail, until a couple of days later when she was passing the Spa shop, where before her very eyes was a life-size dummy modelling her best underwear. To this day, she still has no idea how it got there!

'On another occasion, in fact at two o'clock in the morning of the Friday before Christmas in 2005, one of our female staff thought it would be a good idea to demonstrate her flexibility by climbing into a tumble-drier in our St Elmo accommodation, a party-trick which she had accomplished before. However, this time she was unable to get back out of the thing, so she eventually worked herself into a blind panic and had to be cut out by the Fire Brigade. Happily, she lived to tell the tale, but never tried that trick again!'

Linda and her staff have a very clear understanding of the importance of treating guests with dignity and respect, and of the need to provide them with the highest quality experience possible, irrespective of the circumstances.

'We have to be able to adapt to every situation. If for any reason the boats don't sail and our customers are stranded at Ardrossan, we don't charge them. If they get stuck on the island because of adverse weather and have to stay another night, we give them the lowest rate possible. The tourism pattern has changed dramatically. In the earlier days, the tourist season ran from April to September only. Now it's all-year-round, with us enjoying 90%-plus occupancy more or less the whole time. We're also one of the biggest employers on the island, which means a lot to us. We're a demanding employer, but we treat our staff well.'

So, if customer satisfaction is still so important to the modern-day Auchrannie complex, just how does head honcho Linda know what her customers really think of the place?

'It's very simple. We ask them. Every morning in life, the first thing I do is look at Trip Advisor. Over half of the hotels in this country hate it, because it exposes weaknesses. We work tirelessly to get customer feedback, and when we get it we do something about it, because it helps us to identify potential weaknesses and improve our quality of provision. Honest engagement with our clientele is vital to our whole operation. We are now not only a national brand, but thoroughly international as well. We're right up there with the Gleneagles and Celtic Manors of the day. How do we know? Because our customers tell us. We benchmark ourselves regularly against the other big operations, and we almost always come out on top.

'We have won countless prestigious awards, as have other first-class Arran hotels like the Douglas and the Kilmichael in Brodick, and the Glenisle in Lamlash. And while we're technically in competition, we work together and help each other out. If we're full, we'll direct customers to other hotels, and they'll do likewise. If we run short, we'll lend a side of beef or a barrel of beer to each other.

'In fact, I remember some years ago, the Kilmichael Hotel even loaned us their pet peacock for the day! Not that they knew much about it, though, because it obviously just decided to make an unannounced visit. The first we heard about it was when the guests in our Garden Restaurant spotted it on the flat roof outside Room 29, which overlooks the restaurant. When we contacted the owner to come and retrieve it, he just laughed and said that perhaps the bird had been looking for a better class of hotel!

'Oddly enough, on another day, that same roof also played host to a wee yappy Border Terrier which had jumped out of the window in search of its owners. Yet again, our guests in the Garden Restaurant were treated to a rather unique cabaret act, this time boosted by the antics of our Duty Manager climbing out the window and trying to persuade the poor thing to get back inside.

'As far as we and other hoteliers are concerned, it's all about promoting the island of Arran as a leading holiday destination and giving the customer the best possible experience. The product on Arran is of a very high quality nowadays, which is why we've been voted as "best Scottish island". We're all very proud of what we have achieved, and our customers tell us that they enjoy the experience. And most importantly, they keep coming back to Arran.'

So where does the Auchrannie go from here then?

'Our mission is to continue to promote Arran, and to make the maximum possible contribution to the island's economy. We've become very big now, but we won't ever allow ourselves to get so big that we lose our heart and soul. However, we won't stand still either!'

Nor indeed will they, because the present shareholders have now transferred their shares to a new Employment Ownership Trust, to protect the Auchrannie from the glassy-eyed predators who over the years have tried to buy the Johnstons out and get their greedy mitts on the big prize.

As Linda herself put it, 'employee ownership now gives the whole Auchrannie team a stake in the continued growth of the business. It will also protect the ethos and values that are shared by everyone who works at Auchrannie, and which otherwise might have been lost if the business was ever to have been acquired by an opportunist entrepreneur. And very importantly, it will bolster the Auchrannie's continued contribution to the island of Arran.'

Quite simply, the Auchrannie team don't do 'standing still.' In this exciting new development, team members were fully involved during the transition process, giving them a meaningful stake in growing the business, and they are well represented in the new Employee Ownership Trust.

Ronnie Mann has absolutely no doubt about the impact that the Auchrannie has had, and will continue to have on the island's economy and profile.

'In my opinion, the Auchrannie has contributed enormously to extending the tourism season on Arran, and it is very well positioned to continue to strengthen our tourism industry still further. When we remember that places like the Whiting Bay Hotel once enjoyed a fifteen-week season at best, and consider that businesses on Arran can now achieve at least 35 productive weeks every year, the transformation has been remarkable. I'm pretty much retired myself now, but very proud to have contributed to the success of the Auchrannie. Iain Johnston's bold vision and unrelenting commitment to improve the island of Arran as a leading tourist destination should never be forgotten.'

On a purely personal note, Nan and I, together with our immediate and extended families, have used the Auchrannie facilities more times over the years than we can possibly remember. What wonderful memories we have of our own children splashing about in the very same swimming pool that was Iain's and Linda's great dream, of long, lazy (and often liquid) lunches in Brambles Restaurant and then having to work it all off in the fitness suite the following morning. And more recently, of watching our three young grandchildren having a whale of a time in the play-barn and then creating their own multi-coloured pottery masterpieces on a rainy day.

Many memorable high-profile events have been staged at the Auchrannie Spa over the past few years, including various sell-out concerts by such as The Proclaimers and Abba tribute band, Bjorn Again. On the first of the Edinburgh combo's gigs, the local constabulary and licensing board were so concerned about the influx of an expected 1,500 revellers that they insisted on extra police, ambulance and 'special professional stewards' being brought in to control the mayhem that would undoubtedly ensue. Folklore has it that the only time the stewards had to move in was when one over-excited Brodick lady ripped off her top to display her ample bosom whilst belting out the legendary Proclaimers' chorus, 'I Would Walk 500 Miles'.

Quite simply, the Auchrannie has revolutionised Arran, and while the island can boast many other truly excellent hotels, restaurants and pubs, the jewel of Glen Cloy has now metamorphosed into a veritable honey-pot for all ages in every kind of weather.

And all of this thanks to the courageous vision of Iain and Linda Johnston, who had the tenacity to pursue their dream, but who will forever bestow the Auchrannie's success, not on themselves, but on their fabulous team.

The Magnificent Glen Rosa

Of all the many beautiful glens and burns which radiate from Arran's lofty peaks down towards its rolling sands, the magnificent Glen Rosa and the crystal-clear waters of the Glenrosa Water take first prize. At least in my eyes anyway.

My fond memories of the glen are as indelible as they are innumerable. Strolling up the riverbank with Nan in our student days, before the awful spectre of MS decided to enter the equation. Our two young children throwing sticks into the big deep pool below the Glen Rosa campsite, and giggling gleefully as our first dog, Cindy, launched herself repeatedly off the raised banking in manic pursuit, while Nan sat watching from the car park above. Picnics galore in all sorts of weather, whether sheltering under umbrellas from the latest summer cloudburst or swishing away the dreaded midges with beach towels. Standing in triumph on the ridge of 'The Saddle' at the top of the glen, accompanied by each of my canine soulmates at some stage or other, those who have sadly departed from this life now watching over us protectively from the heavens above. Wonderful memories of happy days set in a truly glorious location.

Well mostly wonderful, anyway. Perhaps less so the day that my then six-year-old son was standing behind me on the riverbank, chucking stones into the Glenrosa Water, when suddenly my lights went out. When I eventually regained consciousness with a bloodstained towel wrapped around my head, I learned that the little sprat had clattered me on the back of the napper with a boulder about the size of a curling stone. He insists to this day that it was all an unfortunate accident, but given the evidence that only a couple of minutes before the heartless assault I had refused to give him a packet of Tootie-Fruities, I've never been entirely convinced. Suffice to say that ever since that day, I have always kept him in my direct line of sight (and, it must be said, liberally supplied with Tootie-Fruities.)

The walk up through Glen Rosa is simply stunning. Heading north out of Brodick and turning left up the 'String Road', which leads cross-country to the west coast village of Blackwaterfoot, a sign immediately on the right points the way. From there, a leisurely half-mile stroll (or two-minute drive) leads to the car park and campsite at the entrance to the glen. The first part of the walk is along a rough tarmac road above the Glenrosa Water, but once through the gate, or over the stile for the more energetic, the path meanders out into the countryside, refusing to leave the burn's side by more than a few yards at any point on its trajectory.

While the same path does undulate somewhat at various locations along the way, the route is generally quite flat up to the foothills of the Sleeping Warrior. However, from those same foothills spring the dramatic mountains that positively dwarf the glen, the centrepiece of which is the sharp-peaked Cir Mhor, otherwise known as 'the Matterhorn of Arran', its Gaelic name meaning 'big comb' and reflecting its uncanny resemblance to a cock's comb.

Alas, the raw beauty of the mountains inadvertently disguises the gruesome historical fact that this was the locus of several tragic deaths during the Second World War. In those desperate times of conflict, both Royal Air Force (RAF) and United States Air Force (USAF) planes regularly took off from their base at Prestwick on the Ayrshire coast, a mere twenty miles east of Glen Rosa. Laden with military personnel and tanks full of fuel to enable them to negotiate the enormous distances of cross-Atlantic flights, some of the less experienced pilots found themselves unable to gain enough altitude in time to avoid crashing into Arran's mighty mountains, resulting in numerous airborne disasters on both higher and lower ground with the subsequent loss of many lives. After each catastrophic impact, the macabre task of recovering the bodies was left to the Arran Mountain Rescue Service. Nowadays, the eerie silence at the head of Glen Rosa pays homage to the sadness of those terrible times, as red deer graze on the heather-covered hillsides and birds of prey hover gracefully in the skies above.

The climb from the foothills up The Saddle, so called because of its distinctive sagging topography linking the adjacent mountain slopes, is long and steady rather than steep and punishing, but the views from the top are truly spectacular. Looking back down Glen Rosa, Brodick Bay stretches resplendently in the distance, while straight ahead lie the beautiful slopes of Glen Sannox which also lead all the way down to another secluded bay.

Alasdair Hendry, one of Arran's most celebrated hillwalking gurus who lives at the entrance to Glen Rosa, has some very good advice for the island's many ramblers.

'When you're out walking, you should always keep one eye on the ground and the other on the hillside. You don't want to stumble and fall, but you don't want to miss a hare or a deer either. And you don't always need to do or say anything. Sometimes you should just stand in silence and take in the beauty of our wonderful island. You should always remember to make the best of your walk and live for today, because tomorrow you could be in your grave.'

Wise words indeed from a delightful elderly gent who spent many years as an expert hillwalking guide … and an undertaker!

Alasdair once famously climbed all of Arran's 'high hills' – Beinn Nuis, Beinn Tarsuinn, Caisteal Abhail, Cir Mhor and, of course, Goat Fell – in one single day, but he certainly wouldn't recommend it to the less experienced walker.

'Fortunately, I'm able to predict the weather ahead from very small changes, like a slight ripple developing on a flat-calm sea or the foliage in the glen suddenly darkening. And, believe me, a changing weather pattern can mean big trouble for inexperienced hillwalkers. You must be prepared to stop and turn back. Turning back is not a sign of failure. If you don't like it, don't do it. There will always be another day.'

Alasdair is convinced that living on an island promotes a great appreciation of our wildlife, and a real sense of responsibility for our environment. He will always remember one particular summer's evening when he wandered quietly down through the hills with his faithful dog by his side, then sat down to listen to the birds singing in the foreground with people chattering away like ants far away in the distance of the village. One little sentence completely captured the mood.

'There was peace in the glen that night.'

On a purely personal note, I have been fortunate enough to witness moments of great peace and serenity while walking with my dogs through Glen Rosa, moments when I've seriously questioned the futility of the manic hustle-and-bustle of daily urban life. Occasionally, though, the delicate balance of wild nature and modern technology will be brought back into sharp focus by the spectacular sight of an RAF Tornado jet suddenly appearing out of nowhere, screaming up the glen and hugging the hillsides on its latest training exercise, inadvertently sending the indigenous hares and red deer scurrying into the cover of foliage.

However, not all of Arran's wildlife is as timid as the hare and the deer. Island vet, Charlotte Clough, is only too well aware of one potential danger lurking in the undergrowth. Britain's only poisonous snake, the adder.

'A hillwalker was out walking with his dog in Glen Rosa recently, when he slipped and fell, breaking his ankle. As he sat on the remote hillside wondering what to do, an adder slithered out of the undergrowth. His dog instinctively ran over and sniffed at it, and the adder pounced and bit the dog on the nose, causing it to become ill very quickly and go into anaphylactic shock. Quite remarkably, and demonstrating tremendous courage, the poor injured walker somehow managed to carry his sick dog all the way back to his car and drive to the surgery, just in time for us to give it a shot of anti-venom. The two casualties then caught the last ferry with literally minutes to spare, the dog ending up in its local veterinary surgery for a few days' intensive treatment and its owner in a neighbouring hospital's A & E department to get his ankle attended to. Thankfully both lived to tell the tale.'

The message is therefore clear. In the extremely unlikely event that you happen to see an adder on your travels, don't be fooled by the mesmeric beauty of the male's grey-and-black zig-zags or the female's two-tone brown, or even try to sneak a closer look. Just leave them alone, and they will leave you alone. Not, though, if you go out of your way to annoy them, as the aforementioned injured hillwalker's dog found out to its painful cost. And as indeed did another hillwalker in Glen Rosa back in 2006, who happened to spot a pair of adders on a footpath and, incredibly, decided to pick both of them up by the tail so that he could have his photograph taken holding them. To his great surprise, the first bit him on one hand and the second on the other, immediately triggering a life-threatening emergency which resulted in the poor misguided chap being airlifted to hospital on life support, where he remained for a whole week before eventually making a full recovery.

All of which does, I suppose, take us back to Alasdair Hendry's astute observation that we are very fortunate indeed to have such a wonderful environment and fascinating array of wildlife on Arran, and so we should treat them with the respect they deserve.

I would thoroughly recommend a leisurely stroll up through Glen Rosa. It will gladden your heart and cleanse your soul. However, if you do decide to pose for a 'selfie' with one of the glen's indigenous residents, you'd be well-advised to choose a rodent rather than a reptile.

Cutting the Mustard

Call me sad, but I will always remember my first ever taste of 'Arran Mustard'.

It was one glorious summer's evening in the early 'eighties, when Nan and I were sitting in the cosy lounge of a self-catering cottage, watching the razor-sharp silhouette of the Arran hills darken against the crystal-clear sky as sunset began to fall over Brodick.

Nan had just laid out three items of local fare on an oval-shaped platter; a neat pile of Brodick baker Wooley's oatcakes, a big lump of Arran Dunlop cheese and a little jar of something called 'Arran Wholegrain Mustard'. We had eaten dinner only a few hours back, and I wasn't all that fussed about the biscuits-and-cheese supper deposited in front of me, but it was an excellent excuse to help myself to another glassful from the bottle of Bordeaux that sat invitingly beside the platter. And as sure as hell, there was no way I was going to contaminate my supper with a dollop of those strange little tadpole lookalikes that masqueraded as wholegrain mustard, into which Nan was already tucking with considerable fervour.

'Try it, Ian,' she commanded me. 'It won't kill you!'

All I could think of at that moment was a most unfortunate earlier experience, this as Nan's new boyfriend, of whacking a great pile of Dijon mustard onto my roast beef dinner just to impress her parents, and the agonising near-death experience which had followed as my eyeballs exploded from their sockets in a tsunami of searing hot tears. That and the revolting sight now in front of me, as the tadpole-thingies stared threateningly at me, daring me to re-live the whole hellish experience once more.

'Try it, for God's sake!'

So, I did, and do you know what? It wasn't half bad. Very tangy, with a slight hint of acidity, it complemented the oatcakes and cheese perfectly, especially when the next gobful of vino collapso hit home. And it was in that very moment that I knew I had matured from boyhood to manhood. Well, at least insofar as mustard consumption was concerned.

However, what I could never have known as the foursome of complementary gastronomic delights washed down my throat, was the fascinating story behind this strange-looking but delicious-tasting concoction that called itself Arran Wholegrain Mustard.

The Russell family had already been making its collective presence felt on the island of Arran for several generations. However, Iain Russell, now sadly departed, whose father had been born on the island, was actually reared in Scotland's capital, the city of Edinburgh. Meanwhile, and unbeknown to him, his future wife, Janet, was busily helping her mother to make her famed chutneys, jams and other quaint preserves at home in the rural countryside of England's Shropshire. It would be several more years before Iain and Janet would meet, and shortly thereafter get hitched and settle down in Britain's second city, the urban metropolis of Birmingham, he as a policeman and she as a nurse.

Then one day in 1973, only a few weeks after the couple had holidayed on Arran, Iain burst through the door from work to inform Janet most enthusiastically that he was sick-fed-up with life as a 'bobby' in Brummie, and that they would be moving over to the island to try their luck in private enterprise. Whatever private enterprise actually meant, that was, because neither had the foggiest idea at the time, other than that the whole adventure sounded very exciting. And so, in a relative instant, Iain, Janet and fourteen-month-old Andrew Russell had upped sticks and kissed goodbye to the paid-job security of city life and found themselves standing on the deck of the Ardrossan-to-Brodick ferry with next to nothing behind them, except the clothes on their backs and the modest contents of an old suitcase lying on the floor.

'We began our adventure by buying the Old Pier Craft Centre in Whiting Bay, and tried our luck at hiring out bicycles,' recalled Janet fondly. 'We started out with only six bikes, all carefully numbered from 101 to 106 to give the impression that we had far more bikes than we actually did! We tried everything to earn a bit of extra cash in those days, from growing vegetables in our own garden to winkle-picking on the beach. I can even remember having to raid the kids' piggy-banks one day to pay the mortgage. By this time, we had added a second son, Duncan, to our family.

'We then bought premises at Brodick Pier, another gift shop which we called The Arran Collection, and which we kept open all-year-round even although it was predominantly a seasonal business. We worked tirelessly and without a break, and it was really hard-going. When birthdays came around, we would just pick an item off the shelf, wrap it up and hand it over to one another as a present, then return it to the same shelf a couple of days later. I vividly remember craving a turkey for our first family Christmas dinner, but having to settle for sausages. One day, I walked along the road to Miller's the butchers, where a local woman was buying a meat joint, and I stood there wondering if we would ever be able to buy proper meat like that. Gluttons for punishment, we then purchased the old Clock Tower in Lamlash, which became our third gift shop.'

It was in 1979 that Iain Russell decided enough was enough. He was determined to get involved in a full-year-round business, rather than having to struggle all year from what he and Janet could earn in the short tourist season alone. So, he bought an old tin-roofed hut at the south end of the village of Lamlash, where the couple set up the Arran Mustard Company.

'We only had one product when we started,' said Janet. 'Wholegrain mustard, which we made in our own kitchen at home and sold in our gift shops. There was nothing like it on the market at the time, and it became very popular, very quickly.'

It was in 1980 that the Russell family's big break came, this at Edinburgh's famous Ingliston Market, which was widely recognised as an excellent venue for small businesses which were trying to promote their wares and seek more ambitious business opportunities, and this finally set the company on the map. Fairly soon, they were receiving some pretty big orders, a number of which came from well-known companies.

One offer in particular really did take young Duncan Russell's breath away.

'Suddenly out of the blue, my dad got an offer for ten-thousand units. I mean, come on, ten-thousand units! And he actually took it! I just couldn't get my head around how we could possibly deliver on an order of this size. But there again, I hadn't figured on Dad's famous mantra ... just say yes, then work out how we're going to do it!

'It soon became obvious that we needed to expand our operation,' Janet recalled, 'so we renovated the old mill at the end of the village and converted it into what was in effect Arran's first semi-automatic production line factory. Before long, we had around fifty people on the payroll, and business was really booming. Iain looked after sales and marketing and I managed production.'

The Russell children, Andrew and Duncan worked in the factory too. Duncan remembers those days well.

'We worked seven days a week, all year round. There were very few health and safety regulations back then, and we were working with searing hot products, protected only by a thin set of overalls and a wee flimsy hat! The family went twelve years without a single holiday, when at last we got away to Cyprus for some winter sun. My next holiday after that was to Florida, nineteen years later. We all grafted hard, very hard indeed.'

And so, Iain Russell had taken the plunge, and the family would never look back. Soon they were trading with some big, well-known multi-national companies, and had become the biggest employer on Arran, providing jobs for around 150 islanders, and lip-smacking treats galore for thousands-upon-thousands of discerning diners the length and breadth of the country, and well beyond.

Building on their considerable success with mustard sales, it was inevitable that the Russell family would eventually diversify into other products as well. Before much longer, an impressive range of other gastronomic delights like chutneys, jams, mayonnaise and cranberry sauce started rolling off the conveyor belts. Clearly the Arran Mustard Company had by then outstripped its originally modest expectations, and in recognition of the range of the products which the Russells were now churning out in bulk, they rebranded the business as Arran Provisions.

'I always saw the products we were making as a natural progression of my Shropshire childhood,' Janet reflected. 'Most were the sort of things we made in our own country kitchen. We also drew inspiration from the old Russell family cookbook, itself created and built up on the island of Arran over many years.'

And that was when the wolves began to circle around the burgeoning business potential of Arran Provisions. One of the country's leading whisky distributors then made a very tempting bid for the company, clearly on a mission to add a range of top quality foodstuffs to its established whisky portfolio, and all of a sudden the Russell family was facing a real dilemma.

Stick or twist? Stay or sell?

Their decision was never going to be an easy one, not least because Iain and Janet now held diametrically opposite views on what that decision should ultimately be. Short of pistols at dawn, there was only one way to resolve their dilemma.

'We decided to toss a coin on Whiting Bay beach!' laughed Janet. 'Iain and I had weighed up all the pros and cons, and we were never going to agree on the way forward. Iain was always the major risk-taker, and I was the safe pair of hands, which led to many an interesting discussion! I wanted to sell the business, mainly because I yearned for financial security after all the years of toil and stress, but Iain wanted to keep it and push ahead. So, we walked onto the beach, and took out a coin. Heads we sell, tails we don't. It was heads. I was delighted, he wasn't! However, we accepted the offer of a lifetime.'

Backed by the same whisky company, the Russell family then built the newer and much larger Arran Provisions factory in 1987, adjacent to the old building at the south end of Lamlash. Typical of Iain's brash approach to things, there was only one person he deemed important enough to formally open the new factory.

'Prime Minister, Margaret Thatcher!' Duncan laughed. 'So, he called 10 Downing street, and he wasn't taking no for an answer. A few weeks went past, then we got a phone call saying that, regrettably, the Prime Minister's diary commitments were such that she simply couldn't do it, but would we like to have the Princess of Wales instead! And so, our new factory was opened by Princess Diana! Absolutely wonderful, and what a difference that made to our official opening, and also to public awareness of our company.'

Arran Provisions had by then become a highly respected national and international brand, selling to such established top-end companies as Boots, Fortnum & Mason, Harrods and Debenhams to name but a few, and in over twenty countries abroad including the United States.

In 1989, the Russell family decided to diversify further and move into the production of toiletries, but the whisky company wasn't interested in departing from their mainly food and drink focus, so the family decided to leave Arran Provisions and bought the site of the former Home Farm at Cladach, on the northern outskirts of Brodick, where they set up a new company. They called it Arran Aromatics.

The Russells then set about converting the Home Farm complex into a visitor centre and courtyard, comprising three retail shops and a coffee shop, all of which were independently managed and operated. Their approach to the manufacture of toiletries was unashamedly based on advice from a lady chemist hailing from the island of Coll, who already had considerable experience in a similar operation and whom the family had invited to stay with them for a month to learn the process. Using as many locally-sourced ingredients as possible, new and exciting bath and body products were soon created.

'Iain loved to court controversy,' laughed Janet, 'so when it came to inviting someone to open our new business, who better than Edwina Currie MP!'

The Russells had done it again. First Princess Diana, and now the extremely controversial 'Eggwina', the Junior Health Minister who had gained fame and notoriety from such outrageous public comments as, 'most of the egg production in this country, sadly, is now affected by Salmonella', and 'northerners die of ignorance and chips'. However, as luck would have it, the Conservative Minister never did manage to open the exciting new Arran Aromatics venture, because her ferry sailing was cancelled in dense fog and she was left stranded at Ardrossan, doubtless like the rest of us to dine in her car on a fish supper and a pickled egg. In the event, it was the island's own aristocrat, Lady Jean Fforde, who stood in for the Junior Health Minister to officiate at the Russells' grand opening. Mind you, in fairness to the much-maligned 'Eggwina', she did catch a later ferry to pay her welcome visit to Arran Aromatics.

Today, the Home Farm centre and its constituent outlets are still a major tourist attraction, the centrepiece of which is, of course, Arran Aromatics, or as it has been recently rebranded, Arran, Sense of Scotland. The company continues to be one of the island's main employers, and it also provides numerous jobs on the mainland in their warehouse and various shops.

'We have had more than a few rocky patches along the way,' Janet confessed. 'However, we've come through them all in one form or another. From 'Banana Wars' in 1999, driving 100% duty on sales to our biggest export market, the USA, and wiping out 40% of the business overnight, to Iain's declining health, then to the 'Credit Crunch' which nearly closed the business for the second time in 2009, we certainly haven't had our challenges to seek. However, with the help and support of many people, we always managed to battle on and save the business.

'New investment in 2013 meant we could take the brand to a new level, but the changing global landscape led to wider differences of opinion, and so for the third time, this in 2016, the business was almost lost. The following year, we found new investors who shared the vision of what Arran, Sense of Scotland could become. It's been an incredibly tough time, and a major health tragedy in the wider family meant we all had to pull together, save as many jobs as we could, and secure the future of the company. Timing is rarely kind. Thankfully, though, the company is back on track to profitability.'

So, what has been the family's recipe for success then, I asked Janet?

'Iain was a natural entrepreneur and would never countenance failing to realise his dreams. I was the balance, in trying to keep his feet on the ground and create a stable home and family.'

Reflecting back over the years, their elder son Andrew also remembers a recurring theme.

'Many of our suppliers and customers were welcomed into our home in Whiting Bay. My father worked so hard in building relationships with everyone he could. "People do business with people," he would say. "You can have great products, but it's the relationships that will support you and the business in the long term." We try to live by this every day, and we're very grateful for all the support we have had as we look forward to the thirtieth anniversary of Arran, Sense of Scotland (Arran Aromatics) in 2019.'

The Russell family may no longer be making the mustard, but one thing's for sure. They're still cutting it.

Brodick Castle and Country Park

And so, it's time to bid farewell to the 'wee town' of Brodick, as it lies peacefully beside the majestic crescent bay with its myriad of anchored vessels sparkling like diamonds in the sunshine.

Driving northwards from the ever-popular Home Farm complex (now known as Duchess Court) at Cladach on the outskirts of the town, two wooden cabins sit regally on the shore. The first and much larger is now the ultra-modern headquarters of the Arran Mountain Rescue Team, this having replaced its rather antiquated predecessor which was formerly located at the old police station in the centre of Brodick. The present-day base now houses the 28 volunteer members of the team whenever the occasion demands, together with their impressive inventory of super-duper high-tech gear. This includes two Land Rovers and two Argocats, the latter being fully amphibious and thoroughly versatile eight-wheel-drive all-terrain vehicles which can whisk the team members to virtually any location on the island, no matter how geographically remote or environmentally hostile. Meanwhile they can all go about their 'normal' day-jobs as usual, but not without mobile phones at the ready, awaiting the next emergency call, doubtless to dash to the rescue of the latest bewildered city-dweller to be found stranded in his shorts-and-T-shirt in the freezing mists of the summit of Cir Mhor.

As we drive on, however, it is to the second of these cabins that my pangs of nostalgia are drawn, a tiny wooden affair which in the late-60s days of my youth was called the Boathouse Grill. Run by Glasgow-born retired Brodick businessman, Alastair Bilsland, the famous old boathouse did precisely what it said on the tin, which was to operate as a splendid eating joint, invariably packed to the rafters during the sultry days and evenings of summer. However, it was only when the sun went down that it really burst into life, re-inventing itself as a 60s-genre disco. The Boathouse Grill might have had no licence and no bar, but it mattered not a jot, because by boogie-time the younger generation would have gotten themselves pleasantly oiled-up in the glass-house of the Ormidale bar before staggering the half-mile or so out to the wee wooden hut, armed of course with their 'cairry-oots'. There they would commence the search for the damsel of their dreams, who would be clad in the standard clobber of the times, flared jeans and psychedelic T-shirt, and one of whom, thanks to the good old Boathouse Grill, would soon contrive to become my wife.

Brought up in the Crosshill area of Glasgow, the redoubtable Alastair was always destined to become a businessman, an entrepreneur indeed, even if he himself might prefer to play the whole thing down.

'I've never had a paid job in my life!' Alastair readily conceded. 'When I was only fourteen, I began a wee venture with my older brother Douglas. We started running dances in the Karioca Club in Bearsden Hall on the north side of Glasgow, which soon became so popular that we could attract some of the leading pop groups of the time, big acts like The Searchers. Then we would come over to Arran for the summer and try our luck there. By 1968, we were hiring the three halls in Whiting Bay, Lamlash and Brodick, and running nine dances each weekend with the halls full to the rafters after 'chucking-out time' at the pubs, which in those days was just after ten o'clock. It was great fun and we did make a bit of money, but the 'sixties were absolutely bursting with energy and we mainly did it for the excitement. And, of course, on a Sunday night, Brodick also had the famous 'midnight raves' at the Electric Hen-Hut!'

The Electric Hen-Hut, to which Alastair was referring, happened to be a wooden shed located in the grounds of The Sheilin, a cottage in the semi-rural Corriegills area of Brodick, which was owned by former Ayrshire farmer's wife, Ann Brown, whose son Robbie continued the story.

'Aye, those were the days, they really were!' laughed Robbie, now long-retired from the lofty heights of his job as Clyde Regional Manager for ferry company, CalMac. 'The Boathouse Grill and the Electric Hen-Hut were Brodick's two nightclubs! The youngsters would get chucked out of the pubs after drinking-up time at ten-past-ten, and hang around Brodick with their carry-outs for a while before making their way up to The Sheilin for the midnight raves, as they were called. The whole route from Brodick to Corriegills would be absolutely littered with people. And because we couldn't get a licence on a Sunday in those days, the raves couldn't start until one minute past midnight, hence their name. We managed to get hold of some of the really big bands of the day, such as Marmalade, while other venues like Lamlash Hall also managed to attract big names like The Kinks and The Yardbirds. There could often be several hundred inside the Hen Hut and another couple of hundred waiting outside desperately trying to get in. Then they would all get flung out about four in the morning and make their way back down to the pier for the 'death boat'. Wonderful days!

'The Sheilin wasn't only about the midnight raves, though. We also operated as a cafeteria during the day. It was a good wee business, although I remember we once got slaughtered in the Daily Record for charging one-and-thruppence for an egg roll! And in the evenings, we were in competition with a few other local eating joints like Alastair's Boathouse Grill, but it was all very friendly and good-natured. Sadly, the poor old Hen-Hut met with a sticky end. It got blown down in the great storm of 1968, and the only two things left standing were the till and the record deck! It was the end of a great era.'

Happily, though, fate has been somewhat kinder to the old boathouse, which still stands proudly on the shore today, although its iconic discos, dances and damsels are now but a distant memory. As indeed is the jaunty little number which will always remind me of those long, lazy and wonderfully carefree summer days on Arran, Mungo Jerry's 'In the Summertime'.

Anyway, continuing our journey north, the sign for 'Brodick Castle and Country Park' stands on the left only a few hundred yards past the boathouse. Heralding a famous old stronghold steeped in blood-splattered history and contemporary intrigue, it is a sign which constitutes an invitation not to be missed. You could, of course, just take a Royal Bank of Scotland twenty-quid note out of your pocket, and there on the back will be a picture of the old castle itself. However, I would seriously recommend that you make the effort, do the detour, and check things out for yourself.

Covering a vast area all the way from Brodick Bay's stunning shoreline right to the summit of the famous Goat Fell, it is the National Trust for Scotland (NTS) which now oversees the whole operation these days. The estate comprises the ancient castle, together with 74 acres of exotic gardens and grounds, the magnificent valley of Glen Rosa, a sprawling 6,600 acres (2,700 hectares) of forests and heather-strewn uplands, and of course the imposing old mountain itself.

Brodick Castle and Country Park currently attracts around 60,000 visitors each year, about two-thirds of whom do the 'castle tour' itself. The operation employs a significant workforce totalling over 50 people of all ages, including tour guides, curators, gardeners, collection officers and catering staff who undertake a wide range of duties. The present experience is expected to expand significantly over the next few years, tapping into and catering for the diverse cultural tastes of the steadily-expanding number of tourists who will visit the island of Arran.

By almost every measure, Arran itself is very much on the up today, and not only are its visitor numbers rising, but the type of visitor is changing too. Clearly, people really know what they want these days, and all connected with Arran's tourism industry are committed to making sure they get it. Brodick Castle's historical and cultural aspects still attract large numbers of tourists, but more and more now participate in physical activities like cycling and hillwalking. So, the aim is to develop a much wider range of high-quality experiences for visitors, and to target those to specific age and interest groups, and to keep changing those experiences. Arran's tourist trade doesn't just want visitors to come to the island. It wants them to come back and keep coming back.

The uniqueness of the castle experience is many-fold. To begin with, this really was a fully functional castle for many centuries. Furthermore, it is located on an island, one to which access can be gained easily by a short sail by ferry from the mainland. And of course, it has quality catering on site, lots to do for adults and children alike, and the country park's attractions keep changing and improving, with the aim that returning visitors will enjoy a whole new experience every time they come back. And to top it all, it now boasts one of the best and most exciting adventure playparks in the whole country, 'Isle Be Wild'.

At the time of writing, the castle itself was undergoing a major facelift, as Stuart Maxwell, NTS's General Manager for Ayrshire & Arran explained.

'We currently have the castle closed for major fire protection works, which are due to finish soon. It will then reopen to the public along with a newly refurbished tearoom in the place of the previous café. We will also have new exhibition spaces in the chapel room, and we're looking to make the castle experience far more interactive and engaging for all. This doesn't necessarily mean the use of technology, but we hope to have more staff and customer interaction and engagement.

'We have also opened our new 'Isle Be Wild' playpark, which has been a great addition to the island. In the gardens, when we reopen, we will have new signage and interpretation as well as silver sculptures and exhibits which aim to bring the theme of the castle's "silver collection" into the gardens. We also plan to enhance and protect the gardens as our main priority for the year ahead. For future years, our focus is all about protecting and improving what we have, in terms of the castle and the collection, the gardens and the grounds, and ensuring that the new playpark stays ahead of the game.'

One of Brodick Castle's great attractions is, of course, its searing history, having been built in the late thirteenth century in a bold bid by the Scottish Crown to establish control in the west of the country. Variously ravaged and occupied by English garrisons and defended stoutly by Scottish forces during the Wars of Independence, the old castle has certainly witnessed more than its fair share of bloodshed. Even after being rebuilt by the Hamilton dynasty in 1510, it continued to be the focus of many a gory battle.

In 1844, the Hamiltons commissioned the major reconstruction works which would see the old stronghold finally being transformed into the modern mansion residence that it is today. Four years later, the 11th Duke of Hamilton had the castle's Bavarian Summerhouse built for his wife, Princess Marie of Baden, who herself set about designing the glorious intertwining walks, trails and drives throughout the castle grounds, many of which are still surviving today.

In 1895, the death of the 12th Duke of Hamilton saw the formally-titled Arran Estate inherited by Lady Mary Douglas-Hamilton Forster, who in 1906 married James Graham, 6th Duke of Montrose. Throughout the 1920s and 1930s, Lady Mary, the Duchess of Montrose, developed the castle's world-famous woodland garden, aided by a whole range of gifts of wonderful plants from such esteemed gardens as Tresco on the Isles of Scilly, and Edinburgh's Royal Botanical Gardens, as well as other exotic treasures from plant-hunting expeditions in such far-flung countries as Burma, Australia and Chile. The castle itself is positively laden with ancient treasures, including the internationally-renowned Beckford Collection of fine furniture, silver and china, once owned by William Beckford, the wealthy magnate who earned his fortune from his sugar plantation empire in the West Indies.

Then in February 1957, Lady Mary passed away, and Brodick Castle together with its entire estate was transferred to NTS in lieu of death duties, by her daughter, the Lady Jean Sybil Violet Graham Fforde, or 'Lady Jean' as she would always be known affectionately by the local island community. The following year, the castle and its magnificent grounds were finally made accessible to the public, and they remain open to this very day. The aristocratic family's devastating loss had suddenly become the public's tremendous gain.

I was honoured to spend a couple of hours with Lady Jean in her Brodick residence, Strabane House, only a few months before her sad passing in October 2017 at the age of 97. As her housekeeper's old dog lay protectively by her side eyeballing me with great suspicion, she recounted some of her many fond memories of a young life spent in and around the splendid old castle.

'We had some great adventures in the castle when we were children, often getting up to things which would lead us into trouble with mother. Playing on the roof of the castle, for example. My two cousins, Prince Rainier of Monaco, and his sister, Princess Antoinette, would spend much of the summer with us, and we were very close. In fact, Antoinette, whom we called 'Tiny', was my best friend. Tiny and Rainier simply loved Arran, because it was so different from the life they knew back in Monaco.

'We used to run up the castle staircase, then climb through a window at the top and down the fire escape ladder onto the roof, where we would play for hours on end. One day, we played an awful trick on our French governess, who was very solemn and very strict. We heard her calling on us from the lawn, but we just hid up there on the roof, giggling. Then Tiny told me to shout out a couple of naughty words at her, which of course I duly did, and we all bolted along to the other end of the castle roof, still laughing. Tiny and Rainier continued to egg me on, telling me to shout this and shout that, which I did again and again. Eventually, the governess could bear it no longer, and burst into floods of tears. However, that was when the fun stopped. Suddenly, we heard a much more serious, authoritative voice bellowing out from the lawn. To our horror, it was mother. "Jean, Rainier, Antoinette! Come to my boudoir! And come at once!" What a terrible row we got. I can still remember it to this day. Much later in life, Rainier married the American actress Grace Kelly, who became Princess Grace of Monaco, and she really was the most lovely and adorable person.

'Things were so different back in our young days. My memories are of long, happy and hard-working days in the castle itself and in its wonderful grounds. Mind you, I have a few less fond memories too. For example, I remember being terribly ill in bed one day, and mother calling for Doctor Buchanan to pay me a visit. We waited and waited for what seemed like an eternity. He eventually arrived several hours later with the most wonderful excuse. "I'm terribly sorry, Lady Mary," he said to mother, "but I've just been at a very difficult calving." You see, in those days, our GPs weren't just doctors, they were vets as well. And so there I was, lying with a dreadful fever and being treated by a doctor whose previous patients had been a pregnant cow and a new-born calf!

'During the Second World War, many children were evacuated from the big British cities to the rural countryside to escape from the bombing raids, many of them coming over to Arran. It must have been a really traumatic experience for the poor souls, being sent away from their families to strange places they had never seen before. However, many of them fell in love with Arran and have been coming over here on holiday ever since. Indeed, some have even set up home on the island, which is wonderful.

'One of my favourite memories was the time we put up a whole family of eight Glaswegians in the castle. They were great characters, and we looked after them very well, or at least so we thought. One morning, the mother complained about the meals we had been serving them. I replied most indignantly that we were feeding them with the very best local produce; fresh fish straight from the sea, meat from our farm animals and even vegetables from our own garden. She just looked at me and replied, "aye that's fine, but what we really want is a jeely piece an' a hauf-pint!"

'When the Second World War broke out in 1939, I was desperate to join the war effort, and I got a job in the Foreign Office. Then I moved to Bletchley Park, as part of the huge team of code-breakers whose work eventually succeeded in cracking the 'Enigma Code' used by the Nazis, which finally helped to end the war. It was a very important job and many of the girls loved it, but gosh I found it dull. We intercepted coded messages from the Germans, and my job was to translate them into individual letters of the alphabet. One letter meant very little, two could have been something like the German word "ja", but three was very good indeed. Whenever you got three letters consecutively, you had to post your little card through a slot in the wall for the men in suits on the other side, but you never heard anything back, so you would have no idea if it might have turned out to be something crucial. It was very frustrating, but I did realise the importance of what we were doing.'

Lady Jean certainly lived a fascinating life, and her contribution to the island of Arran over the last century is incalculable. She will be sorely missed. May she rest in peace.

Returning to the country park itself, a walk with my dogs through the castle grounds is one of my favourite ways to spend a morning, whether in rain, hail or shine. The incredible matrix of waymarked woodland footpaths is ideal for those who prefer to explore the grounds for themselves, and it lends itself perfectly to altering the route on successive visits.

I normally prefer to set off from the beach car park in the centre of Brodick and follow the aforementioned Fisherman's Walk past the delightful Brodick Golf Course to the footbridge over the Glenrosa Water and onto Strabane Beach, where the dogs can cavort around on the lush golden sands and splash in the ocean waves before heading for the mountain rescue centre at Cladach. Then it's dog-leashes on again and across the main road to the Wineport, where we chart the day's route. Sometimes this will be just as described earlier and up through the magnificent forests onto the castle's tarmac drive, finishing with an easy two-mile trek back into the village. However, if the energy levels are bouncing, it might be a much lengthier detour into the pine forests beneath the mighty Goat Fell, before making our return trip to the car park. Whichever route we choose, I have never once failed to be totally energised by the majesty of the experience and rendered completely at peace with the world. Especially when I then find myself sitting at one of the wooden tables on the lawn of the Wineport, a pint of foaming ale in hand and two ravenous dogs by my side tucking into a packet of crisps and slobbering in a bowl of water.

So, there you have it, a very brief snapshot of the history and modern-day delights of Brodick Castle and Country Park, a veritable must-see for every visitor to the island of Arran.

The Mighty Goat Fell

What a pity Goat Fell isn't a 'Munro'. It certainly deserves to be, at least in my opinion anyway.

As every serious hillwalker is aware (you know who I mean, the ones with the designer outdoor gear and the long walking-stick-thingies that they think make them look cool rather than prats), Munros are mountains over 3,000 feet high. Sadly, poor old Goat Fell just fails to qualify, but only by a miserable 34 feet, which renders it a mere Corbett rather than a mighty Munro. I mean, how unlucky is that?

It's still an absolute belter of a climb, though, and I seriously doubt if any of Scotland's alleged 282 Munros will have a better view from the summit. The first time I climbed Goat Fell was with Nan, away back in the summer of 1971 when she was still fit and healthy. It was a real scorcher of a day, and there she was all cosied up in the favourite light-blue cashmere jumper that her dad had bought her for Christmas, which was probably the time of year that he had intended her to wear it. Anyway, that jumper got hauled off less than ten minutes into our sweltering ascent. She hid it under a pile of rocks at the side of the path, intending to retrieve it *herself* on the way back down. Needless to say, we forgot all about it, and by the time we got home it was all *my* fault. Of course it was.

Isn't it funny how we remember little things like that, though? Every time I've climbed Goat Fell since, I've searched and searched for that fluffy blue jumper, or what now remains of it. I have no idea why I've done that, or where it might now be. I suspect that it must have vanished into the ether along with any recollection I once had of my young wife walking this earth.

My second ascent of the famous old mountain was many years later, my companion that day being our eleven-year-old son. It was during one long

'Indian summer' in the month of September, another absolute belter of a day, so we had set off up the slopes in our trainers, shorts and T-shirts. All was hunky-dory until we hit the shoulder of the mountain, when suddenly the icy chill of an easterly breeze began to cut us in half. By the time we had reached the summit, we were frozen to the core. Three guys had beat us to it. They looked like Antarctic explorers standing there in all their pomp, clad in designer outdoor gear and carrying their long walking-stick-thingies, the sweat cascading down their foreheads as they stood gawking at the pair of us chittering in our undies.

'One of us must be wrong!' the eldest of the three exclaimed cheerfully. 'Who's the prat now?' I muttered under my breath.

If you ever decide to climb Goat Fell, you really should only do so when the weather forecast indicates a clear and dry day ahead. There are two very good reasons for this. Firstly, the Arran mountains can quickly become pretty hazardous when the infamous Scottish mists and rain come down. Secondly, it would be an absolute travesty to have dragged yourself all the way up to the summit, only to be deprived of the magnificent views, and for meteorological reasons that could have been avoided with a wee bit of sensible forward planning.

The waymarked track to Goat Fell can be accessed from either the Duchess Court complex on the north-side of Brodick, or from the south-side of the village of Corrie some four miles further up Arran's east coast. The former is the more popular starting point for day-trippers, since it is easier to reach from the ferry terminal by bus or on foot, and the climb is the less demanding of the two. Passing the Wineport restaurant and the Arran Brewery, the route through the castle grounds towards the mountain is clearly signposted. A ten-minute walk leads to a tarmac road, from which a sign for Goat Fell points straight across towards a steep track. This soon reaches a sharp bend to the right, revealing a narrower path which snakes its way up through the wooded foothills, eventually clearing the dense forests and reaching the Cnocan Burn. Looking back from this point, the views across Brodick Bay are simply stunning, and it is well worth taking a few moments to inhale the clean air, absorb the scenery and get the camera out.

Moving onwards and upwards, the track soon merges with another, then leads over a wooden footbridge and through a gate in a deer fence. This is where the terrain starts to get considerably rougher. The same track continues up to the eastern shoulder of the mountain, from which the chill winds can often catch the unsuspecting hillwalker by surprise. Although it can be quite difficult to spot, the hill-path from Corrie also makes its arrival on the mountainside at this particular location, joining the main track which then veers left towards the final ascent, which itself is a much steeper and considerably rockier 'scree' slope.

After a rather strenuous clamber up to the summit, the three-hundred-and-sixty-degree panorama awaiting your delectation is absolutely spectacular. From the towering granite peaks of the neighbouring mountains which along with Goat Fell form the spectacular Sleeping Warrior, down towards the vast glens and sandy beaches which complete the unmistakable topography of the island of Arran, and further across the Firth of Clyde towards the Ayrshire coast and beyond, the views will simply take your breath away.

You then have the option of descending the mountain by the same route, or once you reach the shoulder again, by accessing the path down to Corrie. Be warned, though, the latter is pretty steep and a bit tricky to negotiate, and you will then need to have a few quid in your pocket to catch the bus from Corrie back to Brodick, either that or a friendly face waiting there to pick you up by car. Personally, I would always choose the former descent, not least for the pint of beer and the big plate of fish 'n' chips that will be waiting for me in the Wineport.

All of which may make Goat Fell seem like a really welcoming and hospitable place, which most of the time it certainly is. However, the stark reality is that the mountain and its near neighbours can at times be anything but. This is particularly so in adverse weather, or when the hillwalker is ill-prepared for the rigours that lie ahead.

Former long-serving head of the local mountain rescue team, Stewart Lambie, who very sadly passed away in April 2018, regaled me with some of his memories.

'Goat Fell has been such a draw to tourists over the years that incidents and accidents on the mountain, however rare, are inevitable. On my very first call-out as a team member, we had to go to the rescue of a teenage girl who had fallen on a crag near the summit and bumped her head. Her father, who also happened to be a doctor, came with us. When we got there, the poor girl was suffering from concussion and had lost her memory. Mind you, it must have returned very quickly because it didn't stop her turning up at Whiting Bay dance that same evening!'

It has to be said, though, that not all incidents on Arran's mountains have been the result of mere misfortune. Some have occurred simply because those involved have underestimated the hazards of hillwalking, as Stewart and his colleagues often discovered to their amazement.

'Almost nothing would surprise me after the things I've seen. I remember taking my team up Goat Fell on one of our regular training exercises, when two young kids suddenly appeared out of the thick mist at the summit. They would be about eight or nine years old, and they were all alone. I asked them where their parents were, and the boy replied, "My dad's down the hill at Corrie, with the baby". It was unbelievable. We could hardly see two yards in front of us, and of course there are sheer drops all around the summit of Goat Fell. So, I told them in no uncertain terms to stick to our sides, and we led them back down the mountain to Corrie. And sure enough, there at the bottom was dad holding his tiny baby, with not a care in the world. Well, his ears would be ringing for a fortnight, I can tell you!

'On another occasion, a Boy Scout had somehow become separated from his group and got lost up the mountain. When the alarm was raised, we rushed to the scene and began our search. After a few minutes, Max, a team member's wonderful big German Shepherd dog, got to work. Max was terrific at finding people. When he sensed their whereabouts, his big ears would point forward and off he'd go, leading us straight to them. We found the poor lad lying in the heather with a broken leg, and immediately called RAF Leuchars, who sent a helicopter and airlifted him to hospital. Aye, life on the mountains can be a wee bit tricky at times.'

Likewise, Stewart's colleague Ali Hume, also a long-serving mountain rescue team member and former leader, has many a tale to tell about Arran's most celebrated mountain.

'Stewart Lambie was my role model. Everybody looked up to Stewart, and he taught me everything I know about mountain rescue. Mind you, he could be a wee bit ruthless at times. I remember one day up Goat Fell, we came across a red deer lying in the heather. It was an old stag, and the poor thing was drawing its last. Stewart opened its mouth to examine its teeth, because you can tell a stag's age by the condition of its teeth. They were in a terrible state, rotten to the roots. Just at that, Stewart took out his hunting knife and slit the stag's throat from ear-to-ear, putting it out of its misery. I was in total shock. He looked at me and said, "What's wrong, son?" I replied, "Nothing, Stewart, but I can tell you this. I'll never miss another dental appointment as long as I live!"'

Like Stewart, Ali has often been astonished at how ill-prepared and naive some hillwalkers can be when they set off.

'It's unbelievable, it really is. I've seen men up the mountain with golf shoes on their feet, and girls with hair-driers in their rucksacks. I've even met hillwalkers wearing shorts and T-shirts in the worst of the weather.'

You don't say?

'Many tourists have no comprehension of just how harsh the Scottish weather can be, even during the summer months. Some lose their bearings and get lost, some fail to plan their journey and run out of daylight. I remember two elderly hillwalkers getting into serious bother coming up the mountains from Glen Sannox and trying to locate The Saddle near Goat Fell. The pair of them were doing a "rekkie" for their local walking club. One of them developed chest pains and it soon became clear that he was suffering a heart attack. So, his mate immediately set off in the direction of Glen Rosa to summon help, but lost his bearings and wandered into Glen Iorsa, by which time another walker had raised the alarm. We got there as quickly as we could, and the sick man was helicoptered off to hospital, but despite our search there was no sign of his mate. It turned out that he had gone west from The Saddle instead of east, traversed the whole breadth of the island in the wrong direction and ended up at Dougarie on the west coast about six hours later!

'There was another incident when an uncle and his niece got completely lost in the mists of Goat Fell. He had been desperate to climb the mountain, but she had been scared because she suffered from vertigo, only she didn't want to let him go up there on his own. Anyway, they got split up somewhere near the summit in deteriorating weather conditions, and the uncle scrambled back down the mountain to Corrie, where he raised the alarm. In the meantime, his niece had managed to work herself into a blind panic and started sliding down the slopes on her bottom. By the time we got to her, the backside was completely torn out of her denims. I took one arm and another team member took the other, and we led her down the mountain to safety. For some reason, the rest of the team members followed on behind us!

'On a more sombre note, though, our team doctor was seriously injured one day in a freak accident on one of our training exercises, when he lost his footing in very icy conditions and fell all the way down to the bottom of a steep hill. By the time we reached him, it was clear that he had been very seriously injured. He knew immediately that he was in real bother, but he was so calm and collected. "Right lads," he said, "listen very carefully. I've smashed my pelvis, and blood will start flowing into my pelvic cavity, which will be disastrous, and I'll soon lose consciousness. Make a Spanish Windlass using a jacket twisted tight with a strong stick, and then use it as a tourniquet to push my pelvic cavity back in." So, we did exactly what the doctor told us to do, then stretchered him back down the mountain and rushed him to hospital. I couldn't believe how calm he had been, but it saved his life. Later, he actually wrote a poem about it.'

So, there it is in a nutshell. Paraphrasing Alasdair Hendry once more, by all means enjoy the beauty of this enchanted island, but always treat the environment with great respect.

For what it's worth, you really should take the opportunity to climb the mighty Goat Fell. The whole experience will thrill and delight you, and the views from the top will leave you gasping in wonder. Just choose a fine clear day and heed the information which is available in leaflets from the VisitArran information centre in Brodick and other local outlets.

One little piece of advice, though. Just make sure that you've kept your teeth in good condition. You never know, you might need to call mountain rescue.

The Goat Fell ... Murder?

How would you like to hear about a wee bit of gory island folklore?

I've always fancied myself as a crime writer, you know. The problem is that my publisher doesn't share my enthusiasm. However, I did eventually wear him down sufficiently to allow me to include my own version of this infamous true story. Therefore, given that this might be my first and last opportunity to dabble in the world of blood and guts, I'm sure you will forgive my highly imaginative interpretation of an old tale which was almost certainly much more mundane in its original telling. Here goes.

It was Sunday, 4 August 1889. The Sabbath day. A day of worship, a day of rest. No tennis on the tennis courts, no golf on the golf courses, no washing on the washing lines, and no children on the swings or see-saws. Not even one solitary boat sailing across Brodick Bay. This was nineteenth-century Arran, an impenetrable bastion of regimental tradition and staunch religion.

And yet something strange was happening. Goat Fell, the island's highest mountain, was teeming with people. Over fifty of them in fact, who to the casual observer down at sea level rather eerily resembled an army of ants crawling over an anthill. Yes, something odd was afoot on the Lord's day, no doubt about it.

That 'something' was the islanders' immediate response to a rather unforgettable telegram from a police station in the South London suburb of Upper Tooting near Brixton, more than 400 miles away. As with all manually-generated telegrams, words cost money, and so words were few and far between in the message received by the Brodick police, which was essentially this. A 32-year-old Londoner who had been holidaying on the neighbouring island of Bute and was known to have sailed over to Arran to climb Goat Fell, had failed to return home. He was one Edwin Robert Rose, a builder's clerk in the nation's capital.

And thus, the massed ranks of willing volunteers had been rustled up and were now commencing their orderly search of the island's iconic mountain for what they all instinctively knew could well prove to be a gruesome find. Literally no stone was left unturned, as each nook and cranny found itself being mercilessly probed and examined with forensic attention to detail, whilst every square yard of the vast expanse of purple heather got flicked and prodded with assorted walking canes to avoid incurring the wrath of Arran's most feared indigenous beast, the lethal adder. Every now and again, a cloud of autumnal mist would try its damnedest to engulf the shoulder of the mountain and obscure it from the search party's view, only for the cool sea breeze to send it packing again.

Suddenly, a loud yell split the serenity of that auspicious Sabbath day.

'Over here!' came the anxious cry. 'Over here! There's something inside the howff!'

As hordes of volunteers began to surge frantically through the heather towards the 'howff' – an enormous 42-ton granite rock overhanging Goat Fell's mighty ravine – it was local police officer, Sergeant McDonald, who immediately took charge of the situation.

'Right everybody, hold your horses!' he bellowed. 'And leave this to me. Archie, Bobby, Hamish … you come with me. The rest of you stay put till I tell you different. This might possibly be a crime scene, so I don't want to disturb any evidence. You all understand?'

Heads nodded in unison, accompanied by murmurs of resigned compliance, all consistent with the mood of those distinctly hierarchical times in which the local 'bobby' ruled supreme. The sergeant began marching his three hand-picked conscripts towards the ravine, confident in the knowledge that they were all very experienced hillwalkers who knew the mountain like their own fingernails. Some fifteen minutes later, the team of four had managed to scramble its collective way to the entrance of the small cave-like opening at the foot of the howff. Very strangely, though, they found it blocked with piles of boulders, lumps of fresh turf and recently ripped-out shrubbery.

No sooner had the men set about clearing the entrance to the concave space underneath the howff than a ghastly sight beheld them. It was a body. A dead human body coiled up in the foetal position. And it was dressed only in the traditional male undergarments of the times, a pair of long-johns and a vest, both splattered in mud.

Further clearing operations allowed closer examination, which soon revealed that the corpse was that of a young man. The horrific sight confronting the four men quickly demonstrated that the left-hand-side of the deceased's skull had been caved in from crown to temple, his spine shattered, and his face smashed to pulp rendering it completely unrecognisable. As the sergeant and his three henchmen prepared to secure the dead body on a stretcher for transportation back down to the local morgue, a second party of volunteers was directed to continue the search up the walking track towards the summit of the mountain, in an effort to detect any other evidence which might later provide possible clues as to the cause of the poor man's sorry fate. In the event, the party would discover a cap and a walking cane further up the slopes. Strangely, there was no sign of his outer garments, none at all.

And so began the mother-and-father of all police investigations. Almost immediately, it emerged that a gentleman with a cultured London accent, whom the police quickly established was Rose himself, had been seen by a total of five eye witnesses around 6.20 pm on Monday 15 July at the summit of Goat Fell, which was more than two weeks ago. Rose had been accompanied on his expedition by another young man who had introduced himself to the others as one John Allandale. Very strangely, though, none of the same eye witnesses had come across either Rose or Allandale on their descent back down the mountain, nor had anyone else for that matter.

The police also established that Allandale and Rose had booked a shared room in Brodick's Invercloy Hotel, and that Allandale had been seen buying some drinks in the bar of the Corrie Hotel, located some five miles distant, later that same evening around 10.00 pm. They also learned that Allandale had left his lodgings the following morning without paying his bill. He was then seen by a number of witnesses boarding the steamboat Scotia, destined for the port of Rothesay on the island of Bute. Allandale had a distinctive striped jacket draped over his arm, one which would later be shown to belong to Rose.

The two young men hadn't known each other for very long. Both had been holidaying on Bute, Rose staying in a grand 'hydropathic' hotel along with a few other friends, one of whom went by the name of Rev Gustavus Goodman, while Annandale had been cooped up in considerably less salubrious lodgings.

Both men were rather strange characters, and neither was quite what he appeared to be. Indeed, Annandale wasn't even Annandale. He was actually one John Watson Laurie, a simple 'pattern-maker' with Atlas Ironworks in Springburn, Glasgow. As for Rose, he was a rather camp individual who masqueraded as a 'swell', clad in white flannel trousers and a garish striped jacket, an image very much at odds with his position as a modest builder's clerk.

The pair had first met on a steamboat excursion a few days earlier, a recreational sailing from Rothesay to Arran. It was Rose who had approached Laurie in the first instance, asking him, 'Excuse me, but haven't I met you at the Hydro?' That was when Rose first set eyes upon the majestic outline of Goat Fell, and the sight had completely captivated him. He decided there and then that he wanted to climb the famed mountain, and he said so to Laurie, whom he still believed was called Annandale, principally on the evidence of the name cards he had been distributing to all and sundry from his silver card-case.

Despite warnings from his friends that Laurie appeared to be 'a nasty piece of work', citing quite spectacular mood swings from extremely brash to deeply sullen, Rose proceeded to accompany him over the next few days on a number of walks around Bute. It was on one such walk that they decided to sail over again to Arran to climb Goat Fell. On Sunday 14 July, they booked into their room in Brodick's Invercloy Hotel, in preparation for their expedition the following day. There they met a number of fellow hillwalkers on the way up the mountain, and again at its summit, which was the last time Rose was seen alive. The very next day, following his return sailing back to Bute, Laurie was spotted in the island's main town of Rothesay clad in those now-familiar white trousers, striped jacket, and sporting a yachting cap as well.

Almost as soon as the police manhunt was launched, Laurie disappeared from the face of the earth, leaving Rose's heartbroken family and the islanders of both Arran and Bute to wrestle with one huge conundrum. Did a tragic accident cause the likeable builder's clerk from London to fall to his death … or was he murdered by the decidedly odd ironworks pattern-maker from Glasgow?

Thus, the police were left with a great mystery to solve, and of course completely devoid of the high-tech forensic procedures and electronic paraphernalia that the force enjoys nowadays. Two possible scenarios presented themselves.

Scenario 1: Having by then spent quite a bit of time together walking the moors of Bute and the hills of Arran, and even having shared accommodation and sustenance, Laurie and Rose were getting on like a house on fire. The positive state of their relationship was evidenced by the casual observations of the eye witnesses who had met them on Goat Fell, and who had noted that the pair appeared relaxed and at peace with the world. However, rather strangely, none of the witnesses encountered either Laurie or Rose on their descent of the mountain. This suggested that they might have strayed away from the well-trodden footpaths and headed perilously close to the infamous ravine, either deliberately or inadvertently. There, they might have decided to attempt the risky manoeuvre of crossing the stream which runs through the notoriously slippery Coire nam Fuaran, at one of two exposed drops of ten feet and 32 feet respectively, as a result of which Rose plummeted to his death. Such a catastrophic plunge would almost certainly have accounted for most of his horrific injuries. Laurie, probably in shock, would then surely have clambered down the slopes to where Rose lay, only to find his companion dead. Still in a bit of a stew, but falling short of actual panic, Laurie, a young man with a proven track record of deception, then clocked his big opportunity to perpetuate his alter-ego identity. That opportunity was the acquisition of Rose's flashy clothes, which would enable him to masquerade as a fashionable 'dandy'.

Scenario 2: Outwardly at least, Laurie and Rose had indeed been getting on like a house on fire. However, it was a fire which was about to raze the house to the ground. Remember that it was Rose, the decidedly camp and openly garish fashion aficionada, who had initially approached Laurie with his rather inane rhetorical 'haven't-I-seen-you-before' question on the deck of a steamboat. One crucial question now seems obvious in today's more enlightened times; had Rose actually 'come onto' Laurie, either on the sailing across the Firth of Clyde or at any other time after the two men had become acquainted. Adding fuel to this more sinister scenario was Laurie's own family history, which suggested that he may have been suffering from some kind of mental illness, such as schizophrenia or bipolarity (known in those days as manic depression). Had Laurie then waited for his big chance and battered Rose to death with a rock, in some kind of homophobic temper tantrum? And if so, what better setting than at the top of a remote mountain, where he could then have stripped the London toff of his prestigious outer garments before flinging his prostrate body down the ravine and stuffing it under a giant boulder for Arran's flocks of kestrels and sparrow hawks to gorge upon?

In the glare of nationwide attention, Laurie succeeded in out-running a huge police manhunt for the best part of two months. However, on 3 September he was finally caught hiding underneath a thick copse of bushes in a stone quarry near the Lanarkshire village of Bogwood. As the police officers moved in, Laurie produced an open razor from his jacket pocket and appeared to start cutting at his throat, before he was overpowered and apprehended. When later questioned about Rose's death, Laurie readily admitted to theft but insisted that he did not murder him, a conviction he would continue to hold for the rest of his mortal life.

The much-awaited trial in Edinburgh High Court began on 12 November of that same year. Under the iron fist of a rather impulsive judge, Lord Kingsburgh, it lasted only two days. Laurie's own account of events was self-contradictory and unconvincing. Initially, he argued that Rose had met two other hillwalkers on the summit of Goat Fell and gone back down the mountain with them. He then claimed that Rose had slipped and plunged down the ravine to his death, and that he himself had later robbed his hillwalking companion of his garments, leaving the jury confounded as to how he could possibly have known of Rose's fall if he hadn't been with him on his descent. Furthermore, this version was somewhat at odds with Rose's horrific head and face injuries, and with the enormous effort that would undoubtedly have been needed to shove the corpse under the howff.

The problem for the Crown's case was that it relied almost exclusively on purely circumstantial evidence, principally around the nature and extent of Rose's cranial injuries, compounded by family history and behavioural reports which suggested that Laurie was a decidedly unstable young man. Indeed, the Solicitor General actually based the charge of murder on what he saw fit to call Laurie's 'conduct' and subsequent run from the law.

Very importantly, though, the court failed to establish the precise cause of death. From the outset, the Crown relied to a great extent on the evidence of Dr William Fullerton, a general practitioner from the Arran village of Lamlash, and Dr Andrew Gilmour who had been holidaying on the island at the time. Commendably, both medics had gone straight to the scene as soon as the body was unearthed, and each stated most emphatically in court that Rose's grizzly demise had been the result of blows by a blunt instrument to the head and face. Their account was backed up by that of Dr Henry Littlejohn, chief medical officer and police surgeon for Edinburgh, the net effect of which gave the Crown the ammunition it needed to argue that Laurie had battered Rose to death with a rock or stone. However, under pressure of cross-examination by Laurie's counsel, all three doctors then conceded that Rose's gruesome injuries could also have been caused by a fall, although that collective concession was subsequently refuted by the eminent Dr Patrick Watson, the Queen's surgeon no less.

Crucially, not a single drop of blood had been found on Laurie's clothes, nor indeed had any 'proper' evidence linking him to Rose's demise. Indeed, if there had been a murder, then the murderer had made no effort whatsoever to conceal two vital pieces of evidence, namely Rose's walking stick and yachting cap. In short, neither the Crown's contention that Laurie had murdered Rose, nor the defence's insistence that Rose had merely slipped and fallen were ever satisfactorily proven.

One huge irony remained, though, this relating to Rose's own walking boots, forensic examination of which would surely have provided the court with 'real' evidence reliable enough to point to the cause of his death. However, Rose's boots could not be produced as an exhibit, because an Arran police officer had buried them on a beach 'above the high-water mark', in enactment of a long-held Gaelic superstition that doing so would prevent the dead man's ghost from 'walking the hills' for all eternity.

And thus, in the sad absence of any tangible forensic evidence or persuasive witnesses, the terrible task of making such a momentous decision fell to the fifteen-strong jury. In the event, that jury, under the backbreaking weight of expectation from an impatient judge and a completely engrossed national audience, took a mere 45 minutes to deliver its verdict in line with Scottish law. That verdict was eight votes of 'guilty' to seven of 'not proven'.

Laurie's fate was sealed, and the judge passed his sentence. It was death by hanging.

'The Goat Fell Murder' had held the whole nation spellbound for many months on end, and such was the degree of frenzy on the day of announcement of the verdict, that the police had to be called to quell unruly crowds gathering around news vendors in umpteen locations around the land. No sooner had a date been fixed for Laurie's hanging than a petition began doing the rounds, demanding leniency for Laurie himself. In the face of the petition's tremendous support and taking account of the tightness of the eight-votes-to-seven verdict, the courts subsequently commuted Laurie's sentence from death to life imprisonment. It was a decision which infuriated many people south of the border, leading to several English newspapers hitting out at Laurie's reprieve, and claiming that he had only escaped the noose because his victim had been 'an Englishman'.

Laurie eventually passed away in Perth Prison's 'Lunatic Division', aged 69 and still protesting his innocence, having served a total of 43 years behind bars. Today, Rose's body lies in the old kirkyard in the village of Glen Sannox on Arran's north-east coast, buried 'in loving memory' underneath a mountain boulder.

This, then, remains the conundrum. Did Edwin Robert Rose plunge to his death in a tragic accident … or was he brutally murdered? And was John Watson Laurie a mere opportunist thief … or that same brutal murderer? Alas, we will never know for sure, and today 'The Goat Fell Murder' remains one of Arran's most enduring mysteries.

What is a lesser-known fact, though, is that another serious crime is reputed to have been committed more recently on the summit of Goat Fell. Well, when I say 'fact', perhaps 'folklore' would be a more appropriate term. This little tale is also loosely connected to the island's constabulary, so loosely in fact that no-one should ever feel the need to bother to check the criminal records. Anyway, who am I to doubt its authenticity from an esteemed island worthy, so here goes.

It concerns one of the research scientists who was a member of the world-famous team which cloned 'Dolly the Sheep' in Edinburgh University's famous Roslin Institute, and who allegedly later retired to the island of Arran. The story goes that before he hung up his lab coat, he secretly created an exact replica of himself through the same scientific process of cloning. Apparently, though, his clone turned out to be a rather nasty individual who always spoke to others in the most obscene and foul-mouthed manner.

This quickly became a real problem for the newly-retired scientist, who soon discovered that the clone was being mistaken for himself, resulting in many of his island friends and neighbours refusing to have anything more to do with him. Worse still, and as a result of the clone's disgraceful behaviour any time he was let loose in public, the scientist found himself having to resign from his local golf club and even suffered the indignity of being banned from the village hall.

The situation continued to deteriorate until one day he could take no more, so he decided to lure the clone up Goat Fell. It was a lovely summer's day and everyone walking up the mountain seemed to be in a very pleasant mood. Until, that was, they met the clone, who then proceeded to curse and swear at everyone and everything in sight. By the time the scientist and his identical clone had reached the shoulder of the famous old mountain and were preparing their final ascent up the scree-slope, the former's mind was made up. He had 'had it' and the clone was 'getting it'.

Once alone on the summit, the scientist suggested to his clone that he should take time to admire the glorious view over the cliff edge, which he did most reluctantly whilst standing there effing and blinding obscenities at everything in sight. Seizing his big opportunity, his exasperated creator took a big deep breath and shoved him off the cliff to his death. Unfortunately, this act of desperation was witnessed by a deer-stalker who was plying his trade at the time on the foothills of the neighbouring Cir Mhor, and who immediately reported the incident to the Arran police.

When arrested later that day, the scientist strongly protested his innocence and attempted to convince the police officers that, rather than commit murder, he had merely disposed of his own vile creation for the greater good of humankind. Unfortunately, the cops were having none of it.

'Sir,' the local sergeant said, 'you really don't seem to appreciate the seriousness of the matter. You are charged with making an obscene clone fall.'

And with that, I think we should probably move on to the next chapter.

The North Face

Corrie and Sannox

The four-mile drive from Brodick Castle and Country Park to the village of Corrie on Arran's north-east coast is the longest stretch of level road on the whole island.

As such, it is a perfect route for recreational cyclists, particularly those of a more physically-challenged nature, who on other sections of Arran's notoriously undulating coastal road might seriously struggle to emulate the energy-sapping exertions of the infamous 'lycra brigade'. You know the ones I mean, don't you? Those with the garish skin-tight clobber, pointy hats and protruding eyeballs, who appear to believe that a good day out means straining on the pedals over the island's gut-busting hills, sweat and snotters blinding them, faces contorted in agony. Give me a pie and a pint any day.

How fondly I remember those magical summer days many moons ago, when I would hire a couple of bikes in Brodick, one of child's size for my young daughter, Jillian, and the other an adult-sized contraption for yours truly complete with a little plastic seat welded behind my ample posterior to accommodate her toddler brother, Derek. And off we would set with great gusto along the flattish coastal road in the direction of Corrie, father and son leading the way, daughter in our wake, and mother at the rear of the procession in her Ford Cortina, her omnipresent smiles heavily disguising any wistful thoughts of what might have been if only that terrible disease had left her alone.

Eventually we would arrive puffing and panting at Corrie, where the first inhabitants to greet us would be a pair of donkeys, one of whom was unquestionably male, my astute scientific conclusion having been based on the fact that he had five legs (if you get my drift). Indeed, as I recall, every time we made our entrance into Corrie, whether on two wheels or four, that would traditionally become the very moment when my inquisitive daughter's inevitable questioning began.

'Daddy, what's that thing hanging from the donkey?' she would beseech me, seriously confounded.

'Ask your mother, lass, she's a schoolteacher,' I would respond courageously, before changing the subject.

Wonderful days. It all seems like yesterday.

The picturesque little village of Corrie is something of a paradox, both historically and geographically, as its rather unique profile will readily demonstrate the moment we arrive. While the main residential area of the present-day Low Corrie slumbers peacefully along the shoreline against a spectacular backdrop of 120-foot-high cliffs, there up on the former raised beaches of the clifftops stand the cottages of High Corrie, where their Neolithic, Stone, Bronze and even Iron Age predecessors once witnessed the mighty ocean waves crashing only a few yards beneath their feet. How times change, as many outstanding relics of Arran's fascinating history clearly testify, ranging as they do from innumerable ancient artefacts to a whole incredible array of cairns, standing stones, forts, burial grounds and such like scattered all across the island.

In more modern historical times, Corrie itself was spared somewhat from the worst excesses of the notorious island clearances, at least relative to many other local settlements, including its near neighbour, the charming little hamlet of Sannox. Such good fortune for Corrie was a consequence of the village possessing a much sought-after natural resource, the sedimentary rock that is 'sandstone'. In its white form, the sandstone was quarried from land above the village, while the more familiar red variety was hewn from behind the lower-lying terraced houses.

Also mined in the locale was a colourless crystalline mineral called barytes, which with its barium sulphate base is still used commercially today, principally in the oil and gas exploration industries as a weighting agent to suppress high-formation pressures and prevent gaseous blow-outs. Additionally, there were the village's famed caves, in which lay copious reserves of limestone, another sedimentary rock, this rich in calcium carbonate and therefore a vital source of calcium for animal feedstocks.

The same old limestone caves, nowadays largely stripped of their valued assets, have lain empty ever since, with all the inherent potential dangers that this presents, as the late and much-revered former leader of Arran's mountain rescue team, Stewart Lambie, recalled from a particularly treacherous rescue mission away back in 1969.

'Three schoolteachers decided that they would go potholing,' Stewart told me with a still-disbelieving shake of his head. 'And for good measure, they decided to take a wee dog with them. Bingo, his name was. Believe it or not, the party had gone into the caves armed only with candles for lighting. Inevitably, they dropped the candles, got split up in the darkness and ended up hopelessly lost down in the bowels of the caves. When they didn't return home, the alarm was raised with the local police, who called the coastguard and my own team. The cave network in Corrie is really extensive, with tunnels heading off here, there and everywhere. It was a lovely sunny day outside, but absolutely pitch black deep inside the caves. Just walking to the extremity of the caves took us almost 45 minutes. We had been down there for quite a while and things weren't looking too hopeful, until I suddenly noticed a pair of eyeballs reflecting from the beam of my torchlight, about a foot or so off the ground. They belonged to the wee dog, Bingo. He was very pleased to see us, that's for sure.

'Soon afterwards, we managed to round up the three teachers as well. They were all slumped wearily on the ground, with bewildered expressions on their faces. I asked them why they were just sitting there, rather than trying to find their way back out. One of them replied, "Well, I suppose we thought we'd just wait for daylight." Honestly, that's what he said.'

In days of old, Corrie was one of a number of regular stops for the Clyde steamers which routinely sailed a full recreational circumnavigation of Arran. Passengers were rowed ashore by means of a small rowing boat from what was called the Ferry Rock, located between the village's two adjacent and scenic little quays. The more southerly of the pair is called Sandstone Quay, where several large red sandstone rocks still stand today as a reminder of the halcyon days when this much sought-after building material was shipped to the Clyde ports and beyond. The more northerly is known as Corrie Port, which was traditionally used for assorted shipments to several harbourside locations around Arran and further afield on Scotland's mainland and more distant islands, normally carried by the famous Clyde puffers.

These days, the delightful little village of Corrie still retains its quaint rustic charm, but like all other locations on the island, its population tends to swell considerably during the peak months of the main tourist season, with the arrival of the perennial 'returners'.

Ann Pringle, whose family has been associated with the village of Corrie since the eighteenth century, was Chairperson of the Arran branch of the Scottish Women's Institute (SWI), formerly the Scottish Women's Rural Institute (SWRI), which itself was founded during the First World War in 1917. Ann is very well-placed to reflect on how the village, and indeed the island, have changed over the years.

'Back in the old days, Corrie really was a busy wee village. We had several shops, including a butcher, a grocer, a newsagent and even our own Post Office. We also had two milk-carts, and various vans would visit us daily, selling everything from fish, meat and fruit to hardware and medicines, although my family always grew our own vegetables in the garden. Corrie was always a hive of sea-based activity, with puffers and smacks coming in and going out all the time, carrying sandstone and limestone, and their precious cargoes of foodstuffs, fuel and other essential supplies. I remember one day, my Great-Uncle Donald's smack ran aground on some rocks, and among his cargo were tins of condensed milk, so rather than let them sink to the bottom of the sea and go to waste, he just drank them himself!

'When I was very young, our toilet was outside in the back garden, and our water supply came from a spring which had a tap attached to it. We had a "carbide" unit in the garden too, and this generated gas which was fed through a pipe into the house to give us gas lighting. Our cooking was done on an old solid-fuel Raeburn stove.'

'It's a strange thing, but even today Corrie still draws a lot of its youngsters back again. They leave school and go to university or college on the mainland, graduate and get a job there, but many then return to the island and settle down again in the village of their childhood. Probably, like me, they just think, "this is home".

'Tourism was always very important to the village and to the economy of the whole island, even as far back as the early part of the twentieth century. Corrie's big sandstone houses had smaller outbuildings at the back, and the local families would move into those so that the well-off tourists could take over the main houses for their holidays. I remember that Mister Burrell, of Glasgow "Burrell Collection" fame, used to holiday in Corrie every summer. And, of course, the geologists have been coming here for centuries, and I'm sure they'll just keep on coming back.

'So yes, the village has changed enormously since my childhood days, but it's still a real magnet for tourists. I'm immensely proud of Arran, you know. Proud of today's Arran, of the Auchrannie and Arran Aromatics and everything that represents what you might call the "modern Arran", but also proud of the many traditional little businesses and services that have survived over the years. Arran will always be home, and it will always be a wonderful place to live.'

A leisurely drive through the lower village and around the hairpin bends, then past the old caves, the twin quays and the little primary school/village hall will certainly test your steering wheel, if not your speedometer, after which you will emerge onto a level straight as the A841 hugs the coastline towards neighbouring Sannox.

Named *Sandvik*, meaning 'sandy bay', by the Vikings, you will immediately understand why, as the golden sands on your right-hand-side stretch northwards. Rising to your left lies the stunningly scenic Glen Sannox, where the remains of yet another of Arran's many Iron Age forts is located, as are the remnants of an old settlement which was abandoned in the early nineteenth century in the wake of the infamous clearances which decimated this beautiful part of the island. The old barytes mine suffered the same fate in 1862, when the 11th Duke of Hamilton had it closed, allegedly because its very presence offended his eye. However, it was reopened at the end of the First World War, and a railway and pier constructed for the extracted mineral's transportation, only for its supply to become exhausted in 1938, at which point the mine was closed for the very last time, the railway and pier being dismantled a few years later.

The well-signposted track to Glen Sannox can be found at the north end of the village. One of the most beautiful on the island, this is the glen which gave its name to the old and much-loved ferry now lying in ruin in the humid heat of the Middle East, and of course to the brand-new CalMac ro-pax vessel due to come into service shortly. A couple of hundred yards up the track lies Sannox churchyard, with its peaceful and well-manicured graveyard, in a small discrete section of which lie the remains of the aforementioned 'murder victim', Edwin Rose, protected by a stone replica of the 'howff' under which his battered body was found on Goat Fell all those years ago. Further on, the valley opens up to reveal the most wonderfully scenic countryside, the centrepiece of which is the crystal-clear Sannox Burn with its cascading falls and inviting pools. The site of the old barytes mines lies at the opening to the glen.

So, if it's a gentle hill walk through the most scenic slopes that you're after, then Glen Sannox is the perfect choice. However, if you prefer golden sand under your feet and glorious sea air in your nostrils, then please read on.

Sannox to Lochranza

The village of Lochranza lies at the northernmost tip of Arran.

It can be accessed from North Sannox by a memorably scenic drive over the steep contours of the island's most punishingly steep hill road, the Boguille, which climbs relentlessly beside the dramatic mountains and the eerie recess between their slopes, known as The Devil's Punchbowl. From this exalted vantage point, the enchanted tourist can marvel at red deer grazing on the heather slopes and birds of prey, including the occasional pair of golden eagles, swooping for doomed rodents, whilst beholding the glorious sight of the little village resting in the hollow beneath Glen Chalmadale, separated from the sprawling Mull of Kintyre only by the mighty ocean itself, with the blue-tinted outline of the island of Gigha far away in the distance.

However, there's an even better way to tackle this memorable journey, and that's to use the proverbial Shanks' Pony, expend a bit of energy and take in some of the island's most spectacular coastal scenery. So, if I may be so bold, might I suggest that you just pull on your walking boots, wrap up for Arran's somewhat less than predictable weather, stuff some sandwiches and a flask of tea into your rucksack, and get cracking.

My wife Nan's favourite place on earth is the picnic area on the beach at North Sannox. Never once in all the times we have visited that beauty spot has she ever even got out of her car, but she did once ask the late and sadly-missed Whiting Bay artist, Dorothy DeMay, to paint her a portrait of the scene as viewed from behind her own steering wheel. Today, that elegant painting hangs proudly in our lounge at home, so that whenever the mood demands, Nan can teleport herself back to her 'special place', with the waves lapping on the rocky shore to her left, the grassy picnic field and the rolling waters of the North Sannox Burn straight in front, and the dark imposing mountains of the Sleeping Warrior high to her right. Moreover, she has charged me with the rather daunting responsibility of one day scattering her ashes on that same spot. It is a day which I hope with all my heart will be a very long time coming.

Many who tackle this particular walk decide to start from the picnic area itself, which is well signposted from the main road leading north out of Sannox. However, in order to soak up the walk's full glory, I thought we might set off a bit further back at the car park just before the road-bridge at the north end of the village of Sannox.

Immediately to the right of this bridge over the Sannox Burn, you will find the timeless 'stepping stones', which unless the burn is in spate are very easy to negotiate nowadays, the wobbly boulders of old having been replaced a few years back by big concrete blocks which provide a much more secure footing. A hop-skip-and-jump will take you over the stepping stones in no time, although dogs may choose the aquatic alternative. You can then either walk along the pebbly bank of the burn's estuary or cut up through the gorse bushes onto a narrow footpath, both routes leading out onto the truly gorgeous golden sands of Sannox Bay.

A path then meanders northwards between the sand dunes and a few charming houses on your left, with the first of a series of large navigation masts marking the way, those having been originally constructed so that the lights on top could indicate 'the measured mile' to seafaring vessels sailing from the once-mighty Clyde shipyards, and hence enable them to establish their maximum nautical velocities. The same path winds its way through the ferns and past the Blue Rock, a high and near-vertical cliff-face with an odd-coloured blueish hue, which is often used by abseilers for recreational purposes, and by the Arran Mountain Rescue Team in their training exercises.

A few hundred yards along, and having emerged from a small wooded area, you will soon reach the North Sannox Burn, which if the water level is low enough can sometimes be crossed by means of a makeshift ford, although care would need to be taken to avoid unplanned plunges off slippery boulders (and the subsequent death-knell for your mobile phone when your backside hits the water). Alternatively, you can just follow the path up the side of the burn until you reach another road bridge, then cross over and walk back down the other side to the popular picnic site.

From there, a gate opens onto a rough vehicular track, where for the next couple of miles the views across the Firth of Clyde are truly superb, with the Island of Bute, the Cumbraes and the entire length of the Ayrshire coast stealing the show, while seals and fishing boats bob in competition, and a cacophony of seabird song gladdens your heart.

The track ends at a crude 'hammerhead' and continues along the seashore as a much narrower but still clearly-defined footpath. A few yards along, you will reach a deer fence which can be traversed through a large wooden gate. A few more and you will have reached the Fallen Rocks, a massive pile of very large boulders which many years ago are said to have rumbled down from the cliffs above to the shoreline below. Who 'said' so and whether in fact this event ever happened, I know not, but you must admit that it does make a quaint story.

Having woven your way through the boulders, the path then continues along the shore in a northerly direction for a good couple of miles, with the cliffs on your left punctuated by a number of small caves and one considerably larger, while to your right the glorious sounds of the ocean waves and birdsong are only momentarily disturbed by the sinister hum of the occasional little fishing boat. In due course, you will spot Laggan cottage in the distance, which as you approach ever closer will suggest that this very remote property is actually fully inhabited, thanks to its convincing little windows trimmed with neat curtains, but closer examination of which will soon reveal that those have, in reality, been painted on its stone walls.

Another footpath leads up the steep slope to your left behind Laggan cottage, which I understand is a somewhat shorter but much more taxing climb over the hills towards the village of Lochranza, although I must confess that I have never attempted that particular route. Continuing along the coastline path, you will soon reach the ruins of what was once a commercial salt-mining, panning and milling operation. At this point, the condition of the path begins to alternate between marshy and rocky, and an alternative route deviates onto the pebble-strewn beach.

Further on, you will pass a giant sandstone rock adorned by a waymarked signpost, which leads to the Cock of Arran, originally so-named for its resemblance to a cockerel's head, but sadly no longer recognisable as such. The long-abandoned Cock farm traditionally belonged to the Macmillan family, the two most famous members of which were Daniel Macmillan, who founded Macmillan Publishers, and his grandson Harold, who went on to become British Prime Minister in 1957.

Your next few hundred yards will be more of a scramble than a stroll, as the route climbs uphill over a few more boulders before taking you back down some graded rocky steps once more to shore level, after which the path levels out towards Fairy Dell, which was once the location of a small but fully functional fishing hamlet. You can then wade over the tiny burn, and taking care to avoid wandering off the beaten track, plough straight ahead. Soon you will reach Hutton's Unconformity, which if your memory is holding up, you will remember was the inspiration for renowned geologist James Hutton's revelation that Planet Earth was really an awful lot older than had hitherto been thought, as evidenced by the close proximity of the red sandstone and grey granite rocks which you are about to pass, each of which were originally formed during completely different geological 'ages' separated by many millions of years.

The coastal path then reaches Newton Point, by which stage you will have thoroughly deserved your rucksackful of sustenance and the glorious views across Loch Ranza towards the ancient castle and picturesque little village of the same name. And well done, you.

A Port of Refuge

Until relatively recent times, the very presence of the north-end's mighty mountains, rock formations and landslips, together with the imposing heights of the Boguille to the south-east and the Craw Brae to the south-west, made access to Lochranza from other parts of Arran very difficult indeed. Davie Crossley, who was born and bred in the south-west of the island, remembers those times with fond amusement.

'As children, we hardly ever went far from home, and the other island villages were like foreign places to us. There were very few cars back then, so if you had to travel anywhere at all, it was by bus. You just never went to places like Brodick, never at all. I remember as a wee nipper being told a story about a man from the south-end who had to walk all the way to some far-off place called Lochranza, which seemed an incredible journey to us. A few days later, he sent a telegram to his family which read, "arrived safely". That always fascinated me. Nowadays, I could get to Lochranza and back within the hour.'

Like all the island's villages, Lochranza possesses its own individual character and distinctive ambiance. In all probability, Arran's most northerly village will present to the unsuspecting visitor as a quaint and sleepy little place, one in which time itself seems to have stood still. However, it most certainly has not. Today's Lochranza is a village of contrasts, peppered with traditional old houses, a sprinkling of new holiday homes and assorted buildings of all types, perhaps the most notable of which sits on the driver's left-hand-side, the internationally famed Isle of Arran Distillery, officially opened in 1997 by Her Majesty the Queen, and about which more shortly.

A few yards further up on the right lies Lochranza's rather unique golf course, which if hardly the most challenging of the many spectacular equivalents across a nation that proudly calls itself 'the home of golf', certainly makes up for it in its choice of company. You see, Lochranza Golf Course, together with its adjoining campsite and restaurant, is populated by a herd of wild red deer, sometimes as many as twenty in number, which roam freely all the way from the first hole to the last, grazing on the lush green grass of the fairways and drinking from the quaint little Ranza Burn which runs beside a single-track road that dissects the course neatly in two.

It is this road which leads to Newton Shore, where long-time Lochranza resident and community stalwart, Gillian Langley, still resides today in her grand old house overlooking the magnificent sea loch, Loch Ranza. Gillian's grandfather once owned the field on which now stands the famous distillery. She vividly remembers the vibrancy of Lochranza back in the 'sixties and 'seventies, when the village was still in its prime.

'Back then, we had two churches, both of which were real hubs of the community, a total of five shops, and all the houses along Newton Shore had their very own ports, because in the old days sea fishing was absolutely central to the local economy. The loch was always littered with vessels of all shapes and sizes, from the huge steamers that sailed from Glasgow down to Fairlie on the Ayrshire coast and into Lochranza's old split-level wooden pier before heading off for Campbeltown on the Mull of Kintyre, to hosts of puffers, smacks, fishing vessels and rowing boats. These days, the loch is a much quieter place, although we are still a port of refuge for a good number of vessels which often head here for shelter in stormy weather.'

Gillian has witnessed many a wondrous seafaring sight in the loch over the years, easily the most spectacular of which occurred as recently as the summer of 2016.

'It was a beautiful summer's day, and I was leaning on the garden wall, chatting to my neighbour, when all-of-a-sudden I saw her jaw drop.' "Oh … my … God!" she gasped, as if she had seen a ghost. I felt the hairs stand up on the back of my neck. "What is it?" I said, not totally sure that I wanted to know the answer. "Gillian," she replied, gasping, "turn around to your right … but very, very slowly …" And there gliding silently into the loch was the bow of a huge private yacht. Now this thing wasn't just big, it was absolutely enormous, so much so that it even dwarfed our own CalMac car ferry. It turned out that the yacht was actually the biggest in the world at the time, owned by Russian tycoon Roman Abramovic, and reputed to have cost over £100 million. Apparently, it housed four helipads, various submersibles and even had its own missile defence system!'

Gillian, a former and famously tenacious community councillor who has fought long and hard for Lochranza's cause over the years, is insistent that the village's quiet peace and charm are its most endearing and enduring features. Which is probably why the rich-and-famous keep coming back, because on Arran the high-flyers are all treated as 'Jock Tamson's bairns', just like everyone else.

'As with every other village on Arran, Lochranza has moved with the times and warmly embraced the process of change, but it still retains its quiet, laid-back atmosphere. I'm sure that's why Mr Abramovic keeps coming here, because everyone just leaves him alone and gives him peace. Apparently, he has cycled around the whole island, and made a few visits to our local distillery. My neighbour had heard that he's something of a whisky connoisseur, and so one day when his yacht was in the loch she plucked up the courage to sail out in her kayak and asked his henchmen if she could speak to him. When he eventually appeared, she asked him if he'd be interested in seeing her malt whisky collection. A couple of days later, he visited her and bought the whole collection. And a very decent man he is too. One morning, a tourist was sitting on a child's swing taking a photograph of the yacht, when he fell backwards and thumped his head on the ground. A few minutes later, Mr Abramovic had sent over his own personal surgeon to attend to him. You see, on Arran, we treat people with respect, and it's nice when they respect our way of life too.'

Despite the occasional fleeting appearance of celebrities in Lochranza, Gillian Langley's abiding perspective of her beloved village will always be somewhat more modest.

'To me, Lochranza means red deer roaming on the golf course and rutting in the hills. Seals and otters swimming in the bay. Red squirrels in the trees. The Castle's reflection shimmering in the sea. And peace, perfect peace.'

Continuing our journey northwards, further along on the same side of the main coastal route rests the imposing ruin of Lochranza Castle, preening itself majestically on a little finger of land which stretches out into the shallow waters of the bay, waiting patiently to be accessed by the customary hordes of camera-laden tourists. Built in the thirteenth century by the MacSween clan of Western Isles descent, the once fully-operational old castle was converted some three centuries later to a stately tower-house residence, Arran's own Hamilton dynasty then acquiring it in the early 1700s.

Up until the end of the nineteenth century, Lochranza's compact inner harbour, with the grand old castle as its imposing centrepiece, was one of the busiest and most productive of its kind in the west of Scotland. In those days, the livelihood of local families depended on two main sources of income, crofting and fishing, both of which were very hard-earned, the latter being extremely perilous into the bargain. Alas, the dreaded clearances would bring crofting to its knees and render many families Canada-bound, while the virtual disappearance of herring from our local seas would leave the hardy local fishermen with no option but to seek employment with the Merchant Navy or on the substantial fleet of trading smacks and puffers which delivered general cargo around the various ports of the West Highlands and the Clyde.

Past the site of the castle, a couple of hundred yards will take you around a bend to the far end of the village, where the island's second ferry terminal delivers its continuous vehicle-and-passenger sailing service over to Claonaig on Kintyre, a journey time of thirty minutes, from which a short drive or a brisk walk will lead you into the picturesque little village of Skipness.

And if you think Arran is quaint and rural, you ain't seen nuthin' yet. It was in Skipness that I once saw a note sellotaped to the village's one-and-only shop window, which read, 'If anyone is going into town this week, could they please pick up Mrs McPherson's prescription?' Trust me, Skipness is quaint and rural.

Anyway, as far as I'm concerned, there can only be one good reason for heading overseas from Lochranza, however transiently, which is that the return sailing will allow you to really appreciate the sheer beauty of Arran. The spectacular sight of the Sleeping Warrior dominating the skyline, only this time as a dramatic mirror image of its better-known self, really is something to behold.

As with all other Arran villages, Lochranza's local economy and demographics have changed dramatically over the past century, principally as a consequence of the painful demise of the age-old vocations, crofting and fishing, and the introduction of that new breed of visitor to the island, the holidaymaker. Slowly but surely over the years, the working crofts and fishermen's cottages found themselves being replaced by boarding houses for the well-heeled tourist who wanted it all on the proverbial plate, leading to the construction of annexes and chalets which entire local families would make their temporary homes to welcome the self-caterer. Eventually a plethora of new holiday houses sprang up for those who could afford to build or purchase their summer retreats in this beautiful secluded village by the sea. Make no mistake, the impact of tourism on Lochranza itself and on the island of Arran in general, both over the years and still very much today, would be difficult to overstate.

As far as the loch itself is concerned, its once flourishing fishing fleet, numbering anything up to 100 vessels and 500 local men, has now been completely replaced by another of assorted motorised pleasure craft, ribs and rowing boats of all dimensions and descriptions. Bolstered, of course, by the umpteen private yachts which come scurrying inland to seek shelter from the hostility of the mighty ocean whenever a raging north-westerly storm is about to break. Those who still remember the old and gruelling days of kissing their hardy loved-ones goodbye as they headed off for a death-defying week on the mighty ocean waves, might now marvel at such modern-day progress.

There again, perhaps nostalgia might just have the last word.

Tales of the Sea

One man who well remembers the 'biz' in the port of Loch Ranza is much-revered retired island doctor, Alastair Grassie.

'One night in the middle of the busy summer season, I got word that someone had died on a yacht in the loch. So, I phoned a mate whose own boat was moored in the same bay, and I also got hold of one of the local undertakers. Both were a pair of real characters. We all arrived on the jetty at the same time, where we were met by a couple of joiners who had brought a temporary steel coffin along with them. The night was as black as the Earl of Hell's waistcoat, and we were aware that the bay was teeming with vessels. As we started sailing out into the loch, it suddenly dawned on me that not only had we not been given the name of the boat, but we didn't have the deceased man's name either. So, there we were, in the middle of the loch in the middle of night, shouting up at every boat we came to, "Excuse me, but do you happen to have a dead body on board?" After a good wee while, we eventually saw a light come on and a chap appeared, clearly very upset. He immediately confirmed that, yes indeed, the corpse was on his vessel. When we climbed aboard, it soon became evident that the poor man had suffered a sudden heart attack and plummeted down the staircase. It was so steep and narrow that his prostrate body was still lying there, his head facing downwards and his feet sticking up in the air, a real sight to behold.

'We had one hell of a job getting him into that coffin, I can tell you. First of all, two of us had to squeeze ourselves like contortionists down the stairs past his body. Then we had to turn him around and get him into a standing position. Next, we had to physically haul him up the steep staircase, then dump the body into the steel coffin. And all this while his relatives were sitting there crying their eyes out. Honestly, you couldn't have scripted it.

'Anyway, we eventually managed to put the coffin athwart my mate's boat, but it was a damned tricky procedure because there was a huge swell on the sea, and I had terrible visions of this big metallic coffin plunging to the bottom of the ocean with its grizzly contents, never to be found again. Somehow, though, we succeeded in getting the boat into the shallows, but we then had to wade in up to our oxters and haul the coffin to the shore, where the undertaker's van was sitting waiting. We were completely exhausted by this time, so we just deposited the coffin into the van.

'Since I was still on call, I drove straight home to Shiskine, but the others just high-tailed it back to my mate's house in Lochranza. He always kept a huge suitcase full of whisky under the bed, which was intended to be wheeled out for mourners' consumption at his own wake whenever he eventually popped his clogs. In fact, every time he went to the shop, he would buy a couple of bottles. "One for the suitcase, and one for masel'," he would say to the shopkeeper. So, needless to say, on that particular evening after the drama at sea, they all had a wee dram from the suitcase, and very well-earned it was too.

'Before they knew it, one wee dram had become two, then three, then quite a few, and night-time had become the following morning. Suddenly, somebody remembered that they had left the coffin in the van. It really was a scorcher that day, so the undertaker immediately drove down to the cottage hospital in Lamlash, and deposited the body in the mortuary, or the "bunk beds" as they were called in those days. Honestly, it could only happen on Arran!'

Davie McKinnon, former Station Master of the Arran Coastguard Service, also remembers a major incident in Loch Ranza, one which fortunately did not result in any fatalities, although quite how was more down to good fortune than good seamanship.

It was during the famous 'Tarbert Race' week, an annual sailing event each May which first started back in the mid 'seventies and has been staged every year since. It is one which combines passage-racing with Olympic triangles, and thus competition with a bit of fun and enjoyment for everyone involved. The port of Tarbert itself, resting on the west coast of Argyll, is the perfect venue for the event, providing a safe and sheltered anchorage for the usual armada of boats, and plenty of pubs for the sailors to wet their parched lips and exchange raucous stories after a hard day's work and play at sea, enriched as always by the inimitable 'craic' of the Irish contingent.

Davie recalls one year in particular.

'The Irish boys came over every year for the Tarbert Race. On this occasion, though, and for reasons best known to themselves, they sailed over with their yacht and accompanying cruiser to Largs on the Ayrshire coast. They arrived around late morning and immediately hit the pubs, where they remained until about seven in the evening, by which time they had decided to set sail for Tarbert, very much the worse for wear. Given their state of inebriation, they decided to chart a very simple course, which was to "sail straight out for an hour, and then turn right". Hardly a brilliant navigational strategy.

'Well, as you might expect, things didn't exactly go according to plan. The first bit worked out well enough, because they remembered to sail straight out from shore for exactly one hour. However, it was the second bit that they couldn't remember, and instead of turning right they turned left. Their boat eventually ran aground at Newton Shore in Lochranza. They then set off a flare and the Arran Coastguard Team was called to the rescue, so we duly arrived to oxter them off their boat, every one of them suitably plastered.

'One of our team members, who lived in Lochranza, then decided to take pity on them and offer them accommodation in his own bed-and-breakfast establishment, which they gratefully accepted. It wasn't until the next morning that he discovered they had polished off three bottles of his best malt whisky and scoffed a full fruit-cake that his wife had just baked.

'Mind you, after they returned home from the Tarbert Race they sent a cheque for £150 to the Arran Coastguard Team, so at least they must have appreciated our hospitality!'

The Spirit of Lochranza

You will allow me another moment of sentimental self-indulgence, won't you?

As I stand transfixed in the car park of Lochranza's internationally-renowned Isle of Arran Distillery, watching the latest batch of eager tourists alight from their air-conditioned luxury coach en route to a guided tour and whisky-tasting extravaganza, my pangs of nostalgia immediately take me back to one particular bus journey of my own. I was only eleven years old at the time, and it wasn't just any old bus journey. It was the bus journey from hell.

Do any of you happen to remember the dreaded school 'summer camps', which Scottish local authorities used to bestow upon developing young adolescents? Well, when I say bestow, I really mean inflict. For the fortunately uninitiated among you, Primary 7 children (eleven-and-twelve-year-olds) from each locale were afforded, by school geographical rotation as I recall, the wonderful opportunity to spend a fortnight in a prefabricated dump of a joint situated in the otherwise charming little village of West Linton, located near the city of Edinburgh. It would be good for us, we were told, and how our parents rejoiced at the wonderful social and educational development opportunities from which we would undoubtedly flourish, and the exhilarating thought of two whole weeks of peace without the kids, although not necessarily in that particular order of eagerness.

The West Linton summer camp was sold to us as a kind of custom-built, all-inclusive five-star holiday retreat, while in frightening reality it more closely resembled one of Joe Stalin's dreaded Siberian slave labour gulags, the only discernible difference being that our parents actually had to pay for the privilege.

It all began with that damned bus journey, a gruelling, sun-baked, four-hour torture session in a clapped-out single decker contraption, which as I recall, reeked intermittently of exhaust fumes and children's vomit. As the former freely administered potentially lethal carbon monoxide fumes into our developing young lungs, the latter was being sprayed variously in fine projectile fashion by at least half-a-dozen ashen-faced weans, courtesy of a kind but hopelessly naïve probationer teacher who was last seen handing out cartloads of her granny's homemade tablet. What an eejit.

Home for the entire fortnight was to be a large dormitory held together by sheets of corrugated iron lined with deadly asbestos, and adorned with row-upon-row of sagging bunk beds, which were to creak continuously through each night in fierce competition with the merciless cacophony of relentless snoring orchestrated by dozens of eleven-year-olds who were still waiting to be relieved of their inflamed tonsils and adenoids. A good night's sleep was most definitely not had by all. It was murder.

Which takes us to the food, a term I use very loosely on this occasion. I'm tempted to say that it was nothing to write home about, but to say so would be factually misleading. The thing is that I wrote home about it the very next morning, as did every one of my classmates, save for Butch McNabb who perceived the only practical use of a pencil as being an ingenious means by which to inflict great pain up the backside of whichever unfortunate soul happened to be sitting directly in front of his classroom desk. Three stomach-churned days later, a fleet of articulated lorries delivered several tons of food parcels to dozens of despairing weans, all of whom, like me, had been similarly nauseated by the burnt mince, curdled milk and rhubarb-infested custard with which we were being force-fed. The moment the lorries arrived, we rebelled and lived on homemade gingerbread, digestive biscuits and 'coo toffee' for the rest of the fortnight. It was brilliant.

Thus, we somehow managed to endure two whole weeks of cruel incarceration, heavily sucrose-fuelled but hopelessly sleep-deprived. If I actually managed of a rare evening to lapse into unconsciousness long enough to dream, I dreamt of a quiet bedroom and a fish supper. When I was eventually given a dishonourable discharge from West Linton, I slept for eighteen hours each day and ate for the remaining six.

Anyway, enough of this emotional self-flagellation, so let's join the smiling, camera-carrying, lip-smacking tourists alighting from the big luxury coach at Lochranza's much-lauded distillery, and find out what all the fuss is about.

The Isle of Arran Distillery was the brainchild of Liverpool-born, Second World War hero Harold Currie, who sadly passed away in 2016, aged 92. Much better known as Hal, the Legion d'Honneur recipient went on after the war years to enjoy a brilliantly successful career stretching several decades.

Allow me to give you just one little illustration of Hal's famed business acumen. In the early 'seventies, he was persuaded to join the board of Paisley's

St Mirren Football Club, which was propping up Scotland's second division at the time. Within months, he had been elevated to the position of club chairman and found himself faced with the crucial task of appointing a new manager. As the usual journeymen fired in their assorted CVs, Hal decided to take a chance on a young upcoming coach with very little managerial experience, but plenty of vision, confidence and guts. His name was Alex Ferguson. Suffice to say that this turned out to be an appointment which would do neither Currie's nor Ferguson's career any harm.

Hal Currie then became involved in the drinks industry and was soon appointed as Managing Director of the global giant, Pernod, which had just acquired House of Campbell, the Scotch whisky manufacturer. A few years later at an Arran Society of Glasgow dinner, a discussion took place regarding the island's historical association with whisky production. It was a discussion which sowed an exciting seed in Hal's entrepreneurial mind, leading him to team up with his architect friend and colleague, David Hutchison, whose family connections are said to have gone back several generations to an old illicit whisky still at Knockenkelly, a small hamlet situated high above the village of Whiting Bay on the east coast of Arran. Their brainchild? To design and build Arran's very own distillery.

Historically speaking, Arran has been synonymous with whisky production for centuries. Alas, this particular vocation did not always carry the proud mantle of complete legality. That having been said, the island did formerly play host to three distilleries which were fully licenced by the customs and excise authorities, the last surviving of which near the south-end village of Torrylinn had eventually to close its doors in the 1830s. However, back then the island's glens, nooks and crannies were liberally punctuated with illicit stills, from which many a poor-but-daring crofter would churn out his own particular brand of 'Arran Water', not only for his own personal delectation, but also to generate some much-needed additional income for his beleaguered family. And there at Arran's various ports and burn estuaries, the archetypally brazen amateur distillers would trade their wares for much sought-after commodities like tobacco, coal and salt, or on a particularly good day, for cash as well. No doubt, the Knockenkelly still would have been a very good case in point.

In more modern times and as the 1990s drew nigh, the teaming up of the revered businessman with such enviable connections in the drinks industry and the celebrated architect with strong island connections was a match made in heaven. Now, for those of you who would like to learn a lot more about Hal's and the distillery's fascinating journey, I would thoroughly recommend author Neil Wilson's excellent, fully-illustrated publication, *The Arran Malt: An Island*

Whisky Renaissance. Alternatively, if you can simply make do with a brief potted history from the pen of someone who knows considerably less about the manufacture of whisky than he does about its consumption, then here goes.

Isle of Arran Distillers Ltd was first registered on 11 November 1991. Arising from several years of sterling efforts by co-founders Hal Currie and David Hutchison in their valiant attempts to enlist the support of other shareholders and generate much-needed share capital, construction of the distillery was able to commence just before Christmas 1994. The following summer, whisky production started up while the construction works were still gathering pace, only to be temporarily halted again until the distillery was better positioned to deliver. Around the same time, a large portacabin was situated on site to operate as the distillery's interim 'visitor centre'. Attracting in excess of 20,000 visitors that summer, a second portacabin was immediately added to increase capacity.

The official opening ceremony of the highly-impressive permanent Visitor Centre took place in August 1997, with Her Majesty Queen Elizabeth II doing the honours amid a blaze of publicity. The following summer, the first whisky cask was opened by Scottish actor Ewan McGregor (who had just gained international fame from his brilliant depiction of Renton, the drugs-fuelled wide-boy in director Danny Boyle's searing film, *Trainspotting*).

By 2008, the Visitor Centre at the Lochranza distillery was attracting an annual 'footfall' of over 60,000, this despite the otherwise near-catastrophic effects of the global financial crisis that will forever be known as the 'credit crunch'. Two years later, and with the world's financial institutions still reeling from its dire effects and the assorted Jock Tamsons of the world taking the brunt of its crushing consequences, the distillery celebrated its fifteenth anniversary with unprecedented growth. That same summer saw the birth of the Arran Malt and Music Festival, which would go on to become a very popular annual event.

In 2014, the introduction of RET, and its consequential significant reduction in ferry fares, contributed massively to an enormous rise in the number of vehicles arriving at the Visitor Centre, the increased popularity of the facility leading to the centre deciding to open its doors on an all-year-round basis, very much in sync with the experience of many other tourist attractions and services across the whole island.

March 2016 then witnessed the very sad passing of Hal Currie, whose leadership and determination had driven the project forward from its humble foundations. Hal had realised his dream, and there is no doubt that his contribution to the island's economy has been simply enormous. How he would have loved to see the company's second operation come to fruition, a major 15-

acre development already well underway at Lagg, near the village of Kilmory on Arran's south-end, a mere stone's throw away from the site of the island's last legal whisky distillery. Work on the new Lagg Distillery commenced in February 2017 and the stills will produce spirit for the first time shortly, under the watchful eye of Master Distiller, James MacTaggart.

During the late-eighteenth and early-nineteenth centuries, this area of the island was a hotbed of whisky production, both legal and illicit. Fast-forwarding to today, the next chapter of the story of single malt whiskies produced by Isle of Arran Distillers Ltd will be 'Lagg Single Malt', a whisky heavily-peated in style and reminiscent of the original Arran whiskies which would have been produced all those years ago. The 'Lagg Single Malt' will be quite distinctive from the 'Arran Single Malt' already being produced at the distillery in Lochranza, and which is exported from Arran to over fifty countries worldwide. The casks at the new Lagg Distillery will be the first to be filled on the south-end of the island for over 170 years, representing a continuation of a long and proud heritage of whisky-making on Arran and an exciting new stage in the history of the company.

Faye Waterlow is the distillery's Visitor Centre Manager and Brand Ambassador. Having first joined the company in 1997, she is also its longest-serving member of staff.

'We now attract around 110,000 visitors each year to the distillery, and ever since the introduction of RET our numbers have continued to rise. People come here for a variety of reasons, principally of course to see how our whiskies are made and to sample these for themselves, but also quite simply because we are a very popular visitor centre on a very popular island, and we have excellent catering facilities where visitors can spend a pleasant and rewarding morning or afternoon. People love coming to Arran, which is now a genuinely high-quality holiday destination. Arran is the jewel of the Clyde, and we believe that the distillery is the jewel of the north-end.'

Faye's take on the willing synergy displayed by Arran's constituent businesses chimed closely with the view expressed earlier by former VisitArran chairman, Alastair Dobson. Her enthusiasm could hardly have been more infectious.

'We're an island on the up, and we're progressing and advancing all the time. There's a lot of talk these days about networking, but on Arran it's far more than talk. It's real, and it's about our local businesses and services working together to promote and market the island at home and further afield. Arran has never been more easily accessible from the mainland, hence our tag-line, "island time in no time", and the quality of the product awaiting our visitors is higher than ever. That's why we at the distillery always do our very best, not only to market our own brands but also to work closely with other island businesses to promote the island of Arran, our very own "Scotland in Miniature". And we always strive to contribute meaningfully to the island's many annual social and cultural events, like the Music Festival, "Santa's Sparkle" and the Highland Games. Sure, people visiting from the mainland and abroad want to sample our wares, our food and our drinks, and our various homemade products, but they want to meet real Arran people too, so it's important for us all to get out there and engage with them.'

So, there it is then, distillery tour done and 'Arran Water' duly sampled. And now, suitably refreshed and having negotiated the heights of the famous Boguille to savour the splendours of Lochranza, let's head for the equally imposing Craw Brae and enjoy Arran's dramatically rugged north-west coast.

The Twelve Apostles

Continuing our anti-clockwise circumnavigation of Arran, one thing you may have noticed is just how infrequently you have required to consult your map of the island for directions. Probably, never.

Indeed, by now you will have discovered that your much-treasured, state-of-the-art 'Sat Nav' is about as much use as a snowplough in the Bahamas. All of which is a shame, really, because a decent proportion of visitors to the island hail from the big city, whether that city happens to be in Scotland, south of the border, the European continent or even further afield, and where the same high-tech contraption is deemed to be more vital to human survival than oxygen itself.

And, let's face it, no wonder. I mean, have you ever tried driving in the Midlands, or worse still, in the city of London? Take the British road-numbering system, for example. The country's motorway grid is relatively easy to understand, I'll grant you that, even for a geographically-challenged bozo like myself (although I once famously ended up in Liverpool when I was supposed to be taking my two young children to a birthday party in Rochdale, 42 miles along the dreaded M62 but in the diametrically opposite direction).

No, it's the 'radial route' system which utterly confounds me. Apparently, the six main routes in England and Wales are numbered in order of decreasing importance to their relationship with London, while the three principals in Scotland relate to Edinburgh. Thus in the former, by way of illustration, the A1 runs from London-to-Edinburgh (otherwise known as the Great North Road) and the A6 from Luton-to-Carlisle (also referred to as the A1081, believe it or not), while in the latter, the A7 runs from Edinburgh-to-Carlisle, and the A9 from Falkirk-to-Scrabster (I kid you not). And that's the easy bit. Now get ready for the hard bit.

The single-digit main radial A-routes, nine in total, most of which also possess either alternative numerical designations or pet names (or both), are then supplemented by a whole plethora of double-digit, lesser in status but still commercially important 'trunk routes', which are not centred on London or Edinburgh, but whose number locates them 'radially clockwise' from the parent single-digit route. Then we come to triple-and-quadruple-digit A-routes, and further onwards to the B and C-routes and their countless hopelessly-disorientated offspring, the numbers and complexity of which increase rapidly to exponential proportions, until no self-respecting motorists really know where they are, or even why they have been placed on this planet. And so, it's all left to that great god of the modern motor car industry, Sat Nav, to discombobulate the whole sorry mess and explain existentialism to the bewildered urban driver.

Are you still following all of this? Excellent!

Because it takes us nicely back to Arran (you do remember Arran, don't you?), and to its somewhat less complex road network, which is … well … the A841.

Yes, the A841, the whole 56 mile (90 kilometre) coastal route around the entire island. Which is, of course, why you no longer need a map to get to your destination, let alone your precious Sat Nav. Mind you, to be totally accurate and thereby make a ridiculously simple transport system appear slightly more convoluted than it really needs to be, it is true that a 30 mile (48 kilometre) stretch of the circular road around the island's west and south coasts was declassified in 2007 to C-status, and re-designated as the C147. Factor in the two cross-island routes as well, the 12 mile (19 kilometre) 'String Road' from Brodick to Blackwaterfoot and the 9 mile (15 kilometre) 'Ross Road' from Lamlash to Sliddery, and you might need the bloody thing after all. But not very much.

So now that I've got that out of my system, let's chuck the offending Sat Nav out of the car window and into the choppy waters of Loch Ranza, and head from Arran's most northerly outpost down towards Catacol, a tiny village whose name in the Old Norse language literally means 'gully of the cat'.

As will become strikingly evident once our journey continues, the island's north-west coast presents a totally different outlook from its north-east. Peaceful and serene, the views across the Kilbrannan Sound towards the long, finger-shaped Kintyre peninsula are magnificent. From the forest-lined seaside village of Skipness at the north of the Mull (and let's hope that dear old Mrs McPherson has got her prescription by now), then panning southwards past the secluded little fishing port of Carradale and its much larger harbour-town neighbour of Campbeltown, and finally all the way down to the sandy shores of Southend at its very foot, the panorama from Arran's west coast on a clear day is simply jaw-dropping.

I have holidayed in Kintyre only once before, and that was many years ago in a wooden chalet on the shore at Carradale, accompanied by my two loyal Labrador Retrievers, Meg and Tanna, both now sadly departed from these mortal plains. There we spent a few delightful days in the picturesque little village, hiking over the hills and through the heather by day, and relaxing on the porch of our seaside abode each evening, tucking into the harbour's daily catch of fresh fish, the three of us contentedly exhausted from our exertions.

It really was the perfect little weekend break, one minor but frustratingly omnipresent distraction apart. Straight across the sea from our wooden chalet lay the island of Arran, with the tiny village of Catacol glistening in the sunshine, dwarfed from above by the unmistakeable majesty of the Sleeping Warrior, the glorious sight of which just kept me asking myself over and over again why I was 'here' rather than 'there'. Like so many beautiful locations on Scotland's magnificent west coast, the Mull of Kintyre possesses its own distinctive warmth and charm. However, to me, Arran is Arran, and nowhere else comes even close. Quite simply, the island is like one huge magnet, its pull as irresistible as gravity itself.

The drive from Lochranza down to Catacol takes no time at all. The road skirts the pebbled shoreline all the way, and at high tide you might be forgiven for thinking that the sea is about to lap around your tyres. In fact, many an island motorist has actually witnessed that particular phenomenon, when on a really stormy day the mighty ocean waves have been known to sweep up over the road itself, carrying with them a decent assortment of the shore's boulders and pebbles. Yes, the island's climate may often be considerably warmer and sunnier than that of the mainland, but trust me, when it blows on Arran, it blows.

Catacol itself – and I do hope the locals will forgive me here – is essentially a row of quaint little houses and one hotel situated along the coastal road and facing straight out to sea. Intriguingly named the 'Twelve Apostles', those same houses were built away back in the mid-1860s to cater for the families who lived in an old clachan at the top of the Abhainn Bheag. Each of the cottages had a different and uniquely-shaped first-floor window constructed, to enable the housewife to signal by candlelight to her fisherman husband out at sea, a sign he would recognise by the shape of his own window. Sadly, the same families later found themselves herded out of their homes in the aftermath of the clearances, after which they decided to disperse in protest to various other locations all over the island in search of alternative employment, rendering the row vacant for many years.

Nowadays, the Twelve Apostles play host to locals and holidaymakers alike, their ancient simplicity defining the laid-back ambiance of this charming little hamlet, in stark contrast to the modernity of the enormous but thankfully well-concealed undersea power lines just down the road, which deliver the entire island's electricity supply direct from Argyll's Loch Sloy hydro-electric power station.

Catacol and its Twelve Apostles remain the very definition of the island's rugged north-west coast.

Loch Tanna … and Disorientated Octogenarians

Just south of Catacol, adjacent to a large private residence called Fairhaven House, lies the starting point for one of my own very favourite walks on Arran, the trail up to Loch Tanna, the island's largest and most remote inland loch.

It is also a loch which I have ascribed to be the 'spiritual home' of my wonderful big Labrador of the same name. My beloved Tanna died in my arms one chilly spring afternoon on Arran a couple of years back, and until I started writing this book I simply had not been able to summon the courage to retrace my steps up to that beautiful spot. I suppose my memories of Tanna rampaging gleefully over the rocky terrain and plunging into the crystal-clear pools of the Abhainn Mor were still much too fresh and raw.

And thus, it was with considerable emotional trepidation that I set off from the roadside signpost, marked 'Gleann Diomhan/Loch Tanna', one bright and breezy late-autumn afternoon in 2016, accompanied by my latest pair of canine soulmates, neither of whom will ever replace the inimitable Tanna, but both of whom will always be similarly cherished.

The first part of the walk is remarkably flat, exceptionally scenic and deceptively gentle, deception being the ominous byword. Very soon, the path, which is clearly waymarked from the outset, begins to rise gently over the heather-covered and rock-strewn land before opening up into the imposing Glen Catacol, from the entrance of which can clearly be seen the much more demanding ascent that lies ahead. Put another way, a leisurely stroll in the meadow is about to become a taxing hike up the mountainside. Believe me, though, the whole adventure will be well worth the effort when you arrive at your destination in a couple of hours' time.

What is particularly striking about the walk up to Loch Tanna is the suddenness with which the character of the terrain changes so dramatically, and indeed so often. Relatively gentle slopes on the adjoining hillsides soon transmute to steep climbs, grassy plains to stones and boulders, and Abhainn Mor's gentle streams to cascading rapids, the most spectacular manifestation of which is the glorious Allt nan Calman waterfall, underneath which lies a deep pool of the clearest and purest spring water you will ever have the good fortune to behold. Each time I do this walk, I end up wishing that I'd been raised a keen swimmer rather than a hydrophobic wimp, allowing me to splash like a gannet into that big pool along with the dogs, instead of simply ogling at them in envy from the safety of the banking.

Eventually, after a really stiff climb up an undulating path which never leaves the burn's side, the terrain begins to level out and you will soon come to a cairn, onto the apex of which tradition and superstition demand that you must, of course, place a small rock of your own selection. A gentle walk of a few hundred yards further along and Loch Tanna will then come into view, its clear waters and golden shores wallowing in majesty in the shelter of the bowl-shaped hillsides, with the peaks of Beinn Tarsuinn and Beinn Bhreac in the distance. A slightly boggy final few yards will lead you to the sands on the shore of Arran's most spectacular hill loch, one so large and distinctive that it can clearly be seen from passing overhead aircraft making their descent into Glasgow International Airport, surely the ultimate contrast between technology at its most advanced and nature at its most serene.

Once on the sandy beach of the loch, you will have earned the right to dump your rucksack and ceremonially demolish whichever feast of food and drinks that tickle your fancy, as many a local and visiting hillwalker has felt the need to do after their own exertions. Incidentally, the hardier among them have also been known to resort to skinny-dipping in the loch and sunbathing similarly attired on the sand, in the confident knowledge that Arran's bus service doesn't extend quite that far off the beaten track. However, if you do decide to follow suit, just keep one eye on the hill path for unwelcome gate-crashers, and the other on the heavens above for nosey air passengers armed with high-res binoculars.

As with all other walks on Arran – and I am certainly no expert here - you would be well advised to check out the weather forecast in advance, because things can get rather tasty up there in the hills, even in the summer months. And one other thing. Do allow yourself enough daylight to get there and back safely (four hours absolute minimum for this walk, I would say), about which please allow me to regale you with a little tale.

One early evening during the October school holiday week a few years back, I was making my descent from Loch Tanna with my dogs, when I happened to spot a couple of people in the distance walking up in our direction, and very slowly at that. I looked at my watch and noted that it was just after six o'clock. When our paths began to converge about half-an-hour or so later, I noticed that they were rather elderly (I'm guessing early-eighty-somethings) and dressed as if they were going to a church service rather than about to climb up a mountain. He was wearing polished flat shoes, a suit, shirt and tie, with a golf umbrella under his oxter, while she wore rather dressy shoes, a raincoat and a leather handbag draped over her arm. We exchanged the usual pleasantries, they in their deep Yorkshire accent, me in my even deeper Ayrshire, and the dogs barking for aural superiority. Reminding myself of the lateness of the hour, I decided that it might be sensible for me to enquire politely where they might be going.

'Oop to top of t' mountain, lad!' the old chap exclaimed enthusiastically, as if they were about to conquer Everest.

Now, believe me, I am most certainly in no position to proffer advice to hillwalkers or anyone else on any matter of an even remotely practical nature, but one of the few technical skills which I have managed to pick up along life's way is a surprising competence in telling the time. (Incidentally, I can also tie my shoelaces, although I often need to ask my wife to unknot them for me.) However, that evening, I had this awful vision of Ali Hume and his mountain rescue cronies getting the dreaded call in the middle of the night, and having to confess to them afterwards that I could have prevented this whole impending disaster. So, I decided to tell the old couple that although I admired their pluck, I thought their strategy was somewhat flawed, my reasoning being that it would be dark by about half-eight, and that at their pace they would be doing very well to reach the loch by midnight, let alone commence their descent back down to the car park.

The lady promptly agreed, leaving her husband and erstwhile leader to hum-and-haw for a bit, before eventually coming to his senses. In explanation of his folly, he then informed me that they always had themselves 'A nice little walk oop t' hill to t' cemetery at 'ome, after tea', and he had clearly thought that a similar jaunt up to the remotest hill loch on Arran would have been a like-for-like replacement. As it happened, it took me another full hour-and-a-half to escort them back to their car, by which time he had stumbled twice and fallen once, she had broken the heel on one of her shoes, darkness was already descending, and the dogs were so ravenously famished that they had devoured several kilograms of sheep-shit in *lieu* of their eagerly-awaited dinners.

The moral of this story? If you're going to climb up to Loch Tanna, do it in the daylight. Especially if you happen to be a naive octogenarian with a Yorkshire accent.

'The Dark Side of the Moon'

Next up, a delightfully relaxing journey by car takes us past the rather secretive clachan of Thunderguy, and further on down the west coast towards the village of Pirnmill.

As with most of the island's seaside villages, its homes are built along the coast, the majority with stunning sea views, doubtless in deference to the traditional source of their financial and nutritional livelihood. From the beginning of the twentieth century to around the conclusion of the Second World War in 1945, the thriving but exceedingly hazardous industry that was herring fishing sustained the local families fairly adequately. However, this was in effect a mainly seasonal vocation, the fishermen voluntarily suspending catches from January through to April each year while the herring were spawning, thereby imposing their own astute conservation regime to help sustain the fish population.

The inevitable did, of course, eventually transpire and the numbers of fish began to dwindle, rendering very hard times indeed on the local families. Thankfully, this rather sombre turn of events coincided with the increasing availability of sea travel by steamer and the consequential popularity of Arran as an attractive holiday destination, which served to allow the same families, along with many others across the island, to redefine themselves as providers of accommodation and resources for well-heeled tourists. 'Summer houses' were constructed in back gardens, into which families retreated for the tourist season, with the holidaymakers occupying the main residencies usually for a whole month at a time, and often 'with service', which meant that cleaning and even catering could be provided at a small additional cost.

Scattered around the village of Pirnmill, which itself houses a primary school catering for all the young children living in the island's north-west, are a number of former clachans. From Lenimore, Thunderguy and Auchamore in the north, to Banlicken, Imacher, Whitefarland and Altgolach in the south, to the original settlement of Penrioch above the village, most have proudly retained their ancient place-names.

Liz Dale, a Machrie farmer's daughter, is a long-time resident of these parts. She was born in Lamlash hospital during the Second World War, her dad having to hire a car to take his expectant wife to the delivery room, before returning immediately to milk his cows. Once his chores had been completed, he then headed for the nearest telephone box to find out if he had become a proud father, only to discover that every phone on Arran was down because the British Commandos were conducting a major training exercise on the island at the time. Undaunted, he then hired the same car again and drove back to Lamlash to hear the good news first hand, and greet his new baby daughter.

The deployment of Arran as a wartime commando training ground is probably a lesser-known fact. The island was chosen by the military top brass because of its undulating and at times inhospitable terrain, perfect for the gruelling training exercises that those brave hand-picked young men would have to be put through before they could be let loose on their 'Special Ops' missions across Europe and North Africa. There on Arran's mountains, glens and shores, the commandoes would be pushed to their physical and psychological limits and beyond, before practising every killing technique imaginable, from machine-gun assassinations to brutal knifings and even hand-to-hand slaughter. Frequently-used loci included the tough mountain slopes of Goat Fell, Beinn Nuis and Cir Mhor, which would be mastered on foot and at ridiculous speed, and the often-stormy waters of Catacol Bay on the island's west coast and both Brodick Bay and Clauchlands Point on its east, where the commandoes would secure beach-heads from small amphibious landing craft.

As a tiny baby at the time, Liz Dale would be blissfully unaware of the violence of war which was exploding all around the continent when her parents brought her home to the quaintly rural environment of Machrie, situated on Arran's rugged west coast, where she would live for nineteen more years before moving up the coast to Pirnmill.

Liz is clearly proud of her adopted home village's fascinating history and heritage.

'The village got its name from the old mill and the 'pirns' it manufactured, wooden reels for the thread industry which was positively booming in the city of Paisley. When a sufficient number of pirns were ready, a flag would be hoisted at the mill, and the ferryman – who just happened to be my dad's cousin - would row them out to the steamers headed for the Clyde. He would also pick up any passengers for Arran, and row them ashore.'

The young Liz Dale would receive her education first in Pirnmill Primary School, and then as a consequence of the local authority (Bute County Council) redefining Arran's school delineation arrangements, in Shiskine Primary School. In those days, progression to secondary school for the island's children was far from straightforward. Sure, Arran had its own 'junior secondary' establishment situated in the east-coast village of Lamlash, but that facility catered for years S1, S2 and S3 only, after which pupils aged fifteen would leave school and seek employment. On the other hand, those who had previously managed to fare particularly well in 'The Quali' – the Scottish education system's dreaded 'Qualifying Examination' which unashamedly split eleven-year-olds into various groups according to academic ability alone – had a few other options available to them.

First there was the highly-regarded Rothesay Academy on the island of Bute, where the council's administrative centre was located, all schools on both Arran and Bute managed by the same education authority. Then there was Ardrossan Academy near the seaport of the same name on the other side of the Firth of Clyde, but which was operated by Ayr County Council, and therefore incurred a rather convoluted financial arrangement between both councils, known nowadays as 'inter-authority fees'. Next there was Keil School in the town of Dumbarton, situated on the estuary of the River Clyde, an independent fee-paying school for boys only which would have to wait until the more enlightened next millennium to progress to co-educational status.

Liz, whose late father, Donald Craig, is understood to have been the last-remaining native 'Arran Gaelic' speaker on the island and who actually couldn't speak a single word of English until he first went to school, was offered a place in Rothesay Academy, a real feather in any young Arran lady's cap, if one seriously fraught with the practical difficulties and emotional insecurities of being forced to leave her island home at such a young age.

She remembers those days with crystal clarity.

'I'll never forget the first day I left home for Rothesay Academy. Standing there on the deck of the boat and waving goodbye to my family, in the awful knowledge that I wouldn't see them again for several months. It was a very difficult day for all of us. I was sure I'd be terribly homesick, and that was exactly how it turned out.

'There were no hostels in those days. Rothesay was a busy tourist destination in the summer months, and so there were lots of boarding houses, several of which would serve as my term-time homes over the following five years. We always left Arran on the Sunday, most of the island's pupils sailing from Brodick to either Fairlie or Ardrossan, depending on the time of year, then travelling by bus a few miles up the coast to Wemyss Bay, where we would catch the ferry over to Rothesay. Occasionally, during the summer months, the pupils from the north corner of Arran would take the Lochranza steamer, the *Duchess of Hamilton*, a longer sailing which after a few other ports of call would take us straight into Rothesay.

'There were three school terms, August till Christmas, New Year till Easter, and Easter till summer, and each term meant a long time away from home. There were very few telephones in those days, so I just kept in touch with my family by writing letters, and it was great when there was one lying there waiting for me when I got back to my digs. It was always very sad leaving Arran, but tremendously exciting when the time to return home drew near.

'My very first morning in Rothesay Academy will always stick in my mind. There I was as an eleven-year-old, standing with the massed ranks in the school playground and listening to all the first-year pupils' names being read out by the assistant headmaster, who was called Nelson Blair. Everyone's name, that was, except mine! As I stood there in shock, Mister Blair spotted my predicament and came over to sort it all out. I can't tell you how relieved I was.

'In my first boarding house, I stayed with three other Arran girls, all of whom were senior pupils at the school, and they immediately took me under their wings. That was very reassuring for me, and their guidance and friendship really helped me to settle in. We're still good friends today and we still meet up regularly. One year, the school got burnt to the ground, and we ended up being taught in places like church halls, the local primary school and so on, but we all lived to tell the tale!

'I have mixed memories of my various boarding houses over the years, but the last one I lived in was wonderful. After leaving school I kept in touch with the people who owned it and we became very good friends. Looking back at those days, I suppose it was quite tough being away from my home and family for so long and at such a young age, but I did receive a very good education and I think it helped me to grow quite quickly as a developing young adult.'

Back on her beloved island of Arran, Liz still remembers the quaint simplicity of her formative years,

'There was no mains electricity in those days, and we had to use oil-based *Tilley* lamps. We still keep the *Tilleys* to this very day. In fact, they came in very handy during the "Snowmaggedon" crisis in the winter of 2013. One of my most vivid memories was the "big switch-on" back in 1950, when the Brodick generator finally kicked in. I will never forget that night, standing up on the hillside and watching all the houses and barns suddenly light up. It really was a spectacular sight.'

There is, though, one rather interesting paradox about the wider perception of Arran's west coast, as Liz explains.

'We're often referred to as "the dark side of the moon", but that suits us just fine and we'd like to keep it that way! We don't have many indigenous villagers left these days, mainly former holidaymakers who have made their homes here now, but it's still a great wee village. We have a Post Office, a licensed grocery and a very good restaurant called The Lighthouse, so we all manage just fine, thank you very much. And, of course, we have the best sunsets you will ever see. You couldn't tell that I used to be a tourist officer, now could you?'

The village and its immediate environs are also blessed with a rich, if perhaps understated ancient history. Indeed, several archaeological digs have revealed various treasures dating back to the area's earlier association with the country of Ireland, and even as far back as the Bronze Age.

All in all, the west coast of Arran might well be considerably quieter than its much more commercialised east. However, as any self-respecting astronaut will tell you, there's a lot more to the dark side of the moon than you might think.

4

The Wild West

From Amen Corner to Machrie Moor

You may have heard the name Ben Hogan. There again, you may not.

I suppose it all depends on whether you are a golfing enthusiast or whether you prefer to agree with American author Mark Twain that spending an afternoon hitting a little ball with a big stick constitutes 'a good walk spoiled'. You may also be wondering just what the devil this has got to do with a book about Arran. Patience, please.

As most *aficionadas* of the sport will readily confirm, Hogan was one of the greatest professional players of all time. He was also a renowned playboy, or in his own (slightly sanitised) words, 'If you're not thinking about (sex), then you're just not concentrating'. Widely recognised as the creator of the perfect golf swing, the popular and debonair Texan pin-up boy won all four Major Championships, and nine in total, including the US Masters at Augusta National in Georgia, the US Open at Oakhills Country Club in Omaha, the US PGA at Portland in Oregon and the British Open at Carnoustie in Angus.

And now, here comes the rub. You see, the mighty Ben once actually plied his formidable trade on Arran – on Machrie Golf Course, of all places - a fact to which various photographs on the wall of the adjacent tearoom will enthusiastically attest. So now you know.

Quite what the Texan superstar made of the whole experience, though, one can only imagine. My guess is that he would have loved every minute of it. Temporarily relieved of the artificially-designed azalea-clad greens of Augusta's infamous 'Amen Corner', and the similarly-fashioned gorse-lined fairways which hug Carnoustie's much-feared 'Barry Burn', Hogan may well instead have gawked in astonishment while one of the local sheep trotted off with his precious golf ball (not a particularly common sight at Augusta National, I understand). However, no matter what really did transpire during his round of golf that day in Machrie, I'm certain he would have been completely blown away by the raw beauty and peaceful serenity of his surroundings.

The name Machrie refers not just to the tiny hamlet itself where the golf course resides, but to a fairly large geographical area spread along the island's rugged west coast, comprising four separate districts known as Tormore, Auchengallon, Auchencar and Dougarie, the latter comprising a large country estate whose centrepiece is the resplendent Dougarie Lodge, originally built by the Dukes of Hamilton, but owned in modern times by the Gibbs family, who facilitate shooting parties during the season. Sadly, at the time of writing, Steven Gibbs, the much-respected elderly head of a family which has done so much for the island of Arran, had just passed away.

Historically, the Machrie area had its roots in farming, with sheep and beef its main produce, and it was always a veritable hive of activity. In bygone days, the *Queen Alexandra* and various other Clyde steamers would draw up offshore, to allow their passengers to be rowed ashore in a tiny custom-made ferry, whether to conduct their business, participate in recreational activities or simply return from afar to their rural abodes.

Well-known local resident, Iris Mansfield, and her husband-to-be, John, first came to Arran in 1957, from a farming background in the Dumfriesshire town of Langholm. The couple got married on the island, took a tenancy at Auchencar farm in Machrie, and promptly purchased their first double-seated tractor for the princely sum of thirty quid, this to enable them to work the land and care for their 250 sheep and 40 cattle. Soon afterwards, they bought Balgowan farm in neighbouring Shiskine, where they kept their breeding cows in a barn during the harsh winter months, as Iris recalls.

'We walked the cows from Shiskine to Machrie in the spring, then back again to Shiskine in the autumn, always very early in the morning so that our procession wouldn't hold up the ferry traffic or the school bus. We had many willing helpers, whose job it was to stop the cows from wandering through the numerous open gates and emptying the local gardens. And, of course, we quite often ended up with more cows than we started out with, because some others from neighbouring fields would decide to join the party and we'd then have to return them to their rightful owners the following day.'

Iris, now retired but still a very active member of the local community, is rightly proud of the business that she and her late husband built up. Arising from their experience in the 'tanning' industry back in their Langholm days, the Mansfields were persuaded to try their luck at producing and selling sheepskin rugs on Arran, which they originally made and marketed from their own farmhouse. Building on their early success, they then converted the old cattle byre into a shop, which still flourishes to this day along with a sister outlet in Brodick. The Auchencar complex now also houses Café Thyme, a very popular eastern-European-themed restaurant which was the brainchild of Iris's daughter and her Turkish-born husband. Business aside, though, it has always been the distinctive peace and calm of the island's west coast that Iris cherishes so dearly.

'Arran is a lot more commercialised nowadays, particularly with the tourist industry doing so well. However, Machrie still retains its uniquely quiet and peaceful character. We're an exceptionally sociable little community, you know, and it's a wonderful place to live, work and visit.'

As any self-respecting American superstar would happily confirm.

Stone Circles and Spiders' Webs

One of Machrie's greatest claims to fame derives from the ancient mystique of its iconic stone circles, believed to have been built during the Bronze Age (4,500 – 2,000 BC), with its other huge megalithic monuments following suit up until around 200 BC. The circles and individual standing stones, formed primarily of granite and red sandstone, and recorded and numbered in 1861 by one James Bryce, are thought to have replaced earlier wooden structures which decayed over time. The whole area is steeped in ancient history, and its atmosphere is deep and intense with the sanctity of long-lost souls.

The route to Machrie Moor's numerous treasures is fairly straightforward and not in the least bit taxing, but it can get a bit boggy underfoot at times. Also, if you happen to be a dog owner, leads are essential, because the fields and moorlands constitute a working farm, and sheep roam freely all around.

The walk begins from a well-signposted parking area on the main coastal road, just south of the bridge over the Machrie Water, and can be accessed through a pedestrian gate onto a well-trodden track which dissects the local farm fields. The track veers left and leads to another gate, soon after which the first of a number of cairns comes into view on your right. Further on, the twin stone ring of *Suidhe Choire Fhionn*, otherwise known as *Fingal's Cauldron Stone* in deference to the giant fighting warrior of legend, stands close to what remains of the now-derelict Moss farm. A third gate can then be seen on the right, adorned by a couple of information boards, beyond which the most spectacular standing stones rise in their majestic pomp towards the skies. Further right stands a wonderfully well-preserved and mightily-impressive stone circle, while the narrower path to the left soon reveals a solitary large and imposing standing stone. Continuing further along the main path takes you to the most stunning sight of all, a trio of colossal red sandstone pillars, the tallest of which is almost twenty-feet high. Quite how the mere mortals of pre-biblical times actually managed to lift those huge things into place from wherever they once lay is the stuff of utter confoundment. Meanwhile, all around, the landscape is punctuated with various smaller stone circles, cairns and other assorted remains.

That, then, is the physical anatomy of the walk itself. However, what is much more difficult to put into mere words is the heavy and profound atmosphere which this quintessentially sacred place evokes. Indeed, it is well worth just standing there in peace and solitude for a few minutes, to 'hear' the deafening silence of the moor and absorb the highly-charged aura of searing history.

Buried here are the remains of numerous islanders of yesteryear, hard-grafting and self-sustaining, but not quite as backward a people as you might think. Those irrepressible souls built houses of wood and stone. They grew wheat and barley. They kept cows, sheep and goats. They were hunters, farmers and fishers. They produced meat, vegetables, cheese and bread. They made clothes and fashioned tools from the scant raw materials available to them. They conducted religious ceremonies, the main event quite probably taking place at the summer solstice, from the stone circles which are located in linear alignment with a distinctive north-easterly notch where Machrie Glen splits into two steep-sided slopes, and from which on that most auspicious day of the year the sun would surely rise to intersect the notch and radiate its magical glow on the awe-stricken islanders. A primitive community it may have been in relation to today's heady technological standards, but a fully functional one in every essential regard.

So, for what it's worth, I would urge you to do yourself a huge favour and visit Machrie Moor, if only to experience real peace and serenity for a few minutes, and to treat yourself to a welcome break from today's frenetic pace of life. And here's a strange thing. Not once have any of my dogs ever barked in Machrie Moor, never at any time. That is something which I always found rather odd, and if I'm being honest, a bit unnerving too.

Machrie's other major historical attraction is King's Cave. Folklore has it that the cave once played host to Finn, the legendary Gaeldom cult hero, and much later around the turn of the thirteenth/fourteenth centuries provided a hiding place for none other than Robert the Bruce himself. The famous line of caves sits invitingly just a few feet above the pebbled shoreline on the west coast of Arran, and on the walls of King's Cave, which is recognised as the main one in the line, a number of ancient drawings and carvings can still clearly be seen. The other caves sit adjacent to it, some having been assigned names like The Stables and The King's Larder, and the fascinating site is well worth a visit.

In more recent times, this was also the scene of one of the most bizarre rescue operations ever performed by the hard-pressed Arran Coastguard Team, as former Station Master, Davie McKinnon, recalled with some amusement.

'I got a call one day to report that a wee dog had got itself stranded high up on a ledge near King's Cave, at a local beauty spot called Cosy Den. How it got there I've no idea, but it did, and its owner was frantic. Now, we normally receive anything up to 160 call-outs each year, because we're a coordinating service working with mountain rescue, the lifeboat team, the police and other emergency services, so we're well used to dealing with incidents of all types. However, this one really did take the biscuit ... quite literally!

'So, we got all our gear together and headed off for Machrie, but one of the team members did a quick detour into the supermarket in Brodick to buy some chocolate biscuits, which he thought might help to attract the dog's attention. When we reached Cosy Den, the poor wee thing was running around in circles in a total panic, up there on the high ledge. We knew that we would have to move fast, and we decided that the best strategy would be for half of the team to climb up to the top of the cliff carrying our ropes and an "animal bag", with the other half staying put at the bottom. We then roped up a team member and swung him over the cliff with the animal bag in his arms and the chocolate biscuits in his pocket, and lowered him down.

'He had one hell of a struggle getting the dog to go anywhere near the bag, I can tell you. It just kept licking his face, slobbering all over him. That was when he produced the chocolate biscuits, a packet of Kit-Kats in fact. It seemed to take ages. He just kept shovelling the biscuits into the dog's mouth one after the other, until he eventually managed to grab it and shove it into the animal bag. We were then able to haul the pair of them back up to safety, much to everyone's relief. When we eventually got back down the hill, we asked him how many Kit-Kats he had left in his pocket, and he produced the last one.

'"What?", one of the team asked him. "Did the dog eat the other five that were in the six-pack?" "No," he replied, "eleven of them ... it was a buy-one-get-one-free deal!"'

The walk to King's Cave is relatively easy to negotiate, and there are different ways to plan your route. The caves lie roughly equidistant between the rural car park at Machrie and the charming little harbour village of Blackwaterfoot, a walking distance between the two extremities of roughly five miles. You can choose to leave from the car park and do the circular route towards the caves on the shore, then either re-trace your steps or head up over the hill-track back to your car. Alternatively, you can ask someone (including a local bus driver) to drop you off at Machrie, walk along to the caves then continue straight on towards Blackwaterfoot, to be picked up again at your journey's end. I invariably choose the latter route, Nan chucking me out along with the dogs at Machrie, then meeting me for lunch a couple of hours later at Blackwaterfoot's excellent Kinloch Hotel. So, if you don't mind, this is the route I will describe.

A well-established forest track leads westward from the Machrie car park through the trees, before emerging into open countryside a few hundred yards further on. The track then rises gradually to an elevated vantage point, from which the views of the adjacent Pirnmill Hills and across the Kilbrannan Sound to the more distant Kintyre are simply stunning.

A fairly stiff walk of just under one mile takes you further up the steep hillside track to its highest point, where a decidedly scary drop down to the shoreline will indicate that this would not be a particularly good place to stumble (although I'm fairly sure that the views as you plummeted downwards would constitute a fitting farewell to this world). The track then descends sharply until you reach a steep gully, at the foot of which stands a tall gate, through which the choppy Atlantic waters and a rocky shoreline await. A short stroll along the pebbled beach will soon reveal the outline of the caves up on your left.

King's Cave itself is very easy to locate by the huge metal gate which has been constructed to protect its ancient Christian and pre-Christian carvings, although the gate has been left open in recent years to allow sightseers to investigate the fascinating ancient relics in this cavernous place. It is here that Bruce is reputed to have had his famous encounter with the spider spinning its web, and the inspiration he is said to have derived from its perseverance against all the odds. The neighbouring caves are smaller but still sizeable, and well worth an inquisitive rummage, and the eerie sound of the ocean's echo will tickle your eardrums and imagination in equal measure.

Whether arachnophilic or arachnophobic, you can then bid farewell to the multitude of spiders doubtless lurking invisibly in the long shadows of the caves and continue your walk along the stony shoreline in a southerly direction. Just over a mile to the south of King's Cave, the distinctive cliff-face of Drumadoon

Point overlooks Kilpatrick Shore. Once an ancient sanctuary and near-impregnable fort, the imposing heights of 'the Doon' form an unmistakeable backdrop to the harbour port of Blackwaterfoot. About half-a-mile further along, the path splits, revealing a couple of different routes to make your way past the Doon.

The fork to the left takes you up its very steep contours and over the shoulder of the vast mound to the northern extremity of the beautiful Shiskine Golf Course, allegedly one of the only two 12-hole courses in the entire world. However, one word of warning from bitter experience. This particular route is quite taxing, potentially dangerous because of the near-vertical drops on your ascent (especially so if you have a dog with you), very muddy at the top and completely fenced-off from the golf course, which means that you'll have to climb over a three-feet high barbed-wire fence (and lift your dog over too). Thereafter, a leisurely stroll along the hard-standing pathways of the course, avoiding at all costs any temptation to trample over its precious fairways, will soon lead you into Blackwaterfoot for a well-earned refreshment.

Alternatively, the fork to the right takes you along the shoreline, by virtue of a recently-fashioned path which snakes over and between some fairly large boulders. And while it can be a bit tricky to negotiate at various points, this is a particularly scenic route and leads straight to the same golf course's dramatically-positioned fifth tee, from which a brisk walk along the magnificent sandy beach will then take you into the village.

However, before we leave this truly awe-inspiring walk behind, I owe it to myself to recount a recent experience which now finds itself filed in my ever-expanding folder, entitled, 'Things which will make a funny story someday soon, but not quite yet'.

It was a Monday morning in late-January of 2017. A really beautiful day, wall-to-wall sunshine, but bitterly cold. My son Derek and his family were staying with us in Kildonan, and we decided to do the King's Cave walk, only this time with a difference in terms of transportation arrangements, courtesy of one of his innumerable self-proclaimed 'great ideas'. Essentially, it was this.

We would take both cars. He would park his at Shiskine Golf Course in Blackwaterfoot. I would collect him, his wife Catriona and my one-year-old black Labrador called Rosa, and we would all head to Machrie, where I would park mine. The four of us would then walk the five miles back to the village, pile into his car and he would drive me back to Machrie to pick up my own, after which we would all return once more to Blackwaterfoot and grab some lunch from the village's excellent takeaway shop, superbly named 'On A Roll'.

My offspring was positively beaming from ear-to-ear as he assured us that this was forward planning at its finest, a brilliant strategy that would have been befitting of someone like a legendary war general. In the event, there was just one slight problem. A legendary war general wouldn't have left his bloody keys in the glove compartment of my car. Nor indeed would he then have had to lead his beleaguered troops all the way back from whence they came.

That, then, is my own personal take on the beautiful, secluded Machrie district of Arran's spectacular west coast, although by entering the idyllic little village of Blackwaterfoot we have already strayed into the next port of call on our circumnavigation of God's own island.

The Shiskine valley.

The Good Old Days in the Shiskine Valley

A few miles down the coast from Machrie lies the Shiskine valley, the two areas separated by a sprawling expanse of moorland defined by a rich tapestry of arable land, pine forests, peat bogs and purple heather, all of which provide home to a whole range of fascinating indigenous creatures including red deer, assorted rodents and an incredible array of birdlife.

The Shiskine valley itself is an amalgamation of six discrete districts, namely Balmichael, Shedog, Feorline, Kilpatrick, Torbeg and Blackwaterfoot, the latter being a small coastal village which has served for many years as the harbour port for the whole valley.

The village of Shiskine sits inland in an easterly direction, less than a mile up the valley from Blackwaterfoot. Close to the lofty peaks of Ard Bheinn and Beinn Bhreac, and boasting its very own stone circle of Cnoc Ballygowan nearby, Shiskine takes its name from a derivation of the Gaelic name meaning 'marshy place', since many years ago a great swathe of the area was essentially swampland.

Like all the Arran hamlets, clachans, farmsteads and innumerable settlements of old, those in the Shiskine valley were always firmly in the grip of devout religion, but no strangers either to bizarre superstition and communal tale-telling of ghosts, ghouls and other creatures 'not of this world'. The focal point for the former was the parish kirk, where the minister was traditionally all-powerful, and spent his time lambasting his parishioners each Sabbath day with prophecies of doom, gloom and the fires of hell if they dared to step out of line, while local ceilidhs and social gatherings of that ilk set the scene for the latter, the participants' imagination and enthusiasm often suitably fuelled by copious consumption of illicit whisky.

All sorts of superstition pervaded community and family life in the dark and often troubled times of the mid-nineteenth century. With horrendous infant mortality rates (death by first birthday) in rural and island communities of around twenty demises per thousand being eclipsed only by those in the large inner cities of the British mainland, parents would often go to extreme lengths to 'protect' their children. Putting common foodstuffs like oatmeal on their pillows was one way of fending off evil spirits and the potentially fatal diseases of the time such as cholera, poliomyelitis and smallpox, with other would-be remedies too bizarre to even attempt to describe. Likewise, sheep and cattle would be similarly attired to immunise them against the common ovine and bovine maladies which might otherwise limit their productivity and longevity.

In more modern times, a concerted effort to drain the surrounding areas in the Shiskine valley saw its successful conversion to farmland. Even as recently as the latter half of the last century, crop-farming continued to flourish in the Shiskine valley, most notably during both world wars. The late Lady Jean Fforde remembered with fond affection the incredible productivity of Arran's burgeoning farming industry, particularly during the Second World War effort.

'I will never forget the wonderful countryside all along the Shiskine valley. The fields were laden with healthy farm animals and swaying barley, all encouraged by the war effort. It really was the most uplifting sight. Sadly, though, after the war, our farming industry fell into rapid decline. We still have many hard-working farmers and well-run farms on the island these days, but the industry is now a pale shadow of its former self. I find it very sad when I see the broken fences and undrained fields littered with willows and rushes, where once stood countless herds of cattle, flocks of sheep and rich fields full of golden crops.'

Willie Kelso was raised in Parkhouse farm in the Shiskine valley, the youngest of seven children. He vividly remembers those days of hardship, but the fun and happiness in his upbringing too.

'It was hard going for my mother bringing up a family of nine. She could make a meal out of next to nothing and come dinner time we always had a choice … take it or bloody leave it! I remember writing a letter to Santa for a bike one Christmas and feeling fairly confident that he would make my wish come true. Then I found out who Santa was, and I knew fine well I wouldn't be getting a bike!

'I never had any academic ambition, none at all. I left Shiskine Primary School at fourteen to work on the farm. I've always maintained that I was "destined to shovel shite!" The farmers' markets on the mainland were great fun. When we bought two or three sheep, they would be delivered to us in a wheelbarrow and we would shove them into the rear seat of the car and take them back over to Arran on the boat. If the air got a bit rich, we would just wind the windows down. It was tough going for us, though. There were over fifty milk-producing farms on Arran in those days. We had a thirty-acre farm and about twenty cows, and we soon realised that a farm of that size was completely unsustainable. To be honest, we were making an existence rather than a living.'

Despite the hardship and tough graft of the times, Willie remembers the tremendous community spirit in Shiskine.

'Nobody would want for anything, because we all just mucked in and helped each other out. For example, the postman would deliver the mail first thing in the morning then light the coal fire for us, and he would think nothing of taking a calf to another farm for us in his post van. We always found an excuse for a wee dram … birthdays, anniversaries, every event you could think of. I particularly remember the Hogmanay dances in Machrie Hall, when everyone would pile into Bannatyne's cattle float and then first-foot the locals with their bottles. One year, we ate a whole hen that was cooking in a pot on the stove. However, the farmers were always very disciplined about their responsibilities. For example, when it was time for the cows to get milked, they would just get up and leave the party.

'I remember my pals and me sneaking into Shiskine's Hamilton Arms for a pint when we were about seventeen. It was run by Gordon Yates, and Gordon didn't know we weren't drinking age yet. He even let us join the pub darts team. My mother had no idea we were going to the pub until one day Gordon knocked at the door to ask her if she would let me know that the darts competition was starting at half-seven!

'Sundays were different days though, oh aye. No boats, no washing allowed on the line. We weren't even allowed to watch the telly. Shiskine always had a terrific self-support culture, and it still does. It was nothing to hear your van being driven away by a neighbour in the middle of the night, because you always knew it would be there for you the next morning. One householder at the end of the village used to leave a gallon can full of petrol at the roadside, and it was often taken away but always returned filled up again. The local shop was frequently unmanned, so you just helped yourself to your bread, butter and milk, and put your money in the box. Even today, we still have fresh vegetables and honesty boxes at farm road-ends.'

In short, Willie Kelso's memories of the 'good old days' in the Shiskine valley are laced with hard-earned fun and adventure bathed in warmth and affection. Unsurprisingly, he is not alone with such fond recollections.

It's a Doc's Life

Retired Shiskine doctor, Alastair Grassie, has similar reminiscences of the famed Arran self-support mentality.

'I'll give you a good example,' he told me one winter's afternoon in his grand Inglewood home over a delicious lunch, the highlight of which was a superb still-warm loaf of sourdough bread which his son, George, had just fashioned in his own Blackwaterfoot bakery. 'My wife Libby and I were sitting at the fireplace one night, enjoying a wee dram, when all of a sudden my next-door neighbour burst in carrying a fire extinguisher. All he said was, 'your lum's on fire,' scooted some stuff up the chimney, then buggered off. You see, that's Arran for you. Everyone just looks after each other. No questions asked, no fuss.'

Husband-and-wife medical team Alastair and Libby moved to Arran in the late 'seventies. Both educated in Glasgow University, they first tried their professional luck in London, where he lectured in anatomy and she specialised in child health. They moved to Newcastle for a spell, and then to Dundee where Alastair completed his training as a fully-fledged surgeon, as he recalled.

'By then we had established that hospital medicine was not for us. So, we both undertook further training as General Practitioners, and looked to see if we could acquire a rural medical practice somewhere, a lifestyle which we felt might be right up our street. Libby's only stipulation was, "please, not some bloody island!"'

And as luck would have it, 'some bloody island' it turned out to be. They applied for the vacant Shiskine practice on the island of Arran, and got it. It was advertised as an 'inducement practice', which meant that their salaries would be enhanced by an allowance for such factors as 'rurality' and 'boat time'. This helped to compensate for their much reduced per-capita allowance in comparison to city doctors, who could earn considerably more from their several-thousand-strong patient caseload alone.

For the Grassies, working life on Arran would be tough-going and hard-earned, but immensely rewarding. Their Inglewood premises operated not only as home and surgery, but also as a pharmacy, requiring them to perform the role of dispensing chemists as well. Both salaries were paid into their bank accounts annually, which meant that their income and expenditure throughout the year had to be planned and managed very carefully indeed. In Alastair's own words, it was 'womb-to-tomb medicine', and both he and Libby soon realised exactly what they had let themselves in for.

'On call twenty-four-seven, 365 days a year and every type of treatment you could think of, that was it. There was nothing of an even remotely medical nature that wasn't expected of Libby and me. I even got a wee bit of informal training from a local dentist colleague at one stage, and carried out the occasional dental procedure from time to time. In fact, I was actually the recipient of one such procedure myself. I had been suffering from toothache for some time, and I was so busy that I just couldn't find the time to book an appointment. However, there were three dentists who came to Shiskine every year for their holidays, all of them fairly eminent consultants, and we had got to know them quite well. So, I dropped in on them one night and popped the question. They all had a wee look inside my mouth, a quick fumble around, and hummed-and-hawed for a bit. Then one of them produced a bottle of whisky and a pair of dental pliers. He told me that it was "a bucket job", poured me a huge glass of whisky and commanded me to down it, which I did very willingly. The next thing I knew, the pliers were inside my mouth and the tooth got yanked. "Clean out!", he said as calmly as you like, and flung the tooth into the coal fire. Honestly, it could only ever have happened on Arran!'

In those days, the only other surgery on Arran was in the east-coast village of Lamlash, and the two practices had to cater for the medical needs of the entire island population. The Grassies held surgeries in the mornings, afternoons and evenings. They took their turns at servicing the cottage hospital and made their house calls between surgeries in Shiskine and hospital duties in Lamlash, clocking up some 35,000 miles each year on an island whose entire coastal road measures only 56 miles, and frequently finding themselves being flagged down *en route* by resourceful pedestrians requiring impromptu medical assistance. Alistair once went three whole days and nights without a wink of sleep.

'When I look back, I sometimes wonder how we actually managed it. It's a miracle we had time to go to the toilet. Our surgeries were walk-in, not appointment, so they could be hugely unpredictable. Sometimes people would just poke their heads through the door, take one look at the queues, and if it wasn't anything too serious, walk back out again. One local farmer used to march past the waiting room and straight into our kitchen, make himself a cup of tea and light up a fag, then ask us what the hell had kept us!

'The cottage hospital was an absolute lifeline for emergency cases whom we couldn't get to the mainland. With the last boat leaving Brodick at 4.40 pm in those days, it was often just a matter of keeping them alive till the first boat the following morning, still to this day called the "death boat". We had a part-time consultant back then, and between us we carried out routine operations such as tonsillectomies, appendectomies, limb breakage repairs and so on. However, the one thing we always dreaded was having to perform a Caesarean Section, due to the potential dangers involved and the need to access specialist support very quickly if required, but amazingly we never once had to carry out a single section in 38 years of medical practice.

'I remember one incident in particular, a really nasty road traffic accident. What you have to remember is that, back in those days, not only was drink-driving commonplace, but some folk regarded it as compulsory! One night, a couple of lads were driving home after their work and a good bevvying session in their local watering hole. A few miles down the road and with their van swerving all over the place, the passenger suggested to the driver that he was the more sober of the two, by which he clearly meant the marginally less drunk. After a bit of an argument, they both agreed that they should swap over, which they proceeded to do … while their van was still moving! Hardly surprisingly, their daring manoeuvre failed disastrously, the van hit a telegraph pole at full speed, and they were in serious bother. A passing motorist called 999 and an ambulance duly arrived to rush them to the cottage hospital, where I was on duty. Both were in an awful state, with one of the lads having sustained terrible head and facial injuries, which I quickly established could be life-threatening. So, I immediately fitted a plastic airway on the poor fellow and phoned the Royal Navy base at *HMS Gannet* near Ayrshire's Prestwick Airport, to ask if they could send a Sea King helicopter to take him to the Southern General Hospital in Glasgow.

'The problem was that flying conditions that night were absolutely horrendous, low cloud and mist having reduced visibility to only a few yards. The Royal Navy controller was very reluctant indeed to dispatch the Sea King, which was a wonderful old 'copter but a big brute of a thing, and he told me that he would only do so if it was a matter of life or death. I replied that it absolutely was, and before long I was whizzing across the Firth of Clyde only a few yards above the waves with my patient, a nurse, the pilot, his co-pilot and a navigator. The pilot explained to me that the ridiculously low trajectory was due to the near non-existent visibility, meaning that he was having to fly "on visual" and without the aid of radar.

'The next thing I knew we were flying up the River Clyde, hugging the surface of the water and taking our bearings from the lights of Greenock, Port Glasgow and Dumbarton, while going up and down continuously to avoid hitting the various overhead power cables. I had flown on the Sea King many times before, but this really was hairy stuff. All the while, the co-pilot's voice in my earphones kept asking me, "how's he doing?", and I would give him the thumbs-up. Suddenly, I felt a nudge on my shoulder and the navigator pointed for me to look upwards. And there we were, right underneath the Erskine Bridge. That's right, flying underneath it!

'Anyway, and as they say, all's well that ends well. We made the Southern General just in time, our incredibly fortunate patient lived to tell the tale, and I was left to find my own way home. However, the two helicopter pilots weren't so lucky. They were hauled before the beaks and subjected to the indignity of a formal investigation, and warned within an inch of their careers never to attempt any such act of wanton bravado again.

'On another memorable occasion, I was on duty at the hospital in Lamlash and in the process of delivering a baby. It was about one o'clock in the morning. Just at that, I got a message to say that my wife Libby was on the phone, and that it was urgent. She was at home in Shiskine at the time, looking after our three young children and the family dog.

'There had been a bit of a rabble outside the house, then the doorbell had rung. When Libby opened the door, there stood about seven or eight men, most of them a bit bedraggled and much the worse for wear with drink, and all of whom had clearly been knocking lumps out of each other. Libby immediately checked that, apart from minor injuries, they were all okay. Except one, that was, the problem being that he had a hatchet sticking out the back of his head!

'Libby quickly established that this was a clear "frontline emergency" and informed the gentleman that she was sending for an ambulance to take him immediately to hospital. The guy went berserk. Absolutely no way was he prepared to be put into an ambulance, let alone go to hospital. Despite Libby's repeated attempts to convince him of the urgency of the situation and the need for him to receive immediate emergency treatment, he was still having none of it and demanded that Libby treat him right there and then in our own surgery. And, of course, that was when she phoned me.

'So, essentially the situation was this. Here I was in Lamlash delivering a baby, and there was Libby on the other side of the island looking after three kids, one dog and a man with a hatchet in his head, the latter still refusing point-blank to go anywhere near an ambulance or a hospital. So, we discussed the matter on the telephone and quickly came to the view that she really had to take action and just do her best in the circumstances, since doing nothing simply wasn't an option. We quickly agreed a plan.

'First, she should give the patient a good dose of local anaesthetic and remove the hatchet from his skull. Next, she should do her best to clean out the head wound, which would be no easy matter. Then she should sew up the wound and give him hefty inter-muscular injections of antibiotics and a tetanus shot. Having absolutely no time to lose, Libby got started immediately while I phoned a neurosurgeon in Glasgow's Southern General Hospital for further advice, which thankfully confirmed that our intended course of action was spot-on.

'In the event, everything worked out hunky-dory. I delivered a fit and healthy baby in the cottage hospital, Libby performed her heroics in our surgery at home and then discharged the patient minus the offending hatchet. And a few days later, the guy removed his own head stitches at home … with a razor blade!

'So yes, I suppose that just about sums up our lives as doctors on Arran. Extremely hard work and a bit scary at times, but very, very rewarding.'

Into the Soup

Since the turn of the nineteenth/twentieth centuries, tourism has been a vital source of income to the island of Arran in general, and to the Shiskine valley specifically.

The changing pattern is a familiar one, with in the old days well-off families renting the same properties for a whole month year-on-year, while nowadays a much more diverse social and cosmopolitan tourist cohort tends to check itself into hotels and B & Bs, or rent from a huge selection of self-catering premises ranging from the humble-but-comfy to the ultramodern-and-swish.

Blackwaterfoot's Kinloch Hotel is a very good example of a family-run business which has adapted extremely well over the years to the increasing expectations and quirky whims of today's much more demanding holidaymaker.

Owner Robbie Crawford, who has run the hotel for the past 25 years, was born and brought up in the little west-coast harbour village.

'Blackwaterfoot was a great wee place for a child to grow up. There was a big bunch of us, lads of my age. We were educated in Shiskine Primary School, and we had complete freedom to roam and play after school and during the weekends. It really was great fun.

'My grandmother originally came to the village from Glasgow in 1954, to what was then an eight-bedroom guesthouse, and between her and my own parents they gradually built up the hotel bit-by-bit. What made the Kinloch really special was that we were one of only three hotels in the whole of Scotland with a swimming pool. Down through the years, we have continued to build, extend, refurbish and improve our facilities to what you see now. In fact, over the past few months, we have just completed another major refurbishment programme, and today's hotel now has a 95-bed capacity, which is vital to the infrastructure and economy, not just of Blackwaterfoot itself, but of the whole island.'

Robbie's late father, Lawrence Crawford, is now well-and-truly embedded in island folklore, in deference to the ebullience of his character. The tales of Lawrence's antics are the stuff of legend, although in those earlier days of more liberal 'industrial language', their *verbatim* telling in this book might be a bit *risque*, so if you don't mind I'll just give you a couple of examples containing a few blanks, which you can then fill in for yourself. One of Lawrence's trademarks was that he famously called most people 'darling', male and female alike.

Possibly the best-known of Lawrence's exploits occurred one lunchtime when a regular sales representative was sitting at the bar having ordered that well-known Scottish delicacy, tattie soup. After a few sips of his soup, and clearly disappointed, he piped up, 'Excuse me Lawrence, but there are no potatoes in your tattie soup'. Unperturbed as always, the bold Lawrence nonchalantly grabbed a couple of boiled potatoes off the big plate of mince-and-tatties being ravenously devoured by an adjacent local worthy, plopped them from shoulder-height into the rep's soup, and said, 'Well … there's f----n' tatties in it noo, darling!'

Continuing on the 'soup' theme, another of Lawrence's classics relates to a summer's day also in the Kinloch's ever-popular public bar, where a visiting tourist was about to order his pub lunch and had just spotted the words 'Soup of the Day' scribbled on a blackboard behind the bar. 'Excuse me, barman,' he enquired of Lawrence, 'but what kind of soup is it?' to which the great man shook his head in annoyance and retorted, 'Och, it's just f----n' soup, darling!'

Alas, the latter tale lends itself to a rather sad epitaph, but one which is steeped in the raucous humour of the late and much-missed Lawrence Crawford. At the reception in the hotel immediately following the local legend's funeral service, a lovely spread had been laid out for the peckish mourners, and there in a large pot sat the chef's own piping-hot soup-of-the-day, with a familiar inscription emblazoned in big bold letters - 'Just F----n' Soup'.

'Yes, my father was a real character!' Robbie laughed, fondly recalling some of his now-legendary antics. 'However, in those days things were a bit more rough-and-ready, especially in places like public bars, so I suppose he just spent his time trying to live up to his reputation. He was one of a kind, that's for sure!'

Robbie is very optimistic about Arran's capacity to continue to deliver an increasingly high-quality holiday experience for the island's steadily-growing tourist numbers. Tellingly, though, he is also very proud of his childhood village.

'Blackwaterfoot really has everything you would need to live on a day-to-day basis, a self-sufficient community if you like. We've got a butcher's shop, a grocery store and off-licence, a bakery, a newsagent, a hairdresser, a restaurant, a garage, a takeaway food outlet, a primary school, two churches, a health centre, a golf course and the hotel itself with our two bars, restaurant and the largest function suite on Arran, and of course our own swimming pool. In the old days, the local area had six separate licensed premises – the Hamilton Arms, the Rock, the Greannan, the Blackwaterfoot Hotel, the Barn and the Kinloch – but as with most of the island's villages, not all have survived. However, it's is still a great place to live and work, and an idyllic holiday destination too.

'As far as the hotel itself is concerned, we're more popular than ever. For example, we've been full all this weekend and it's the middle of November. RET has been huge for Arran and for villages all across the island, because with cheaper ferry fares, more and more people are now bringing their cars over these days. In the past, we used to rely almost exclusively on the main tourist season, but now we're an all-year-round hotel and our guest numbers are up significantly.'

As a major hotelier on the island, Robbie has witnessed many a change in social habits and trends over the years.

'There is no doubt that people's attitudes and expectations have changed dramatically over my 25 years of running the hotel. Take drinking, for example. Many years ago, things were much more relaxed and liberal. Nowadays, people are very reluctant to take even one drink when they're driving, which is of course much more socially responsible. One unfortunate knock-on effect, however, is that many now prefer to stay at home and keep in contact with friends and neighbours through social media, rather than popping into their local pub for a pint and a chinwag, which is sad in a way.'

Of course, the island's hotels and hostelries still play a very important role their communities, particularly during times of crisis. And, as previously rehearsed, seldom if ever has the island of Arran had to deal with a crisis on the scale of 'Snowmaggeddon', which occurred in March of 2013. Robbie remembers that time only too well.

'The entire Shiskine valley was a total white-out, with ten-foot-high snowdrifts all over the place and miles of power lines down, leaving many local families completely stranded and without electricity for seven days and nights. Fortunately, we have a generator at the Kinloch, so we were ideally placed to operate as an emergency hub and to provide ongoing support to the local community. Anyone who needed a hot meal got a hot meal, and anyone who needed a warm bed got a warm bed, simple as that. And yet, despite the seriousness of the situation, the community spirit was incredible, and we had many a laugh. At one stage, the television crews were lining up local residents to do live interviews, and out they would troop one-by-one to appear on the telly. Meanwhile, everyone else in the bar had been watching the live proceedings on our own TV screen, so as soon as each interview was over and the latest conscript had high-tailed it back into the bar for a pint, they would get a thunderous round of applause and then be given "marks out of ten" for their performance! It was a very difficult situation for the locals, but they're a great bunch and we all just made the best of it.'

As indeed did Robbie Crawford, his family and his staff in making certain that the community they serve came first in those most demanding of circumstances. And proving yet again that when something needs done on the island of Arran, the islanders never roll over and expect the authorities to do it for them.

They just roll up their sleeves and do it for themselves.

Dynamic Dynasties

Up until the 1930s, a more expansive district known as Shedog, which took in the village of Shiskine itself together with the immediate surrounding area, was a veritable hub of local industry. Indeed, within a mere square-mile stretch, there stood the local church, a primary school, a public hall, a police station, a library and a whole range of public/commercial premises including a saddler, a tailor, a dressmaker, two joiners' workshops, an undertaker, a post office, a hotel and pub, a transport garage, a blacksmith, a doctor's surgery, and a couple of shops selling everything from paint to porridge.

Before the end of the nineteenth century, Blackwaterfoot, operating as the port for the Shedog/Shiskine and surrounding populace, had its own inn and shop. A 'packet boat' made regular sailings over to Campbeltown on the Kintyre peninsula, this vital service subsidised by local residents who paid fees for the privilege.

There are many colourful characters in the Shiskine valley, all of them undoubtedly the product of its historically rich heritage and culture.

Local worthy Charlie Currie is the 'middle' son of the late Rev James Currie, himself a renowned man-of-the-cloth and brilliant after-dinner speaker, whose parishes ranged from Renton in Dunbartonshire and Pollok in Glasgow to

Dunlop in Ayrshire, and famously extended to the distinguished role of Chaplain for Glasgow Rangers Football Club. Charlie has tried more career and business ventures than he cares to remember, including a spell as manager of Drumadoon farm back in the barnstorming days of the early 'seventies.

'My grandparents owned the farm, which had been in the family for well over a century. When my parents took over, my mum drove the tractor and ploughed the fields with the horses. However, I was actually raised on the mainland, where I was educated in Bellahouston Academy and then in the High School of Glasgow, but Arran was always where my heart lay.

'In the late 'sixties, my mate Dougie McLean and I borrowed a hundred quid each from our dads and set up a mobile disco unit. In 1968, we founded the 'Shiski Diski', a disco-with-a-difference located in Shiskine village hall, which soon grew arms and legs. At its peak in the summer months, there could be a couple of hundred people inside the hall and another hundred outside waiting to get in. We invited some high-profile DJ's to the 'Shiski Diski', including Tiger Tim and Richard Park. I remember the first time that Tiger visited he was accompanied by two bouncers, both huge big guys who thought that their job would be to control the unruly crowds. Needless to say, the Arran crowds were anything but unruly, and one of the bouncers got so drunk that he fell in a ditch on his way back to the hotel and slept there till he woke up the following morning!

'We ran our mobile disco until 1971 in various venues on the mainland, and also on Arran during the summer months. I remember one weekend at the 'Shiski Diski', we added vintage cider to the soft drinks menu. Not only did it liven up the proceedings, but we also made an immediate profit of £150! When I then became farm manager at Drumadoon, it was back to beef cattle and hill sheep rather than Mungo Jerry and The Bay City Rollers. The funny thing was that I never at any time saw myself as a farmer who did disc-jockeying for a hobby, but as a DJ who farmed for a living!

'My big break as a DJ came when I joined Ayr's Radio West Sound in 1982, and happily my one-hour-a-fortnight slot on air soon graduated to three-hours-a-week. That was when I invented the first-ever "live pub quiz", which I called the Arran Waves Quiz. It really was a hoot. We would set up a live link in the studio with two island pubs each week, and they would compete against each other over the airwaves, most of the contestants suitably lubricated, of course. Honestly, it could only have happened on Arran, but what a laugh we had!

'Sydney Devine, the famous crooner who was absolutely adored by the ladies, did an early-morning show for West Sound around that time, and he had a slot for children to phone in with their jokes. Now please remember that this was in the days before we had the now-standard "seven-second delay" technology in our live broadcasts. I was actually in the studio on the infamous occasion when a wee lad called in with his joke, asking Sydney, "What vegetable makes your eyes water?", to which Sidney replied, "Well, I would say … an onion". "Naw," the youngster retorted, "it's a turnip." The great man immediately dived straight in and asked him, "So tell me then, son, how does a turnip make your eyes water?" And the wee nipper replied, "Have ye ever been hit on the b---s by a turnip?" Needless to say, we had seven-second delay technology installed the very next day!'

It was in the late 'eighties that Charlie Currie was then lured back to his beloved Arran.

'I moved into my parents' house in Blackwaterfoot in 1988 and became a tourist officer with the Isle of Arran Tourist Board three years later. My next crazy invention was on a Tourist Board visit to Newcastle, where we staged the world's first "Indoor Highland Games" in the Metro Centre! We even made a rubber caber for the contestants to toss, and the whole gig went down a storm. While I was down there, I spotted a boating lake with pedalos for hire, so we got permission to get hold of one and converted it into a "Loch Ness Monster". Again, the locals thought that this was great, and turned up in their droves. We also ran a mini Burns Supper each day in the Metro Centre, complete with the *Address to the Haggis*, toasts with malt whisky and haggis-tasting. We were always trying to come up with something novel, just for a laugh.

'A few years later, I ended up in Aberdeen and found another position as a tourist officer, this time with the National Trust looking after Castle Fraser. However, I then felt I had to do something to lose some weight and get fit, so I got myself a job as a postman. I suppose that's why I've always had sympathy for posties, because although it's a great job, it's physically demanding and can be a wee bit dangerous at times too, especially when angry dogs are around. In fact, I've even been bitten twice myself. I remember one Arran postie getting bitten by a dog at a farm in Machrie, while he was delivering the mail. He immediately complained to the farmer, who just handed him a loaded shotgun and said, "Here, shoot him!". The postie replied in horror, "Oh no, I couldn't possibly do that!", at which point the farmer said, "Well suit yoursel' son, I'm no' bloody shootin' him!", grabbed the gun back off him and slammed the door in his face!'

After one final spell as a postman on Arran, Charlie has now retired to his idyllic Blackwaterfoot cottage facing the mighty Kilbrannan Sound. His life is now somewhat quieter than in the frenetic 'Shiski Diski' years, but the fun-loving legacy of the inimitable Charlie Currie still continues to enrich the spirit of the Shiskine valley.

Another long-time local resident is Neil Arthur, who spent many a happy holiday on Arran with his family in his younger days, before enjoying a varied career with the fire service on the British mainland. On retirement, the self-confessed 'ferry-louper' then moved to the Kilpatrick area at the south side of Blackwaterfoot, where he set up his own garden maintenance company. Now fully retired, Neil's experience of working on the mainland allied to his long-standing love affair with the Shiskine valley places him in an excellent position to run the rule over the many demographic and social changes which he has witnessed over that period.

'Arguably, the biggest change in recent times has been the demise of so many small farms on Arran, and notably so in the Shiskine area, most of which had become financially non-viable and were then forced to buy or rent other land to make it work. We now have only two dairy farms left on the island, the remainder being mainly beef cattle and sheep businesses.

'From post-war times up until the 1980s, one of the area's main employers was the Bannatyne family. At one stage, they provided jobs for almost thirty local people, courtesy of their haulage and delivery lorries, their Bedford TK trucks and assortment of buses, all of which had a driver and a conductress. Bannatyne Motors also provided work for local people in the garage and in the Blackwaterfoot office. A great many locals have worked tirelessly to make the village what it is today, but in my view the contribution of the late Donald Sillars Bannatyne, known locally as DS, and Donald Ebeneezer Bannatyne, or Don, has been immeasurable. Equally, the efforts of Robin and Lawrence Crawford and their families in developing the Kinloch Hotel have to be recognised. With their considerable entrepreneurial skills, those two families did a great deal for the development of the village and the valley, and many other local families and individuals have since made their own significant contributions.

'One of the most colourful characters of them all was Lawrence Crawford. To say that Lawrence led an interesting life would be putting it mildly. He was brought up in Singapore, educated in Glasgow Academy where he was school captain, and went on to become captain of Glasgow Academicals' first XV rugby team. Lawrence then served his country in the Korean War, before going into hotel management, after which he and his mother bought what was then the Kinloch Guest House, to be joined by brother Robin. Between them, they gradually built up the hotel and ran it for more than forty years. In much the same way as the Bannatyne business served Blackwaterfoot's economy for many decades, so too did the Crawford family's hotel operation, and happily it is still thriving today.

'Looking back, it is hard to imagine what might have happened to Blackwaterfoot without the Crawfords developing the Kinloch Hotel and the Bannatynes expanding their haulage, bus and contracting operations. Had neither of these businesses been set up in this small community of ours, who knows what might have happened here? They were both highly significant employers and key service providers in the days when the village was a lot smaller than it is today.

'When Lawrence's brother, Robin, passed away in 1999, their partnership was described as "Robin's Ernie Wise to Lawrence's Eric Morecambe", a real class double-act which made its patrons laugh out loud. Lawrence's legendary one-liners were simultaneously outrageous and hilarious. A man with a public-school education, his polished accent was only betrayed by his liberal use of expletives.

'Many people will have heard his famous "soup" stories, but there are umpteen others too. Like Lawrence greeting an elderly returning guest with the line, "Oh I see you're back, I thought you would have been six-feet under by now!". Or the time a resident was having an argument with him in the public bar and demanded to speak to the manager, at which point Lawrence slipped away, put on a tie, and met the annoyed guest at the hotel reception desk with the beaming welcome, "Hello, sir, I heard you wanted to see the manager, well that's me!" However, perhaps his most infamous tale involved the cleaning staff finding a resident dead in his bedroom. Completely undaunted, Lawrence immediately gave his instruction to the cleaners. "Just shove the body under the stairs, and we'll sort it all out later!"'

As for Blackwaterfoot itself, the size and social fabric of the village may well have changed dramatically over the years, but Neil still insists that it's a great little place to live and work.

Who better to ask, then, about his family's legacy than Blackwaterfoot's very own Duncan Bannatyne. Born in the cottage hospital in Lamlash back in 1955, the home of his childhood would be 'Holmlea', situated right in front of the Kinloch Hotel facing the sea, where he still resides today. There he was raised by his father, Don, and mother, Nancy, along with siblings, Karine, Anne and Stewart, together with their assorted family pets.

Having contracted that dreadful and progressively debilitating disease, *Multiple Sclerosis*, in his early twenties, Duncan has been physically disabled for many years now. However, he remembers his childhood and formative years in Blackwaterfoot with great affection. A skilled raconteur, he is determined to write his own book one day soon, in celebration of those wonderful days. In the meantime, he was happy to share some of the nostalgia with me.

'We lived right on the beach, and it was a great place to play. Whenever we went to the seashore to play in the rockpools, we had to wear our wellies. As we got older and the wellies got longer, we could wade further out into the deeper water before they eventually filled up. Even if the wellies had gone up to our necks, we would still have found a way to fill them. A day at the beach normally required three dry pairs of trousers and three dry pairs of socks. Of course, we could always opt for total immersion, when everything had then to be changed from head to foot. After a day at the shore, there was always a basin on the back green filled with various creatures crawling around in the sea water, which we were then told to return to their natural habitat the following morning.

'In those days, you never went outside your own village. In fact, I remember that when it was time for our Sunday School trip in the summer, we went no further than places like Kildonan and Brodick! I attended Shiskine Primary School, which had only two composite classes. Primary one, two, three and four were taught in the "wee room", and primary five, six and seven in the "big room". Our school dinners were brought up from Kilmory in big metal drums. School was great fun. At Arran High School in Lamlash, my favourite subject was Geography, mainly because we had a great teacher, and great teachers make you want to learn, don't they?

'Our first dog was a white Boxer bitch called Rae. She was a happy dog, and she liked following the tourists along the beach. Unfortunately, she developed a similar liking for male dogs whenever she was in season, which was ultimately her downfall as she died giving birth to her third litter of pups. Our second one was also a Boxer, a brown male dog called Chiel, who was nothing short of a lunatic. Deeply protective of us, he could easily frighten away any strangers or "nogoodnicks" who ever came near us. His favourite person, apart from us, was the driver of the butcher's van. Chiel would sit there at the window waiting for the van to arrive, then bark furiously whenever it did, to let mum know that it was "bone time". When Stewart was about four, he decided that it was unfair for Chiel to be the only one who got a bone, so eventually he got one too and would sit with it in the back garden beside the dog!

'We also had a cat called Lucky, but why it was called Lucky I'll never understand. As well as having to live with a psychotic Boxer, there were also our two rabbits, Samson and Delilah, neither of whom was a male, something which my dad only eventually realised when they both escaped from their hutch one day and got themselves impregnated within about five minutes of freedom.

'One day my bike tyre got a puncture, which seemed a simple thing to fix since my dad owned the local garage. I must have been about eight years old at the time, but the thing was that we all suffered from "shoemaker's wean syndrome". You see, shoemakers' children were historically unshod, and likewise we could never get our own mechanical things fixed. So, I just got hold of a universal bicycle spanner and began the frustrating process of removing the offending wheel myself. After about fifteen minutes of trying, it still wouldn't budge, so I flew into a tremendous rage and flung the spanner onto the concrete floor, where it bounced and crashed straight through the bathroom window. To my utter horror, there was my mum sitting on the toilet.'

The Kinloch Hotel once belonged to Duncan's parents. Indeed, his father, Don, was born in the hotel back in 1921 and lived there until he sold it to the Crawford family.

'The Kinloch was the first hotel on the west coast of Arran to get a full licence, and the public bar was opened. This stopped all the local men going to Brodick for strong drink and curtailed the infamous parties at the top of the String Road that were often held on the return journey. Then in the late 'sixties, the Kinloch and the adjacent Montana guesthouse building were finally joined, which was when the Crawfords built the swimming pool.

'Just up the road from the hotel, the building which is now Cameron's shop and post office used to be the Bank of Scotland. When I was still an eight-year-old, the bank manager tried to advise me that my entire life savings, which amounted to some five-pounds-sterling, would be much safer with them than in my own bedroom. However, they hadn't realised that I was very well-versed in the ways of bank robbery from the many TV programmes I had been watching, so I figured that my fiver might potentially be available to any gun-toting masked robber who might be passing through Blackwaterfoot, and just kept it to myself.'

Another vital village facility which is still thriving today is the local garage, formerly part of the Bannatyne 'dynasty', but now owned and run by the Cameron family.

'In the 1890s, my granny and Uncle Johnny were born and brought up in the Blackwaterfoot Hotel. After the turn of the century, it was renamed the Blackwaterfoot Temperance Hotel, which I am told was a valiant attempt by my great-grandmother to stop my great-grandfather drinking. I am also told that it was singularly unsuccessful. Straight across the road from the hotel was the garage, which was owned and run by my dad and Uncle Donald, better known as 'DS'. They had a fleet of buses and lorries, they sold vehicles and petrol, and they carried out all sorts of mechanical repairs.

'The main attraction for me as a child was that the garage was a particularly filthy place. I couldn't walk past it without becoming oily, because the dirt and I had a very strange attraction. Any time I went near the building, I ended up having to get bathed when I returned home. It was something that never left me. Even today, whenever I enter that same garage, which is now run by Colin Cameron, I simply cannot leave without smelling oily. Strange, but true.

'Another odd thing about the garage was that although the nearest building to it was Cairnhouse, a dairy farm in those days, the men always put 'Carnation Milk' in their tea at tea-break. They opened the tin by shoving a screwdriver twice through the lid, although if the srewdriver was particularly manky, they might wipe it first with a similarly manky old rag. The tea was made from loose PG Tips tea-leaves, never from tea-bags, with lots of sugar added before the Carnation Milk got poured in. It was an acquired taste for the mechanics and drivers, but absolutely detested by almost every other member of the human race. This tradition went on for many, many years and no ill-effects were ever recorded by any of the tea-drinkers. Nurse Sinclair, our much-loved district nurse, often remarked that the garage was simply far too dirty for any germ to have the slightest chance of survival.

'The garage was also the venue for one of the most important events in the annual calendar, Hogmanay. At lunchtime on the last day of the year, all work would cease, the teacups would be washed out and the kettle filled with clean, fresh water. Bottles of whisky would then start appearing from all directions, signalling the start of the "garage party". This was an annual all-day event, and the rules were very simple. It would continue until all participants were clinically comatose. However, some did eventually manage to make their way down to the Kinloch in the evening, clutching teacups which had not seen tea since ten o'clock that morning, but few if any of whom would ever survive long enough to bring in the new year. It was for that reason that the wives eventually got the infamous garage party banned altogether, bringing a sad end to a great tradition.'

When Duncan reached the age of sixteen, he decided to leave the island of his birth and head for the big city, where he studied Engineering at Glasgow's College of Nautical Studies.

'I had lived all my life right across from the beach, and I had watched the boats sail past our windows, so it was hardly surprising that one day I would want to try my luck on the ocean waves. After leaving college, I worked at sea until I was 21, but then decided to return home to Arran, and got a job in the garage. When I was 24, I was diagnosed with MS. I knew how serious the disease was, and all about the prognosis which was very gloomy, but I was determined to work on. I then got a job with Shell for a time in Aberdeen, and that included offshore work which I wouldn't have been allowed to do if they knew about my condition. So, I just forgot to tell them.

'You see, that's the thing about disability. You must never allow your illness to take over your life. There's absolutely no point moaning about it or feeling sorry for yourself. You just have to continue doing what you're doing to the best of your ability and get on with it.'

I wondered where I had heard that one before.

In recognising the influence of the Bannatynes and the Crawfords on the economy of the Shiskine valley, many local residents were also at pains to highlight the vast contribution made to the area in more modern times by the Cameron family. I met Colin Cameron for a coffee in the Kinloch Hotel one breezy afternoon in late February.

'My parents bought the garage over twenty years ago, and I've worked there since I was sixteen. While the site of the garage might potentially have led to further development opportunities, my dad realised its importance to the local community and economy. For example, if it had ceased to function as a filling station, the local folks would have had to drive over the String Road to Brodick for their petrol. Quite possibly, many of them would then have popped into the Co-op and other Brodick premises for their messages, rather than shop in Blackwaterfoot. That would have put real pressure on our own local businesses, which might have set the village on a downward spiral. Thankfully, my dad had the foresight to recognise this.

'The family now owns the garage which I run, the shop and post office which my sister Nicola manages, and our food takeaway shop, 'On A Roll', which is very popular with locals and holidaymakers alike. There are still several other very good shops and outlets in the village too, which makes Blackwaterfoot a really attractive place to live, work and visit.

'As for my own garage business, we sell fuel, we do MOTs, and we carry out mechanical repairs mainly for the islanders, although we would never see our visitors stuck either. In fact, I remember one night a few years ago when I got a phone call from a friend in Shiskine to come to the aid of the driver of an articulated lorry who was completely lost. When I got there, it quickly became evident that he couldn't speak English, not a single word. From the signage on his lorry, we established that he had driven all the way from Estonia. Now, I learned many things during my time in Shiskine Primary and Arran High, but speaking fluent Estonian wasn't one of them. So, I phoned down to Robbie in the Kinloch Hotel to see if any of his employees happened to understand the language and might perhaps come to our rescue as a translator. However, none of them could, and we were left trying to make some kind of sense out of what the poor guy was saying to us, and where he was actually trying to go with his artic lorry.

I gestured to him to open the back door of his trailer, and saw that it was full of shopping trolleys! He then pointed to his Sat Nav, and I could see that he had entered the correct postcode for Shiskine. It was only when he handed me a wee piece of paper with an address written on it that the penny dropped. It read, "Shiskine Road, Glasgow", and the shopping trolleys were for the local Lidl store!

'Anyway, we eventually got him sorted out, turned him around and directed him back over the String Road to the terminal in Brodick, where CalMac moved heaven and earth to get his lorry back onto the next ferry. A few days later, a big hamper arrived from Lidl thanking us for our help. Honestly, it could only happen on Arran!'

So, there it is, then, the Shiskine valley in all its rustic charm, as told through the words of a few local worthies. However, before we move onto the next chapter of our travels around this enchanted island, let us first do a short but necessary detour.

Thomas Telford's Finest Hour

The Shiskine valley on the west of the island is connected to the main ferry port of Brodick on the east by the famous String Road.

Back in 1817, it was Thomas Telford, the legendary Scottish civil engineer from Eskdale in Dumfriesshire, who designed 'The String', the first road between Brodick and Blackwaterfoot capable of taking wheeled transport. The String immediately became a vitally important cross-island link for the islanders and their businesses alike. A motor bus was subsequently introduced to the route, but since the various existing bridges were too narrow and fragile, its passengers had to alight and cross them on foot while the driver drove the bus with painstaking care across a succession of shallow fords which had been fashioned for that very purpose. Sadly, the iconic old bus was commandeered by the government at the outbreak of the First World War in 1914. Remarkably, though, it was then bought back at the end of hostilities in 1918 and restored to its former glories, where it would go on to transport the islanders between the two vital ports for many years to come.

Paradoxically, the String's very existence soon began to have the effect of shifting the balance of commercial harbour traffic from Arran's west coast to its east, the latter being much more conveniently placed to accept cargoes from other West of Scotland ports and, of course, from the mighty Firth of Clyde. Up until the 1930s, fleets of smacks and puffers carrying heavy cargoes such as metal, coal and cement had traditionally docked at Blackwaterfoot, where they were met at the mouth of the river at low tide by horse-and-cart, their goods then being taken over to the weigh-house (which is now the car park adjacent to the Kinloch Hotel), before being transported to destinations all over the island. Sadly, for the little harbour village, the bulk of the sea freight would then shift to the island's eastern ports.

Around this time, the Shiskine valley's main population centre of Shedog had its very own landing strip too, this capable of taking light aircraft in order that the more well-heeled Arran residents could ask to be uplifted to or dropped off from the regular Glasgow-to-Campbeltown service. It was a wonderful facility for those who could afford their five-shilling (25p in today's money) journey to the city to be reduced in duration from several hours by ferry and road transport to a mere 35 minutes by air. In more recent times, several laudable attempts have been made by local business leaders and community stalwarts to facilitate another landing strip on Arran, but so far to no avail.

A drive from Blackwaterfoot across the Telford-constructed String Road to Brodick, which is of course technically a diversion from our chosen circumnavigation of the island, is thoroughly recommended at some point during your stay. There are three very good reasons for making such a detour. Firstly, as you meander up through the glen with its towering hillsides on either side, you will immediately realise just what a phenomenal feat of engineering the great man himself achieved in the construction of this remarkably undulating and commercially vital cross-island link. Secondly, you will be able to marvel at the sight of red deer grazing on the adjacent slopes, especially if you remember to bring your binoculars. And thirdly, as you approach the long drop down into Brodick itself, you will be completely blown away by the jaw-dropping view from the top of the String down towards Glen Shurig and Glen Rosa in the valley below, with the distant Ayrshire coastline shimmering across the Firth of Clyde, one of the most spectacular vistas of all on an island which is blessed with so many.

Anyway, please don't take my word for it, just check out 'the String' for yourself and I'm sure you won't be disappointed.

Loch Cnoc an Loch

This is a fairly demanding walk of about 7 miles in distance (and a good two-and-a-half-hours in duration), which is best tackled after a dry spell, since you'll need to cross a fast-flowing burn *en route*.

Your starting point is on the aforementioned String Road just on the east-side of the village of Shiskine. Simply cross the road-bridge over the Clauchan Water, and turn right up a tarmac road leading to the local cemetery, after which the surface turns to forest track. Following this track eventually leads to a small burn, which if you have judged the weather conditions carefully, you should be able to cross by means of a makeshift ford. However, if your judgement has been misplaced and the water level is high, crossing could be quite dangerous and you'd be well advised to cut your losses, head back to base and leave things till another day.

Once across the ford, you'll see a path leading from the banking up through the trees. This path winds its way upwards through the forest, until it eventually reaches a clearing, where a waymarked signpost points you to the right and a further climb up the arduous slope, which eventually begins to level off, rendering the surface quite marshy. This is the trickiest stage of the whole walk, since not only can the underfoot conditions become fairly sodden, but what now remains of the path is strewn with dead trees, so you'll need to follow the footprints and take the scenic route into the forest for a bit. Personally, I always pop the dogs on the lead at this juncture, to prevent them from cavorting around and getting themselves injured by protruding branches poking out of the undergrowth.

You will soon reach another small burn which is easily crossed, leading to a gate at which you should bear right and head downhill alongside the forest through the most accessible parts of the waterlogged moss, this route taking you towards Loch Cnoc an Loch (and try saying that after a couple of wee drams). Simply plough on over the moor between the forest and the loch, until just before the southern shore of the latter you will spot a track diving into the forest, which widens out a short distance further on. A left turn followed by a right then lead you onto a clear path towards another small burn, and down the slope to a gate at the end of the forest. Once through, you will find yourself walking along a valley towards the next gate where a signpost points you up the incline leading towards Cnoc Ballygown, yet another of Arran's ancient hill-forts, from which the views over the Mull of Kintyre are terrific.

Continuing along a clearly defined footpath and through a succession of gates, you will eventually emerge at Balgowan farm, where a stroll past the farm buildings and down towards the red-sandstone St Molio's Church will lead you back onto the String Road at the west-end of Shiskine. A right-turn and a final half-mile walk through the village will then return you to your starting point.

However, you have been suitably warned, because even on a good day your trousers and footwear will inevitably end up saturated. Nevertheless, this is a cracking walk which will provide you with some wonderful photographic opportunities and another unique perspective of the raw beauty of the island of Arran.

And so, from the splendours of the Shiskine valley, let's now head for the island's 'deep south'.

The Deep South

The District of Kilmory

The extensive geographical area known traditionally as Kilmory - old spelling 'Kilmorie' - is based on the island's long-established demarcation system of church parishes.

It stretches all the way from Corriecravie on Arran's west coast to Craigdhu on its east, Arran's main coastal A841 road linking the villages and hamlets of Sliddery, Lagg, Kilmory, Torrylinn, Shannochie and Bennan. Much of its coastline is rather rugged, in sharp contrast to the breathtaking Torrylinn Beach, which lies just off the village of Kilmory itself, easily the longest, loveliest and most secluded of Arran's many golden sands, and to which we shall return very shortly.

The district of Kilmory lies just to the south of the village of Blackwaterfoot, from the western end of which the main drag sweeps sharply to the right, taking you through the hamlet of Kilpatrick where many years ago a ferry used to sail passengers to and from the Kintyre peninsula. As you climb to the apex of the road's steep gradient, the views of Kintyre on a clear day are glorious, with little Sanda (or 'Spoon') island at its toe, and Island Davaar rather jealously concealing the harbour town of Campbeltown, itself once a whisky-distilling mecca of global proportions, and which can be accessed by boat from the adjacent sea-loch. Indeed, if you are of a 'certain age', then you may, like me, fondly remember the lyrics of the jaunty little number which the immortal and ever-kilted Scottish folk singer, Andy Stewart, used to belt out on the hugely-popular BBC programme which graced our television screens back in the 'fifties and 'sixties, *The White Heather Club*.

> Campbeltown Loch, I wish you were whisky,
> Campbeltown Loch, och aye.
> Campbeltown Loch, I wish you were whisky,
> I would drink you dry.

Continuing the journey southward, you will soon come to the rural community of Corriecravie, which despite its relatively isolated location (or indeed, because of it) houses a fire station of all things, this to serve the emergency needs of the island's west coast. However, perhaps the most striking landmark on the journey is the site of an ancient fortified farmstead near the village of Sliddery, which can be accessed on foot by a path leading from the main coastal road down towards the sea. The famous remains are known by the Gaelic name of Torr a' Chaisteal, and they rest on top of a natural outcrop above yet another of Arran's spectacularly raised beaches.

Further south, and just a few hundred yards short of the village of Kilmory, another track leads down towards the seashore. However, this is no ordinary seashore. This is Cleats Shore, an official naturist beach, believe it or not. The advertising blurb proudly proclaims that 'clothing is optional', but knowing how the wind can blow on Arran even on a bright summer's day, you'd be well-advised to bring along your winter woollies just in case. Put another way, should you choose to participate in the noble art of skinny-dipping on Cleats Shore, your chances of being arrested for indecency are considerably less than those of being hospitalised for hypothermia.

And here's another interesting consideration. High up on the hill above Arran's sole nudist beach now sits the aforementioned Isle of Arran Distillery's brand-new sister site, with its hordes of inquisitive visitors no doubt preparing to peer seawards, free taster-glass of whisky in hand. So, you may wish to factor that thought into your deliberations, as you stare in horror at the pigmentation of your shivering skin racing along the visible spectrum from infra-red to ultra-violet, and your favourite appendages shrinking to infinitesimal proportions.

The main drag then decides to leave the coastline for a few miles, dipping down into the little village of Lagg, where a big white hotel of the same name stands resplendent, complete with its superbly-located beer-garden nestling invitingly beside the gently-flowing Lagg Burn.

It was during the long and ridiculously hot summer of 1976 that the same beer garden provided the backdrop for one of my own wonderfully mirthful memories, the mirth only serving to illustrate the limitless boundaries of my exceedingly warped sense of humour. Nan was heavily pregnant at the time with our daughter, Jillian, and her neurological condition had already stolen most of her ability to walk, to the extent that she was by then shuffling around uncomfortably on a pair of wooden walking sticks.

Picture the scene, if you will. There she was, sitting in the sunshine on a plastic seat in the beer garden, and holding our fun-loving Labrador, Cindy, on a leash to prevent her from launching herself into the burn in pursuit of the half-dozen mallard ducks which were paddling contentedly in the cool, clear waters. And there I was, returning from the hotel bar with a tray of drinks. The moment that dog spotted lord-and-master, off she bolted in my direction. Holding onto Cindy's leash with admirable pluck, one of the back legs of Nan's chair slowly began to sink into what transpired to be a parasol-hole in the grass. By the time I got there, her head was almost touching the grass and her feet were sticking straight up in the air. The guy at the next table immediately leapt to her assistance. Amazingly, it turned out that he was an obstetrician on holiday. In deference to the spirit of this book, I will refrain from telling you what he said, although I'm sure you can work out the general thrust for yourself.

The whole character of the interior of the island's south-end has changed dramatically over the years, from an area once fairly peppered with small villages, farming townships and crofts, to one now lined with forests and only sparsely populated by the occasional farm and cottage. The main catalyst for this stark metamorphosis was, of course, the infamous island clearances in which the wealthy landowners abandoned the tried-and-tested run-rig system of land allocation for the lure of much richer pickings from the introduction of sheep farming and the like. As previously rehearsed, Arran's once booming dairy industry, in which milk was uplifted from over fifty farms, is almost a thing of the past with only two still producing the white stuff. Happily, though, Kilmory's iconic Torrylinn Creamery, opened in 1946 and visited by King George VI and Queen Elizabeth the following year, and exporter of its famous Dunlop and other fine cheeses all over the world, is still using good old-fashioned Arran milk to churn out its delicious products.

Around the middle of the nineteenth century, the old parish of Kilmorie was served by three schools, one in the village itself and the others at Sliddery and Bennan. Schoolmasters were paid around fifty pounds a quarter, a pretty decent salary in those days, and qualification depended on him (yes, almost always him) being able to teach Latin. The subjects available to local pupils included English, Arithmetic, Bookkeeping, Latin and Navigation, the availability of which were totally dependent upon the ability of hard-grafting parents to cough up fees of between two and five shillings (10p and 25p today) per annum. Nowadays, the entire 'deep south' of the island is served by one single school, Kilmory Primary, which was rebuilt by the former Strathclyde Regional Council in 1975.

Folklore has it that the good folks of Kilmorie parish were at one time particularly gifted in a certain rather *risqué* vocation, the fine art of smuggling. Not that the villagers were ashamed of their prowess, though. Far from it, they considered smuggling to be a most honourable form of employment, and one proudly handed down through the generations, even if their coastguard, customs & excise and police contemporaries took a somewhat dimmer view. With the sea only half-a-mile away through the undulating forest-lined terrain, the crafty smugglers of the locale had more nooks, crannies and hiding places available to them than a colony of rabbits in a field full of warrens. In short, this place was smuggling heaven.

Unsurprisingly, the two vocations of illicit whisky distillation and smuggling were inextricably linked, not just in Kilmory, but across the entire length and breadth of the island. Both continued to grow in popularity around the beginning of the eighteenth century, when taxes were introduced on spirits like gin and brandy as well as whisky itself, and duty was also imposed on the malt which local people traditionally used to make their home-brewed ales.

Production of barley, an important ingredient in the distillation of whisky, was very high on Arran, principally because of improving agricultural practices, but the fruits of the farmers' labours were very difficult to transport to the more lucrative markets on the mainland. As a consequence of being stuck with excessive stocks of barley and the need to generate additional income in the face of steadily-increasing rental charges from unscrupulous landowners, many farming communities turned to the illicit production of whisky, while the professional smugglers arranged its transportation to their waiting seafaring vessels under cover of darkness.

However, whisky wasn't the only locally-produced commodity to be smuggled to pastures new for tidy profit. Around the same time, the government introduced a tax on salt, also manufactured in various locations around the island, and salt smuggling soon began to generate very rich pickings as well. Because of the island's unique terrain, topography and extensive coastline, Arran soon became a veritable haven for smuggling, with local farmers and seamen growing particularly skilled in their nefarious techniques, while exasperated customs & excise officers tore their hair out trying to stem the flow of illicit whisky and salt to an eagerly-awaiting market.

Many tales of derring-do, ingenious resourcefulness and violent clashes pepper Arran's historical records, on an illegal trade which drew a great deal of public sympathy for poor islanders being unjustly penalised simply for using their own raw materials as a means to survive, while the 'gaugers' chased them all around the island, pistols at the ready. Indeed, in the year of 1817, one infamous stand-off in Arran's south-end resulted in two local men and one woman being shot dead by an over-enthusiastic exciseman who was immediately charged with murder, only later to be acquitted by a court in Edinburgh for 'simply doing his job'.

The demise of the illicit whisky-distillation trade and the closely-associated art of smuggling became inevitable when the introduction of less draconian government tax measures soon led to the construction of large and completely above-board distilleries, with the result that the illegal whisky stills were then squeezed out of the market.

Well ... most of them.

Halcyon Days in the Deep South

As for the south-end's individual villages themselves, much has changed. For example, in terms of population, today's Sliddery is a shadow of its former self, which up until the mid-twentieth century was a bustling little village complete with the obligatory range of shops and businesses, including a blacksmith, joiner, butcher, draper and such like. And indeed, as octogenarian Davie Crossley recalls from his childhood, a rather unforgettable cobbler with an uncanny ability to 'multi-task', as we would say nowadays.

'Many Arran farmers took up shoemaking when they retired, and the shoes they made were so good that they were sold all over the world. Twelve-and-sixpence a pair, and you could stand in the burn without getting your feet wet. When I was a wee boy, one of the local men went to the cobbler for a pair of shoes, suffering from toothache. The cobbler measured him up for his shoes, then gave him a big glass of whisky and yanked the rotten tooth out with his cobblers' pliers. The poor man immediately fainted and had to be revived with another shot of whisky!'

Davie's memories of his south-end childhood are indelibly engraved in his still razor-sharp mind. The youngest of seven children, he was born and bred on a farm in Shannochie but has spent the vast majority of his life in Kilmory.

'I had a great childhood. Life was all about your own village, and every village had its own school, even wee places like Sliddery and Bennan. During the Second World War a lot of children were evacuated from the big mainland cities to Arran, so it was nothing unusual to see fifteen or twenty new faces on a Monday morning, most of them crying their eyes out. They stayed with the islanders in their own homes, and while the householders received an accommodation allowance and the children's clothes got sent on, they still did everything possible to make the kids feel happy and secure.

'Life was simple back then, and although there was very little money around, it was a good life. All the Arran villages had their own shops, even tailors and shoemakers, and there were umpteen vans that delivered straight to your door. Believe it or not, there were five butchers' vans on Arran, and a whole range of grocers, bakers, chemists, fishmongers and so on. Some vans carried an amazing variety of goods, everything from fruit and vegetables to bread, paraffin, dungarees, garden tools, wellington boots … you name it. I remember one day my wee pal very nervously asked the woman in the chemists' van for a tube of toothpaste. She just glowered at him and said, "You got toothpaste yesterday son, so here, have these!" and flung a packet of condoms at him!

'The island's transport system was completely different in those days. The boat came from Fairlie on the Ayrshire coast, berthed at Brodick to let the north-enders off, sailed to Lamlash and onto Whiting Bay, then headed back to Fairlie. Every village had its own privately-owned buses, all with their distinctive colours, and the roads always seemed to be littered with buses but very few cars. For example, Brodick had Ribbeck's and Newton's, and we had Stewart's in Kilmory. Some of them carried newspapers, which would get chucked from the bus door into individual driveways. Some buses even carried livestock at times.'

Working life soon beckoned for Davie, but like all other aspects of living on an island, nothing was ever straightforward, and everything was very hard-earned.

'I became a farm-hand and ended up in Rothesay on the island of Bute for eighteen-shillings-and-sixpence a week. My father wrote to the farmer and asked him to put it up to a pound. He reluctantly agreed, but pulled me in the very next day and said to me, "And you'd better bloody work for it"!

Davie then returned to his native island of Arran, but soon afterwards in 1954 got called up for National Service.

'When I came out of the army, I returned to dairy farming. I remember thinking that I could do a lot better than the four-pounds-six-shillings a week I was getting as a farm-hand, so I moved out and got myself a job at Torrylinn creamery for nine-quid a week, only to find that by the time I had paid for my food and electricity, I was worse off than ever! In the early 'sixties, I started working for Howie of Dunlop at the sawmill in High Kildonan, cutting down huge 140-year-old larch trees with a saw, an axe and my bare hands. The wood was then made into planks and stabs. A few years later, I was working for the Forestry Commission, planting trees in High Kildonan. Life was pretty tough in those days, but a lot simpler than it is today.

'The job I liked best was when I worked for the council on roads maintenance. I remember one day I was grafting away up the Ross Road, and I started to feel quite ill, coughing and spluttering all over the place. Then I saw Doctor Buchanan's car coming up the hill, so I waved him down. He just stuck his head out of the car window, instructed me to pull up my jumper and sounded my chest with his stethoscope. He told me I had a chest infection and that he'd give me some antibiotics, then asked me if I'd still be working up the Ross the next day. Sure enough, the following morning, the Post Office van appeared out of the mist and the postman handed me my medicine. I took a couple of pills out of the bottle and just washed them down with a big slug of water from the Sliddery Burn.

'They used to say, "You can only be ill on a Wednesday", because that was the day Doctor Buchanan did his rounds in Kilmory. He regularly performed operations on the kitchen table, removing tonsils and procedures like that. He treated animals too, nothing was a bother to him. Nowadays, if you staved your thumb, they'd send you over to Crosshouse Hospital!'

And so Kilmory has seen many a change over the years, sometimes but not always for the better, as witnessed through the eyes of Davie Crossley who had one final astute observation to make.

'Aye, the village has changed quite a bit in my time, and the people have changed too. Gone are most of the south-end's traditional trades and lifestyles, and many of the old local families have been replaced by incomers. But I'll tell you what, Kilmory is still a great wee village. And someone will always have made sure that my daily newspaper will be sitting there waiting for me in the village hall every morning. You see, that's the thing about Kilmory. We look after each other down here.'

The Big Yellow Bus

One recurring theme which visitors to Arran readily pick up, and frequently quote back in the 'comments book' of their holiday hotel or on their chosen social media forum, is the noticeably strong community spirit which defines the island and its individual villages.

I remember stopping one rainy morning to assist a damsel-in-distress who had just punctured a tyre on one of the coastal route's many notorious bends, this between the villages of Sliddery and Kilmory. The fact that she was a gorgeous, sun-tanned blonde had, of course, absolutely no bearing on my decision to interrupt my journey and come to her rescue, nor indeed did my motor-mechanical incompetence even enter the equation. In the event, an off-duty bus driver also stopped at the roadside a few minutes later, so I just delegated to him the puerile task of changing the tyre, while I subliminally assumed strategic command of the whole operation and chatted to her about her holiday on Arran.

'Do you know something?' she said to me. 'You're the third person to stop this morning and ask if I need help, and he's the fourth. If this had happened to me back home in the Midlands, I'd still be standing there yet, wondering what to do.'

Which takes us back to Arran's outstanding self-support culture, and the islanders' in-built conviction that they must always be ready to spring into action whenever someone's luck runs out. This unwritten philosophy was never better illustrated than back in March of 2013, when that infamously catastrophic snowstorm – 'Snowmaggedon' - suddenly hit the south-west of Scotland, seriously affecting many areas, the Kintyre peninsula and the island of Arran in particular.

The snowfall on Arran was incredible, but so too was its pattern of distribution, with the vast bulk of the island engulfed under several feet of snowdrifts, while a few coastal areas never saw a single snowflake. Perhaps the most striking example of this great anomaly manifested itself in the south-end, where the low-lying seaside village of Kildonan was completely snow-free, yet less than two miles west on the heights at Auchenhew, the A841 suddenly metamorphosed from a clear tarmac road to something resembling an Olympic toboggan run, complete with ten-foot walls of snow on either side.

Oddly enough, the main source of the problem occurred not on Arran itself, but on the Kintyre peninsula opposite the island's west coast. There, the sheer volume and dead-weight of the incessant snowfall brought umpteen massive electricity pylons crashing to their knees, cutting off the power supply right across the peninsula, and of course, over the length and breadth of Arran too, the island's electricity being fed from Kintyre by undersea power cable. The net upshot was that the areas affected would be without electricity for a whole week. And for Arran in late winter, a whole week without electricity is a very long time.

Literally overnight, the normal everyday challenges of island life shot up exponentially. Suddenly, the power supplies to some 1,500 homes and most of the island's businesses were completely severed. Villages were cut off from each other, with all except Brodick being denied access to the ferry and the mainland's essential lifeline supplies.

Schools and most other community services were closed until further notice. Local residents were stranded without food supplies and had few or no cooking facilities anyway. Households were completely without heat, save for those who happened to have their own back-up gas-fired contraptions, and residents were consigned to living in freezing temperatures, placing the elderly and infirm in a perilous situation. Telephone, television and internet connections were severed, rendering most forms of communication dead in the snow. Vulnerable people had to be rescued by the coastguard service or airlifted to hospital. Farmers worked tirelessly around the clock to save their new-born lambs from freezing and starving to death, often with little success. In short, Arran was in serious bother, and so too was its four-and-a-half-thousand population.

And that's when the famed Arran community spirit kicked in. In each and every one of the island's beleaguered villages and across the vast whiteout of its rural countryside, people waded waist-deep through the snow to check on their neighbours, to share their rapidly-dwindling food and auxiliary fuel supplies, and to offer much-needed moral support and friendship. The island's hotels and village halls sprang into action, with local people removing their once-frozen, steadily thawing joints of meat from their redundant freezers and bringing them along to anywhere that had a communal gathering place, cooking facilities, and with a bit of luck, an emergency generator as well. Meanwhile, the farmers continued despairingly to scour the Alpine-like terrain for their bewildered, dying livestock, while the energy company's dedicated staff and Arran's magnificent emergency services kept toiling around the clock until they were fit to drop.

This was community spirit at its best, and the island and its people lived to tell the tale. It was by no means the first crisis ever to hit Arran, and it certainly won't be the last, but one thing is for sure. When the islanders find themselves facing a challenge, up go the sleeves and it's all hands to the pump. That's the way it has always been on Arran, and that's the way it will always be.

I asked Phyllis Picken, a highly-respected community stalwart from a long-established indigenous farming family in Arran's south-end, to explain the self-support culture in her local village of Kilmory, which is commonly lauded as an excellent case in point.

'I'll give you one good example. The village has suffered a number of setbacks in recent times, with the loss of our public bar, local shop, tearoom and Post Office. Strangely enough, losing the bar was the biggest blow, because that's where the local workers would gather for a well-earned pint and a blether after a hard day's work, many of them still wearing their boots and dungarees. The bar really was the hub of the community, a communal gathering place where local issues could be aired and resolved, and the world set to rights. So, when it was closed a few years back, that really was a devastating blow for Kilmory and the surrounding area. Then losing our local shop, tearoom and Post Office were further terrible setbacks for the village, and we were all suddenly facing a real challenge. How could we possibly sustain the livelihood and spirit of our community, now that such important amenities had been taken away?

'So, we did what we always do in Kilmory and everyone just pulled together. Fortunately, we still had the excellent facilities available in our village hall, which gave us a number of possibilities. We began by converting the hall's meeting room into a bar, applied for a drinks licence and appointed a bar manager to oversee it all. We then formed the "1934 Club", a social club named after the year in which the original hall was built, and before long we had signed up a very respectable number of members. Today, the club is really popular, providing a welcome service to the people of the village and neighbouring areas, and also making visitors very welcome. So yes, I would contend that the "1934 Club" is an excellent example of community sustainability in action.'

While, characteristically, Phyllis prefers to play down the vitally important role that she herself has performed in the village's battle to preserve its spirit and identity, one thing did make her eyes light up. And that was Kilmory's iconic 'Community Bus', which for many years now has been a hugely valuable asset, not only to the village itself, but across the whole island.

'Oh yes, I'll admit it, the bus has always been my "baby"! It all started some 25 years ago. At that time, we had ten girls from the local area who wanted to go every week to the Girl Guides in Shiskine. We only had two main drivers, so everyone just piled into a couple of cars, which were full to the gunnels. The Outdoor Centre in Shiskine, formerly the Hamilton Arms Hotel, had a minibus for sale at £1,500, so back in Kilmory we got ourselves organised and raised the money to buy it, mainly from coffee mornings and other fundraising events. It was a modest start, but at least we were up-and-running. The local girls could get to their Guides meetings in safety and comfort, and soon we were running people to various other events on the island. Before long we needed a new minibus, and our next one turned out to be a big yellow ex-prison bus!

'However, our biggest break came in 1995. I'll never forget that day. It was Monday 23 of October, and a letter had just arrived from the National Lottery, which had only recently started up. The committee had applied for funding for a new minibus, and that letter gave us the news we had been desperately awaiting. Twenty-three-and-a-half thousand pounds, that's what we got! It was fantastic news. The champagne corks fairly popped that night, I can tell you!'

Phyllis credits much of the success of the 'Kilmory Bus' project to the sterling efforts of her fellow committee members and other key local individuals in the community, although they would be the first to attribute that success to her determined leadership and drive. 'Drive' also being the key word when it comes to the various Kilmory minibuses which have since hauled countless local people around the island of Arran and well beyond, some even as far afield as the Scottish Highlands. And thanks, of course, to Phyllis and her other willing community volunteer colleagues beavering away unselfishly behind scene and wheel.

These days, Kilmory's very own and highly distinctive 'big yellow bus' provides a service which is so important to the local and wider community that it would hardly be an exaggeration to call it a lifeline. It takes schoolchildren to swimming lessons, elderly residents to the shops, women to breast cancer clinics, budding Rembrandts to art classes, mourners to funerals, guests to weddings (including a bride herself, would you believe?), walkers to various locations around Arran, and innumerable locals to umpteen other island facilities and amenities.

Little wonder, then, that the Kilmory Hall project received the prestigious 'Queen's Award' some five years ago at Edinburgh's Holyrood Palace, and from Her Majesty Queen Elizabeth II in person.

All of which just goes to prove that when the going gets tough in Kilmory, the tough really do get going.

The Giant And The Anvil

Speaking of toughness against the odds, now to a tale of sheer guts and determination.

David Ballantyne, or 'Big Davie' as he is more affectionately known around these parts, is a gentle giant of a man standing six-foot-four and weighing in at eighteen stones of pure muscle. He is also one of the nicest guys you could ever have the good fortune to meet. Which is just as well really, because with biceps like prize marrows and a handshake that can bring grown men to their knees in floods of tears, even the thought of being on the wrong end of a right-hook from Davie has a strangely diuretic effect, if you get my drift.

Born in Glasgow's Duke Street Hospital and reared in Lanarkshire's East Kilbride, Davie remembers his formative years with fond affection.

'East Kilbride was a wonderful place for a young lad to grow up. It was nothing like the huge modern "new town" it is these days. Back when I was a wee nipper, East Kilbride was all open countryside, a great place for playing in the woods and the open fields for hours on end. I suppose that was where I developed my love of the outdoors.'

And it was the pull of the great outdoors that would forever dominate Davie's life choices and ultimately lead him to settle down on the island of Arran, but only after a period of disappointment and frustration. Having completed an HNC in Biological Surveying, only to discover that opportunities in the career he craved – that of 'forest ranger' – had all but dried up, Davie decided one summer to set sail over the Firth of Clyde to Arran with his then girlfriend. There they pitched a tent in a campsite in the village of Kildonan, a well-known beauty spot located on the island's most southerly tip. Davie instantly fell in love with the island, and despite having to return to the mainland for another spell to earn his corn, he knew instinctively that Arran was where his heart now lay.

A couple of years later, he packed his bags, bought a one-way ticket on the CalMac ferry crossing from Ardrossan to Brodick, and began looking for digs and work on the island, the latter with one non-negotiable stipulation. It simply had to involve outdoors work. For the highly-intelligent, well-educated big Davie Ballantyne, pushing a pen for a living would always be a fate worse than death.

Davie quickly picked up a job as a farm labourer on the island's south-end, where his main duty was shepherding. Soon afterwards, he met a young Dutch girl called Anneliese, or 'Liese' for short, with whom he then settled down in the village of Whiting Bay. A few years on, Davie and Liese had a baby daughter, Roisin, who immediately became the centre of their universe. They later moved on to their present home in Kilmory, where they were a family blessed.

'Roisin was always a happy, healthy wee girl,' recalled Davie with unashamed pride. 'She soon developed a great fascination for nature and wildlife. She took that from me, I suppose. I loved reading about nature, and we were always watching wildlife programmes on the TV, so it was probably inevitable that Roisin would also develop a love for the outdoors. In fact, two of the first words she ever tried to say were, "David Attenborough!" It was hilarious, this tiny wee lassie trying to pronounce a name like that! One day, I sat her down on the grass beside three adders that were wriggling about only a few yards away. Roisin had no fear of wildlife, none at all.'

Then just after her ninth birthday and quite out of the blue, the family was hit by a veritable bombshell. Roisin was diagnosed with Type 1 Diabetes, a serious disease in which the body's own immune system, which normally fights harmful bacteria and viruses, mistakenly destroys the insulin-producing 'islet' cells in the pancreas. Ever since that diagnosis, Roisin, now thirteen years old, has had to self-administer insulin injections four times every single day in life simply to control her sugar levels, and her whole attitude to managing her own condition has been exemplary.

For some time, and unknown to his wife and daughter, father Davie had been giving very serious thought to raising funds for the Juvenile Diabetes Research Foundation (JDRF) charity.

'I just wanted to put something back into our healthcare system, after all the wonderful treatment that Roisin had received. But I knew that whatever it was that I eventually decided to take on, it had to have something to do with a mountain, because I've always loved the mountains. And it had to be a real challenge. Not just something very difficult, but something almost impossible. Something that at the end of the day I might actually not be able to achieve. You see, Roisin had been facing an enormous challenge with her illness, and I wanted an enormous challenge too.'

Hardly surprisingly, the challenge which Davie ended up choosing would be one with such an outrageous degree of danger and difficulty that it soon had the whole island of Arran tut-tutting and head-shaking at the sheer folly of his utterly madcap idea, and the near-certainty that it could only result in failure and despondency.

However, the doubters had forgotten one thing. This wasn't just anybody they were talking about. This was big Davie Ballantyne. A man on a mission. A mission for his cherished wee girl. The mission of a lifetime.

So, what exactly was the challenge that Davie eventually chose to tackle? Simple. To haul, single-handedly, a nineteen-and-a-half stone (124 kilogram) blacksmith's anvil up to the summit of southern Scotland's highest mountain, the famous Goat Fell. A huge, odd-shaped lump of solid metal, much heavier than even his own very substantial body weight, which most fit and healthy adult males would seriously struggle to budge a single inch.

Davie Ballantyne had redefined the meaning of the word 'challenge'.

'I could see Goat Fell every day on my way to work, this beautiful big mountain which towered over Brodick Bay. Then one morning, I happened to notice an old anvil lying in a yard, and the idea just came to me. So, I said to myself, "See this anvil sitting here, Davie? Well, I'm going to haul it up that mountain over there. And I'm going to do it for my wee Roisin".'

Before much longer, what had started out as a fanciful idea soon grew arms and legs, and became a monster in Davie Ballantyne's fired-up mind.

'Every day I went to work, I could see Goat Fell and I couldn't get it out of my mind. I became consumed with the challenge of pulling that anvil up that mountain, totally obsessed. But I decided to keep it to myself because I knew that everybody would just think I was daft. And I kept thinking, "Well, maybe I am daft!" Eventually I had to tell my family and friends, and the whole thing quickly became public knowledge. Everybody thought I was off my head, and nobody thought I could do it, which was fine because I honestly didn't think I could do it either.'

While this would clearly be an extremely gruelling and lung-bursting physical challenge, Davie also recognised the huge psychological pressures he would face all along the way, and so he very wisely enlisted a bit of companionship in the form of his trusted friend, Fraser Aitchison. An Ayrshire man with a similar passion for the great outdoors and a skilled photographer to boot, it would be Fraser's job to keep big Davie sane and focused throughout his gruelling ordeal, and to bully and cajole him as each occasion demanded. Oh yes, and a few good photographs for posterity certainly wouldn't go amiss either.

So, between Davie and Fraser, a masterplan was hatched. Anticipating that the whole thing would take several days, possibly even running into a week or so, Davie would ask his employer if he could take his full annual leave entitlement at the one time. His thinking was that this would enable him to make a start in early May of 2016 and give him enough time to complete his mammoth task.

Now, for those of you who are not familiar with the climb up Goat Fell, there are two recognised main routes (as described earlier in this book), the 'easier' climb from Cladach near Brodick, and the 'harder' one at Corrie further up the coast. Predictably, Davie picked the Corrie route, which is the much steeper and rockier of the two.

For several weeks prior to the climb, Davie spent countless hours in a local gymnasium getting his mighty frame tuned up for action. He also carried out considerable research into dietary requirements, exercise and sleep patterns to give himself the best chance of getting through his ordeal. 'Carb-up before the daily climb, and protein-up afterwards', that was the theory. And, of course, always leaving just enough space for a couple of his favourite indulgences, a pint of lager and a wee fag.

The plan was this. Davie and Fraser would set off from home at half-seven in the morning and begin their ascent at eight. Davie would start each day's 'big pull' - on a length of thick rope wound around the neck of the mighty anvil - whenever he reached the spot where he had abandoned it the previous afternoon. That would allow him to commence his gut-busting torture session early in the morning, thus helping to keep to a minimum both the heat of the summer sun and the inevitable questions from the usual hordes of inquisitive hillwalkers. Then at the end of each day, Davie and Fraser would 'case the joint' by scrambling a further hundred yards or so up the mountain, in order to plan their trajectory and set their target for the next morning.

The prep work was done, the time was nigh, and Davie Ballantyne was as ready as he would ever be. Easy-peasy. It was time to boogie.

To say that things did not immediately go to plan would be the understatement of the millennium. On the first day, Davie, wearing the pair of fingerless gloves that he thought would be tailor-made for the job, had managed to pull the anvil a mere fifty yards, and ripped his fingers to the bone in the process. The following day, wearing 'proper gloves', he succeeded in doubling that distance, but pulled the bicep in his right arm as a direct consequence of the awkward, jerking movements which he had to deploy in hauling the dead-weight of the anvil inch-by-inch up the steep and rocky slope of the mountain.

That evening, when the normally calm and placid Davie Ballantyne lay stretched out in the hot bath of his Kilmory home, he was anything but calm and placid. Lying there with every muscle in his body aching, his right bicep throbbing in agony and his fingers still seeping blood into the bath water, he felt utterly despondent. A hundred-and-fifty yards, he kept muttering. A hundred-and-fifty bloody yards. Suddenly an idea came to him, the genius of which lay in its simplicity.

'A stick!' Davie said aloud to himself. 'A wee stick! I'll get myself a wee wooden stick and twist it around the rope, then use it as a handle!'

And in the event, it was that little stick which would turn out to be the difference between success and failure. Hardly rocket science, but as simple as that.

On the third morning, Davie tried out his crude invention, and it worked a treat. Sure, his muscles still ached with every enormous upward pull of the weighty anvil, and his heartbeat continued to thump in his ears like a rock band's bass drum as the sweat poured down his cheeks in the summer sunshine, but at least he could now get a proper grip on the rope without ripping the skin off his fingers. The 'wee stick' was working. It was doing its job and his confidence was rising at last.

'Every day was different,' Davie recalled, 'and it soon became obvious that casing the joint and setting targets for the next day were a complete waste of time. Some days we got on like a house on fire and managed 200 yards, while others were just pure frustration from beginning to end and we'd be lucky to do fifty. It all depended on the steepness of the slope each day, and how rocky the surface was, so we eventually decided just to turn up every morning and get on with it. No goals, no targets, just get on with it.'

'Day Eight was a real killer. We had reached a part of the mountain where the gradient was almost vertical. No kidding, vertical. I pulled and pulled, and I felt I was getting nowhere. I became more and more frustrated, then I just lost my temper completely and started hauling the thing in ridiculous jerking movements. And that was when I tore the intercostal muscles in my ribcage, the ones that control your chest expanding and contracting when you breathe. It was agony, and at that moment I really wondered if that was it, game over. But it wasn't, because I got that anvil up the vertical. I still don't know how I did it, but I did. And do you know the funny thing? That was the very first time I was able to see the peak of Goat Fell. Mind you, it still looked miles away!'

What really took Davie by surprise, though, was the sheer extent of the psychological pressure of the mammoth task, not just the physical exertion.

'I just couldn't get the whole thing out of my mind. It became totally obsessive. I would think about the mountain and the anvil and the rope and the stick all day long, and all through the night. I'm a light sleeper anyway, and I would wake up every couple of hours thinking about it. I kept thinking, "Can I really do this?" The only time I wasn't thinking about it was when I was actually doing it, because the effort and the pain just took over.'

Davie's next target was the Corrie Burn, also known locally as the White Water, which cascades down the mountain towards the village of Corrie.

'Fraser and I agreed that crossing the Corrie Burn was a critical milestone. If we could get the anvil over that burn, then we knew we could make it, because to be dead honest, I was never really confident until I managed to cross it. Once I did, my confidence started to grow, and I thought, "do you know what, Davie, you might actually manage this".'

However, even after this major milestone had been accomplished, one further and very considerable factor was coming increasingly into play, and that was this. Davie had by then pulled the anvil so far up Goat Fell that every morning now entailed a lengthy and challenging mountain hike before he even got started, and every afternoon would require another muscle-jarring descent back down to sea level. And, of course, the walking distance was increasing day-by-day.

By the time the final week was approaching, Davie, and also to a significant extent, Fraser, were really suffering.

'We were both in a hell of a state,' said Davie. 'The weather was scorching hot by the last week of the pull. Fraser's feet were badly blistered, and he had to go and get himself some special socks. My own hands were throbbing, my feet were in agony, my knees were on fire and I could hardly breathe because my intercostal muscles were goosed. I could only manage wee shallow half-breaths, and my chest ached. Sometimes after a really heavy pull, I thought I was going to stop breathing altogether. My diet was out the window by then and I could hardly eat a thing, never mind stick to a proper scientific diet, and I had lost three stones in weight. Everybody kept telling me to go to the doctor, but I knew that if I did, that would have been the end of it. Any doctor worth his salt would have told me I was mad, and that I was going to kill myself if I kept going.'

Then one morning, the strangest thing happened, something which would give Davie a whole new lease of life, something which he himself described as 'a truly spiritual moment'.

'It was one early morning during the last week of the pull, and we were on the shoulder of Goat Fell in glorious sunshine, looking up at the final part of the climb to the peak. Fraser decided to wander off and take some more photographs, because the views of Brodick Bay down below and over the Firth of Clyde were spectacular. Suddenly a mist came down, and within seconds it was like pea soup. I honestly couldn't see two yards in front of me, so I just sat down on the grass. And there was this silence, this complete and total silence. I looked down, and there beside me was this beautiful wee wild mountain flower, with tiny beads of water dripping from it. And that was the only sound I could hear, the drip-drip-drip of the water drops from its petals. It was a magical moment. After all the grunting and sweating, here I was engulfed by mist on a mountain, and I was at peace with nature, completely at peace. And that was when I knew I would do it. I would get that anvil up that hill for my wee Roisin.'

Davie and Fraser will be forever grateful for the great support and encouragement they were receiving from other tourists and hillwalkers, many of whom had no doubt been aware of the publicity and decided to do the Goat Fell climb to see things for themselves.

'The support we got was tremendous. However, there was a downside to it as well. Almost everyone we met stopped to talk to us, and some wanted to take photographs and "selfies", and it was really slowing us down. So, we decided that for the final few days we would start even earlier in the morning, to try to get up onto the mountain before the hillwalkers. Mind you, they would always catch up with us, because they weren't pulling an anvil!'

Then came D-Day. The very last day of the 'big pull'. Incredibly by then, the whole thing had now taken a total of 24 days.

Two further enormous problems now lay in wait for those intrepid action adventurers, Davie Ballantyne and Fraser Aitchison, problems which they really could have done without.

'Day 24 was a Sunday, and because I had taken all my holidays at the one go, I had to get back to work on the Monday morning. The first big problem was that I was going to have to do a "two-day pull" to get the anvil up to the peak of Goat Fell, because of the distance remaining and the steepness of the final part of the climb. The second problem was water, or to be more exact, the lack of it. You see, the Sunday was a boiling hot day, and we were running out of drinking water. The hillwalkers would always stop and give us some of theirs, but that particular day was so hot that even they had run out. Fraser and I could only carry so much water with us because of the weight involved, and we had only one bottle left, but we knew we would need that one at the top. You see, there was a bottle of whisky waiting for us on the summit, and you wouldn't expect us to drink our whisky neat, would you?'

In the event, Davie's and Fraser's wee celebratory dram with the dozen or so friends who had plodded their way to the mountain top in anticipation of their eventual triumph, would be even harder earned than they had expected.

'That last pull, at least two days' worth, nearly killed me', admitted Davie. 'The heat was tremendous, I was dehydrating fast, and I pulled for a total of six hours. At one point, I sat on the slope and lit up a fag, then leaned over for a drink of water and pulled a muscle in my shoulder. The pain shot right up through me and I thought, "That's it, I've fallen at the last hurdle". But I kept telling myself that there was no way I was going to be beat after coming this far, so I just kept pulling. It was absolute agony. At one point, I physically couldn't budge the thing at all, but I just kept hauling on that rope and eventually made it.'

The scenes which awaited Davie and Fraser on the mountain top were ecstatic. Through its many centuries of welcoming exhausted hillwalkers to take a well-deserved rest and marvel at the breath-taking panoramic sight before them, the peak of Goat Fell had never seen anything quite like it.

'I'll never forget that moment as long as I live,' smiled Davie, clearly proud of his fantastic achievement. 'Andy Errol was playing the bagpipes. Liese and Roisin were there to welcome me, and some of my pals as well, the press too. And I'll tell you this. I've never seen a bottle of whisky disappear so fast in my life!

'However, it was a different story on the way down. Everybody was so emotional, but I was far too exhausted to feel any emotion, and I knew I just had to get off that mountain, and fast. My feet and my knees were killing me, in fact my whole body was screaming. There was hardly a word spoken on the way down. When I eventually got home, I went straight into the bath. I must have lain there for over an hour, my body in agony and my head in turmoil. I had done it, I had actually done it, but I was much too tired to even think about celebrating.'

Yes, the gentle giant had indeed done it. He had overcome the most phenomenal physical and psychological challenge, and all for his beloved little princess, Roisin, raising an amazing £16,875 for the JDRF charity in the process.

When I asked Davie for one final reflection on his superhuman effort, he just stroked his chin for a moment before giving a reply which was as understated and deadpan as I really ought to have expected.

'One final reflection?' he pondered. 'Well … it's a bloody good way to lose weight.'

Sand, Sea and Solitude

The site of Kilmory Village Hall provides access to one of my very favourite spots on the whole island, the magnificent Torrylinn Beach.

For reasons which will soon become obvious, the walk to the beach is best done at low tide. The path, known locally as Lovers' Lane, leads from the rear of the hall past a solitary windmill and along the raised banking above the Kilmory Water. It soon merges with another path leading up from the Lagg Hotel, and a couple of hundred yards further on reaches Torrylinn Cairn, one of a set of Neolithic chambered cairns in which skeletal remains and ancient artefacts, such as flint knives, have been unearthed in past 'digs'.

The elevated path continues parallel to the coastline and leads through a gate, after which it soon narrows downhill in undulating fashion until it reaches a wider track descending towards the pebbled shore. A sharp left turn at the shore will lead you past a large rock formation, and from there you will catch your first glimpse of the most spectacular sandy beach, one which at low tide is almost a mile long and occupies an area which could easily accommodate four or five full-size football pitches.

The golden sands seem to stretch for ever and the shallow sea is perfect for a therapeutic paddle. So secluded is this magnificent beach that you will probably find yourself in splendid isolation, save for the company of seagulls swooping overhead and oyster-catchers toddling along the sand by your side.

You can continue your walk along the beach for as long as you wish, this after all being an integral part of the Arran Coastal Way, but once you reach a line of large rocks jutting out into the sea and little Pladda isle comes into view, easily identifiable by its shimmering white lighthouse, you'll probably find that you have walked far enough. At that point, you can then either re-trace your steps in their entirety, or instead of climbing back up the original hill path towards Lovers' Lane, continue straight up the wider track until you meet the main road near Torrylinn Creamery, then turn left and return to the car park at Kilmory Hall.

As far as I'm concerned, Torrylinn Beach is the most spectacular and awe-inspiring of its kind on an island where you will find yourself mesmerised for choice. There again, maybe I'm just hopelessly biased, such are the many wonderful memories I have of strolling along those same sun-kissed golden sands, with the glorious scent of sea-air in my nostrils and the incredible cacophony of birdsong in my ears, watching my beloved big dogs cavorting along the beach and crashing through the waves.

Very poignantly, though, this was also the scene of my wife Nan's first reunion with the seaside since she became unable to walk more than forty years ago. That most unexpected privilege was courtesy of our incomparable Kildonan neighbour, Alastair Yates, aka 'Slats', giving his own Land Rover a radical makeover to facilitate Nan sitting in its rear in her own wheelchair, then whizzing both of us along the sands at outrageous speed, much to her delight and my terror. The occasion did, of course, call for a bottle of chilled champagne to be cracked open in celebration of the impossible just having been made possible by a local worthy who lives by one of the island's defining mantras.

It could only happen on Arran.

The Magic of Kildonan

A leisurely four-mile drive eastwards from Kilmory will take you through the farmland areas and rural settlements of Shannochie, Auchenhew and Bennan, towards the village of Kildonan, which occupies a prime location right on the southernmost tip of Arran.

As you approach the right-turn that will take you down to the village, the view from the heights towards the coast will have you gasping. To avoid plummeting over the cliffs in wonderment, this would be a very good time to stop driving. So just pull into the side of the road, get your camera out and live to tell the glorious tale.

Panning from the left in a clockwise direction across the Firth of Clyde, you will marvel at the sight of over one hundred miles of dramatic contours and rugged coastline, all the way from the distant symmetrical peak of Ben Lomond to the quaint little islands of the Cumbraes and down the entire Ayrshire coast to Loch Ryan in Galloway. On this side of the firth stretches Kildonan Bay, with in the foreground little Pladda adorned by its towering white lighthouse, while in the background some twelve miles further beyond lies its more sinister cousin, Ailsa Craig. This huge 1,000-foot-high granite rock was once dubbed 'Paddy's Milestone' by the maritime Clydesiders, in deference to its half-way location between Glasgow and Belfast. Panning further clockwise, the dramatic clifftops of Northern Ireland's County Antrim can just be made out, then the southerly toe of the Mull of Kintyre, off which lies little Sanda, or Spoon Island as it prefers to call itself nowadays.

Trust me, the sight of this wonderful vista in the early morning sunshine is one you will never forget.

Kildonan itself was named after sixth-century disciple, St Donan, who accompanied his more illustrious colleague, St Columba, on a mission to convert the once-heathen Arran community to Christianity.

The former's remains are reputedly buried in the grounds of Kildonan farm, where the remnants of a chapel have been unearthed by the droves of contemporary geologists who still invade the island with amazing regularity. In the village's infancy, Kildonan Castle was the very heart of the community. An official royal residence until 1405, the Castle was then bestowed by King Robert upon one John Stewart of Ardgowan, in whose family its ownership remained until the seventeenth century when it eventually became the property of the Hamilton family, numerous contemporary descendants of whom still live on the island.

Around that time, the great majority of local residents were farming families scattered across a whole plethora of tiny 'clachans' which punctuated the landscape of both High and Low Kildonan. Each of the local farms supported around ten families apiece. Like all of Arran's farms, they operated on the aforementioned run-rig system, narrow strips of ploughed and cultivated land being allocated to each tenant by 'lot and rotation' in order to provide everyone with their fair share of the best and the worst of the land. Sustained mainly by a staple diet of barley, oats and potatoes, the wider Kildonan community swelled to nearly 600 in those days. Times were good, if very modest and exceedingly hard-earned.

The village's first church and school were built in the nineteenth century, in the aftermath of much controversy concerning such things as the chosen denomination and location of the former, and the preferred social and pedagogical philosophies of the latter. In the late nineteenth and early twentieth centuries, the church congregation grew to an amazing 700-plus, while by the beginning of the 1920s the pupil roll of Kildonan School topped 60.

Edna Picken, a born-and-bred 'sooth-ender' and farmer's widow who sadly passed away just a few months prior to the completion of this book, will always be much revered for her larger-than-life personality and immense contribution to island life. Edna was born in Kildonan in 1924 and raised in the croft at Kildonan Castle. She was kind enough to share with me some fond memories of her developing years.

'In those days, the Post Office was located up at Dippen, which was a real hive of activity. My memory of Dippen is one of majestic houses surrounded by beautiful gardens, the place teeming with people from the neighbourhood walking back and forward to the Post Office, and the farmers and tradesmen arriving in their horses-and-carts. Everybody knew each other, and everybody spoke to each other. It was a simple life, but a happy life.'

Edna's infancy and much of her childhood revolved around her beloved Kildonan, the birthplace she will always hold dear to her heart. She remembered the village layout as if it were yesterday.

'There were several buildings around the Castle where we lived, and a few more along Shore Road towards St Donan House and the Kildonan Hotel, both of which are still standing today. Further along and on the other side of the road you came to Kildonan School with the headmaster's schoolhouse beside it, and then to Drimla Lodge where the Clark family (the celebrated shoe-makers) lived. The United Free Church was originally located at Yellow Port on the south side of the village, after which Kirk Kildonan was built on what we now call "Church Brae", half-way between High and Low Kildonan, in order to satisfy the residents of both parts of the village. In the 'twenties and 'thirties, almost everyone went to the Sunday service, and just about all of them walked there and back, sometimes for several miles in the pouring rain. After the service, the young ones like myself attended Sunday School. Church on a Sunday really was an institution, the hub of the community.

'Yellow Port (Porta Buidhe) was a proper working harbour, with motorised "smacks" sailing in and out all the time carrying their cargoes of timber, cement, paraffin, all sorts of foodstuffs and, of course, coal which fuelled everything in those days. The horses and carts would start arriving when the tide was out, so that the carts could be backed right up to the side of the smack to avoid any coal being lost. From there it would be taken across the road to the weighing station. I seem to remember that the Breadalbane Hotel and Drimla Lodge used to share a 40-ton load of coal between them.'

However, it wasn't just the smacks which intrigued the young Edna. In fact, it was one seafaring vessel in particular which really caught her eye.

'The *Queen Mary* used to sail right past us on the far side of Pladda, sometimes in the middle of the night. Whenever my parents knew she was due to pass Dippen Point, my two big sisters and I would get a knock on our bedroom door to come and see her sail past. She really was a magnificent sight, all lit up from bow to stern, absolutely majestic. I also remember that she was due to make her appearance one particular summer's morning, and all the tourists flocked to Corrie to see her, armed with their binoculars and cameras. However, it was a very misty morning and they never saw a thing. By the time the skies eventually cleared, the *Queen Mary* was sailing right past our window in Kildonan. I'll never forget her emerging out of the mist into the sunshine, a truly spectacular sight.'

As far as Kildonan School was concerned, teachers' salaries in those days were about twenty-pounds-per-year, paid for in full by parents' tuition fees, which as previously rehearsed started at two-shillings-a-year for reading, increasing by sixpence (or a 'tanner') if you wanted your child to learn to write as well as read, and a further tanner if arithmetic was thrown in too. Finally, school fees could peak at an astronomical one-pound-sterling for those very few parents who could afford to have their children taught in the fine disciplines of navigation and book-keeping.

Edna's lasting reminiscences of her childhood would always be of a humble, happy upbringing bereft of the excesses which many youngsters now take for granted but blessed with a real appreciation of the simple things in life.

'Much of our time as children was spent playing on the cliffs at Kildonan Castle, just watching the boats go by. I was always fascinated by the sea and the range of vessels that sailed past. And I was always impressed by how well the emergency services on Arran all worked together whenever there was a crisis at sea or on land – the police, the coastguard service, the lifeboats, the mountain rescue team, the medics and all the volunteers on the island.'

Given her self-confessed fascination with the mighty ocean, perhaps it is no surprise that Edna would go on to serve on Arran's Lifeboat Committee for practically all her adult life, working with fellow volunteers to raise many thousands of pounds in the process for this lifeline service. Yet again, proof positive about the essence of island life. If something needs done, the islanders don't automatically look for the authorities to do it for them. They just get on with it and do it for themselves.

Wonderful memories from a wonderful lady. Edna Picken will be sorely missed.

Former schoolteacher and farmer's widow, Mamie Stewart, who first came to Arran away back in 1947, is another much-respected elderly Kildonan resident who has witnessed the changing face of her beloved village over the decades.

'I met first Johnny in Kildonan Hall. We got married in 1960 and moved into Craigend farm. I had no hesitation about leaving my teaching career and becoming a farmer's wife. I loved the life. We reared turkeys, we had cattle and crops, and life was great. Nowadays, though, it's much tougher for farmers to make a living, with milk prices in particular stifling the business. Kildonan has changed dramatically over the years. It has gone from being a small, tight-knit community to a much bigger and more up-market village. We warmly welcome the tourists who are the life-blood of our island, but what really upsets me is the ever-increasing number of big modern holiday homes being built, many of which lie empty half the time.'

Mamie fondly remembers her late husband's eye for an opportunity and his wicked sense of humour.

'Have you seen that big standing stone in the car park down at the foot of the drive at Craigend?' she asked me with a wry smile. 'Well, it used to be in our field, but the tourists kept climbing over the fence to see it, and Johnny had to keep mending the wires. He was also getting fed up with them stopping to ask him about its origins, so one day he decided to hatch a plan. He moved the stone to the other side of the fence, where it still is today, and made up a story just to give the tourists something to think about. His story, which soon grew arms and legs and had everybody talking about it, was that the standing stone marked a famous chambered cairn, underneath which lay the remains of a beautiful Scandinavian princess. Honestly, within weeks they were flocking in their busloads to see it. It seemed to keep them happy though. And it certainly kept them away from Johnny's fence!'

Anything that Mamie doesn't know about the seafaring life around Kildonan simply isn't worth knowing.

'In the old days, there were four cottages on Pladda. The lightkeepers lived there for six weeks at a time, then got a fortnight off, while their wives and families lived in the big buildings on your left as you come into Lamlash. The keepers manually logged every single vessel which sailed past, a lonely job but a very important one. The coastguard base was down near the Kildonan Hotel, from where they would launch their rockets and flares to let the other team members know any time there was an emergency. Even today, you can still see the remains of the old observation tower up at the castle. In those days, it was manned 24-hours-a-day, 7-days-a-week, and the coastguard men used 'semaphore' to communicate with each other. I remember that a big rope hung from the top of the tower down to the ground, so that the duty coastguard's wife could bring a basket of food for him to haul up for his lunch. Life was very simple back then, but it all worked remarkably well.'

Larger-than-life local character, Finlay Cook, is a born-and-bred Kildonan man and very proud of it. His great-grandparents built Cook's Stores, situated along the coastal track at the western extremity of Kildonan, surely one of the most scenic locations of any shop in the entire country. Looking out from its sea-facing windows, the local customers and tourists alike would marvel at the seals basking on the rocks of the calm bay in summer, and the mighty ocean waves crashing onto the shore in the winter, as they prepared to lug their assorted provisions homeward. Cook's Stores was a much-valued local enterprise which was run by the family for an astonishing 125 years.

'The day came when it was left to my two brothers and me to take over the business. So, our job was to run the shop and also a travelling van, both of which were always busy. The main holiday season was really hectic. The holidaymakers would phone in their orders in advance and expect them to be delivered to their front doors on arrival. We sold just about everything you could imagine, from food and drink, to haberdashery, to paraffin oil, to dungarees, wellies and wire netting. You name it, we sold it.

'It was a very honourable trade, though. There were many small businesses and travelling vans on the island in the old days, but we always respected and helped each other out, never standing on anybody's toes. Hogmanay was always my favourite day of the year. We would shut up shop at half-past-five, and the local farmers and quite a few of the villagers would turn up for the party. I'll always remember the banter and laughter as we sat on the lemonade crates with our wee drams, mulling over the year that was about to come to a close, and toasting the one that lay ahead.'

Some of Finlay's stories are now part of Kildonan folklore. Like the party in Drimla Lodge, at the conclusion of which he and a few cronies decided to jump into a tiny rowing boat, armed of course with their 'cairry-oot', and set sail for Pladda, only to discover that they had forgotten to put the 'bung' in, at which point the boat began sinking and they had to swim back to shore. Or indeed, the time Finlay attempted to negotiate his way home from a raucous night in the Breadalbane Hotel, the mere 200-yard walk taking him all of two-and-a-half hours, including a one-hour nap on the beach. As Finlay himself put it, 'I was so drunk that night, my troosers fell doon!'

Like many an elder statesman on the island, he too has observed the changing pattern of tourism over the years, from month-long lets on a year-after-year basis for the same, mainly British families during the July/August holiday season only, to weekly or fortnightly breaks all year round for an ever-changing and increasingly cosmopolitan clientele.

'In the old days, you got to know the holidaymakers quite well, because they tended to come back every year at the same time, but nowadays the pattern is completely different and there are new faces all the time. We're still a thriving wee community, though, and the village remains a very, very popular tourist destination.'

Kildonan Village Hall was originally constructed during the Great War of 1914-18, principally as a 'reading room' but also to provide a more fit-for-purpose venue for the dances, whist drives and numerous other social events which characterised village life, and which up until then had been held in Kildonan School. The hall was originally funded from the public purse, and in more recent times it was extended to become the impressively functional building that it is today.

Kildonan worthy, Alistair 'Slats' Yates, has witnessed many a change in the village's fortunes over his 28 years in office as Chairman and Vice Chairman of the Hall Committee, and as local Community Councillor.

'Yes, Kildonan has certainly changed quite a bit over the years. When we first moved here in the mid-eighties, the majority of residents were indigenous to the south-end, and there was a very powerful "community feel" to the village. Everybody helped each other out as a matter of course, and nobody wanted for anything. For a small community, we were very well served by having two good hotels – the Kildonan and the Breadalbane – a village hall, and our wee shop which will always be known to the islanders as "Cook's Stores". The sale of the Breadalbane Hotel was a huge loss, particularly now that the building has been demolished for yet more property development. The village has got a good bit bigger in recent years with lots of incomers buying up property, so I suppose it was inevitable that the community dynamics would change. As Hall Chairman, I find that it's a bit harder to get people involved nowadays. However, I will say this. If there's ever a crisis or something important that needs to get done, the Kildonan people still turn out and work together to resolve it. A lot of things may have changed over the years, but we still have a great wee community, and village life still works remarkably well.'

Today's Kildonan may have developed a more modern twenty-first century 'feel', but it still retains a great deal of its quaint laid-back atmosphere and unique magic. A leisurely drive, cycle or walk through the village will illustrate this paradox in spades.

Near the Castle ruins, Craigend farmhouse sits on the left, opposite which is a small car park complete with the late Johnny Stewart's famous standing stone, and from which a steep set of concrete steps leads down to one of the most beautiful and secluded beaches on the whole island, the perfectly-named Silver Sands. As its name implies, it is a wonderful beach on which many a sun-kissed sandcastle has been built on a glorious summer's day, and from which many a daring New Year's Day 'skinny-dip' has been launched into the icy waves. A short walk along Silver Sands will take you past some big black rocks onto a narrow coastal path which soon winds up the hill towards the ruins of Kildonan Castle, where a large information board describes the ancient castle's history. Another short stroll will then complete your circular route back to the car park, from which the views across Kildonan Bay are simply gorgeous.

Looking due south, the pear-shaped Pladda will appear so close that you'll feel you could throw a stone onto its long, narrow jetty. Defined spectacularly by its tall ivory-white lighthouse, the tiny island radiates a strange mystical charm. First illuminated by a single small lantern away back in October 1790 to warn seafaring vessels to steer clear of its perilous rocks, it was upgraded to a much more powerful and effective 'group flashing-light' system in 1901. Boatmen ferried provisions to Pladda, and also took the lightkeepers themselves to 'mainland' Arran and back four times each month, two on Sundays in order that they could attend church. By 1972, a helicopter was being deployed to perform this function, and by 1990, the lighthouse service had been fully automated and the lightkeepers withdrawn altogether. Nowadays, the lighthouse, along with its many distant siblings scattered around the coastline of Scotland, is operated and monitored remotely by the headquarters of the Northern Lighthouse Board, based in far-off Edinburgh. However, modern technology notwithstanding, Pladda lighthouse's uniquely distinctive 'triple-flash' every thirty seconds over a glorious moonlit Kildonan Bay is something which, once seen, will never be forgotten.

Seeking Sanity

While I have attempted to be as objective as possible in writing this book, I do hope you will allow me at this point to wallow in another of my little self-indulgences. The fact is that I feel I must now blow my cover and confess that Kildonan is my favourite location on the whole island. Indeed, if truth be told, it is my favourite place on Planet Earth.

I can honestly say that nowhere relaxes me more than Kildonan does. Ever since we set up home in the village over a decade ago, the stresses and strains of professional and domestic life just always seemed to evaporate into the clean salty air every time we arrived at our haven-by-the-sea. As indeed did modern living's innumerable irritants, which being much more prevalent amid the hustle-and-bustle of mainland life often managed to wriggle and burrow their way right under my skin. My 'pet hates' I call them, although my children always preferred the term, 'bees in dad's bonnet'.

Take recreational cyclists, for example. Particularly those brain-dead numpties who ride two (or even three) abreast on Ayrshire's rural roads, blethering away to each other and merrily oblivious to the fact that a council bin lorry, two Stagecoach buses and nine cars are queued up behind them trying desperately to get to their destination. Perhaps a local byelaw ought to be introduced to permit frustrated drivers to mow them down (always humanely, of course). Just saying.

And television news reporters. You know the ones I mean, don't you? Those who begin their lengthy monologues by introducing their first point as '1', then drone on for ages without '2' ever getting a mention (or alternatively (a) rather than (1), with (b) enjoying no more success than (2) did). And their football pundit bedfellows too, especially former players, whose big new word these days seems to be 'fortuitous' when all they really mean is 'lucky', in a laughable attempt to convince us that by using a four-syllable word they have somehow transmogrified overnight from bustling centre-forwards into suave intellectuals.

Please allow me to give you one very recent example. 'Real Madrid were very fortuitous there, because Ronaldo was clearly offside.' No, I'm sorry, but Real Madrid weren't fortuitous! They were just lucky, plain and simple! I mean, what's wrong with the word, 'lucky'? For example, would a legendary gun-toting New York gangster ever have gained the same notoriety if his name had been 'Fortuitous Luciano'? Or would Kylie Minogue have bagged her first Number 1 hit with a song called 'I Should Be So Fortuitous'? I rest my case.

And what about couples who go into restaurants and share a scone? Or worse still, the really disgusting ones who buy a pudding between them and slobber over it using the same spoon? What's that all about? Do they do it to save money, or to reduce carbohydrate intake, or to infect each other with lurking micro-organisms or what? Perhaps they too should be subject to the new byelaw applying to multi-abreast cyclists, thereby addressing all their financial, calorific and hygiene-related issues in one fell swoop.

Then there's the 'nanny state' in which we have now found ourselves gasping for freedom to breathe. The politicians, doctors and assorted academics, who with increasing frequency and fervour, delight in telling us what we can and cannot do. Now, I'm all for promoting sensible lifestyle habits, but I really didn't need the advice of the NHS bozo who came on TV recently to say (and I kid you not), 'There's nothing wrong with having a small glass of red wine when you come home from work on a Friday evening'. Good grief, not only are they still sanctimoniously wittering on about what we should and shouldn't drink, but they're now even telling us what colour it should be and on which night of the week we should drink it. I need a beer. And right now.

And while I'm on a roll, let's look at people on waymarked walks who don't like dogs. I mean, what do you expect to find up there in the woods? A teddy bears' picnic? Sure, Scotland's rural countryside is a hillwalkers' paradise, but it's also a dog-walkers' paradise as well, as our tourist literature and route maps make blindingly obvious to anyone who can be bothered to read them. So, if you don't like dogs, might I suggest that you just stay clear of the hill paths and forest trails which are certain to be full of them, because they sure as hell don't like you either.

Anyway, that's my rant over, you'll be glad to know. Clearly, I'm writing this particular chapter on the mainland at the moment, and my frustration is beginning to reach very worrying proportions. I really must jump into my car before it gets out of control and head straight back to Kildonan immediately.

Rectilinearly-orientated cyclists, beware.

The Healing of the Hidden Valley

I find that one of the most successful ways of cleansing my soul is to shove on my walking boots, stuff my pockets full of dog biscuits and head for Loch Garbad with my canine companions.

Loch Garbad, aka 'The Black Loch', is an incredibly tranquil hill-loch situated high above the village of Kildonan. I normally walk the full way there and back from our home on Shore Road, but if you're just visiting the area, it's probably best to start from the car park located immediately across the A841 from the steep 'Church Brae' which leads up from the village. There you will find an information board and a newly-constructed cafeteria, courtesy of the most impressive 'Eas Mor Ecology Project'.

The project's mantra captures its ethos perfectly - 'Always believe in your dream, for it's a beautiful dream, and without your dream there can be nothing.'

The 'Hidden Valley' of Eas Mor ('great fall' in Gaelic) is located in the forests above the western extremity of the village of Kildonan.

It was so named because the sheer density of the woodlands once rendered it almost completely obscured from view, meaning that the people of the locale were only obliquely aware of its existence, but totally unable to access its well-hidden secrets. Indeed, it is said that many Kildonan residents were even blissfully unaware of the valley's most spectacular feature, the magnificent Eas Mor, which at 103 feet is the highest single fall on the whole island. Just try to imagine, if you can, a waterfall of such magnitude and incredible beauty, yet one so tragically concealed from all human delectation.

However, that was then, and this is now. Today, the Hidden Valley and its constituent treasures attract an annual 'footfall' of some 20,000 visitors. And all of this thanks to the vision and determination of one man in particular, the larger-than-life character that is Albert Holmes. Or, as the Eas Mor Ecology website proudly proclaims, 'In the beginning, there was a forest, a fall, a man, and a dream.'

Born and reared in the Ayrshire town of Maybole, Albert first made a start to fulfilling his dream of 'healing the forest' away back in 1983. It was always going to be an incredibly ambitious and arduous task, but his commitment was boundless.

'This place was truly beautiful, but in need of tender loving care. Although Eas Mor was just over three quarters of a mile (one kilometre) from the village of Kildonan, the waterfall and the forest surrounding it were so inaccessible that many never even knew of its existence. So, along with others of like mind, I would return from time to time and start the long hard healing process. We would crawl into the depths of the forest, and it was from there that the healing began. We then created the only place in the whole forty-acre site where you could actually stand up, and that was where we situated 'Base Camp'. Over time we have thinned out the trees, and let the light touch the forest floor for the first time in many, many years. Good nights were enjoyed around the fire at Base Camp, with our hard work giving us heat, light and talk of the possibilities for Eas Mor.

'More than fifteen years later, Eas Mor was still elusive to many, and as the new millennium approached I decided that the whole valley should be accessible to all, showing what a beautiful and special place it is. Otherwise people would never be able to appreciate the therapeutic benefits of being out in a relatively wild forest, one in which they can find rare orchids, an oasis of indigenous deciduous trees, some of which are many hundreds of years old, and also red squirrels and water voles, as well as a plethora of birds and other woodland creatures.

'And so, in 1998, and with part-funding from "Millenium Forest for Scotland", a core group of eight of us set about undertaking the mammoth task of building a path around the waterfall for people of all abilities, which would end up at an eco-friendly library in the heart of the forest. The magnitude of this prospect was awesome, but with a limited budget and a total belief in each other, we completed our task in May of 2000. However, the work never stops, and every day since then something is done towards fulfilling the Eas Mor dream.'

Over the years, Albert and his team of willing volunteers managed to complete the construction of a basic log building with a turf roof on a clearing high above the waterfall, using wind-blown timber from the infamous storms of 1998, and developed it into a library and interpretation centre with an ecological theme.

Albert has always had a crystal-clear vision of the library's potential.

'It is a place where everyone can learn about their environment, and where children are encouraged to draw pictures of what they have seen when coming face-to-face with the nature that is all around them. The whole project is a perfect example of recycling, with nothing being removed from the site and everything being re-used for construction.'

In Albert's own words, the project is 'a labour of love'. A forest can need almost constant attention, and the vast forty-acre woodland at Eas Mor is certainly no exception. It has involved some really heavy-duty work too, such as the quarrying of many tons of 65-million-year-old lava-flow stone to create the bottom path network, a process which over time has left a horseshoe-shaped 'amphitheatre' next to a large firepit to be used for various outdoor gatherings. The process to thin out the lower and mostly dead branches of the trees to around seven-feet up the trunk is called 'brashing'. This allows natural light to get through to the ground, encouraging the trees to grow upwards. A lot of the work involves removing wind-blown plantation trees and re-planting indigenous species.

'At Eas Mor, large areas of woodland are being brashed to allow for future play areas where children can climb and play without parents having to worry about them hurting themselves. With the lower branches cleared, the pine-needle-covered floor makes an ideal surface for play, much better than any man-made material could provide, and it costs nothing. Once the trees have been trimmed, there are many piles of branches left lying on the forest floor. These are not wasted, but instead are recycled to build hedges to keep the site secure, and they provide a natural habitat for the local wildlife. However, building these hedges is a long process requiring patience and knowledge of specific construction techniques. Two people working for eight hours might struggle to clear more than fifty trees, and the enormity of the project only comes into perspective when you realise that there are many thousands of trees requiring attention. Building the hedges will take longer, as all the branches have to be collected and moved down to the areas where they are being constructed, but by the time this part of the project is eventually finished, there will be many miles of hedges.'

A major strand of the Eas Mor Ecology Project was 'planning a truly green source of sustainable power', through the construction of a hydro-electric energy facility. Since the approval of the original application to develop a smaller hydro scheme, additional land stretching a further quarter of a mile downstream alongside the Allt Mor was subsequently acquired, thereby increasing the scheme's overall capacity, and its connection to the main electricity grid was also accepted. The 100-kilowatt hydro scheme is now fully operational, providing an income stream which fulfils even more of the 'dream'.

An attractive new cedar-lined building has now been constructed adjacent to the Eas Mor car park, located at the junction of the island's main A841 circular road with Kildonan's Church Brae. Due to be opened in 2019, this will operate as a small reception and information area for the site, the new 'Forest of the Falls' cafeteria, a disabled-friendly toilet block, and a store for the project's intended 'Tramper Mobility Scooters', which together with communication handsets will be available for use by visitors with limited mobility to enable them to explore the natural delights of the forest. In addition, a roadside shelter has already been constructed, and a yoga pavilion and two additional footbridges are planned, with the site's many intertwining paths being upgraded continuously.

However, perhaps most impressive of all will be Eas Mor's proposed woodland 'Ecology Centre', which will serve as the 'hub' for the whole project. Designed to merge with the surrounding countryside and to reflect the topography of the nearby dome-shaped Auchenhew Hill, the new building will be constructed as far as possible from on-site materials, including stone from

Eas Mor's very own quarry. It will be powered by 'green energy', specifically hydro, solar and wind power.

The Ecology Centre's main purpose is to provide a facility for people of all abilities to stay on site, thereby maximising their appreciation of the uniquely beautiful woodland surroundings, and to learn and enjoy hands-on experience of environmental and conservation practices. Its lower floor will comprise a central kitchen, a solar-heating glasshouse and seven bedrooms, with at its centre the 'Forum' and its welcoming open fire, which will be used for conferences, lectures, meetings and a whole host of activities. Staff and visiting lecturers will be accommodated on the upper floor.

Albert's dream has now become a reality, but his commitment to taking the Eas Mor project to the next level is stronger than ever, as encapsulated in the words of one of his own poems.

> I am the wind in the trees, the rain in the leaves,
> A sunset in June, a crisp autumn moon,
> A son yet unborn, a great one long gone,
> That tear in your eye, the river that runs by.
> ***
> I am these things in us all.
> Tour of life, and life to all.
> ***
> But you poison me in droplets, and you poison me in streams,
> You poison me in oceans, and poison your own dreams,
> When the first step of reincarnation is evaporation then precipitation,
> Never be frightened of the rain, it is only those who've been before you.
> ***
> This tour of life.
> This life to all.

Returning to the 'Black Loch walk' itself, the tree-lined track up the hill from the Eas Mor car park is quite steep. To the left, the rolling farm fields are populated by flocks of sheep as they munch contentedly on the lush green grass, while low on the right lie a couple of stagnant ponds, the second of which once set the scene for one of the most excruciatingly embarrassing moments of my entire life.

Accompanied that lovely spring morning by my now sadly-departed Labradors, Tanna and Saffy, it was the latter and decidedly crazier junior of the two who decided to plunge into the slime-infested pond for no particular reason, other than to perform the role of 'class clown' as usual. It was unbelievable. When she eventually decided to heed my command and extricate herself from the pond, her golden-yellow coat had turned a manky-green, and tiny gunge-covered creatures were clinging to her coat, some of which may have been mere tadpoles but the rest of which looked almost extra-terrestrial, and the stink was appalling.

Just at that, a family of three came wandering down the hill-track, mum and dad holding hands, their toddler daughter wandering a few yards behind and licking an orange-coloured lollipop. A vision of impending horror engulfed my psyche. It was right to do so.

As our paths converged, the parents began to pat and fuss over the much more mature and sensible Tanna, but as soon as the pea-green monster-from-the-deep came gallumphing into view they dissolved in hysterical laughter. Saffy took that as an invitation to join in the social discourse, and immediately bolted towards them, shaking herself furiously to rid herself of the jelly-like effluent that clung to her coat like some kind of sinister ectoplasm, at which point the toddler let out a blood-curdling shriek.

The next scene seemed to unfold in slow motion. The youngster decided to protect her lollipop by thrusting it high up above her head. Interpreting this as an offer of sustenance, Saffy leapt and grabbed the lolly, saturating the poor wee soul from head to toe in green gunk. As mum and dad carried their traumatised daughter screaming back to their vehicle, doubtless to administer a full change of clothes and tut-tutting in disgust, my apologies fell on deaf ears. My humiliation knew no bounds.

Anyway, back to the walk itself. A few hundred yards up the slope, the track soon levels out above the gorge below, the basin of which at this point will be completely hidden from view by the tall pine trees. Another hundred yards along the track you will arrive at a viewing platform, from which you will be able to wallow in the most incredible vista. To your left, the fast-flowing waters of the Eas Mor cascade dramatically over the precipice and crash onto the rocks below, while straight ahead the cavernous cliffs drop vertically from the site of the wood-built 'ecology library' down into the valley. Meanwhile to your right, the same valley opens up to reveal the whole expanse of Kildonan Bay, with the beautiful Pladda and its unmistakeable lighthouse dominating the foreground, and Ailsa Craig providing a distant backdrop. If ever a panorama was designed to tickle your camera's fancy, this was surely it.

A few yards further along, the track forks left towards Loch Garbad and right to the ecology library and the lower forest. If you take the former, which is clearly signposted, you will soon find yourself meandering alongside a tiny tree-lined burn. The path then climbs out into the open again, where you will reach a sharp left turn at a wooden stile. This leads down to the farm in Ballymeanoch Glen, which is the route I would normally choose when walking from Low Kildonan. However, ignore this stile, keep left and continue along the footpath into the woods, where an 'Arran Angling Association' sign confirms that a well-stocked loch awaits any anglers keen enough to trek all the way up the hill to try their luck. The path then takes you across another burn, shallow enough to cross without getting your feet submerged, and into a much denser pine forest. A steep climb of about half-a-mile then brings you out into a clearing, and although you won't be able to see the loch at this point, the level topography on the summit ahead gives the game away. A few steps further up the slope, and the still waters of Loch Garbad suddenly reveal themselves.

'The Black Loch' is very well-named, its deep-dark depths fully in synch with its slate-grey bottom. A fishing boat lies moored to your left, while straight ahead you will be able to negotiate a walk along the steep banking for a good few yards before it becomes rather inaccessible. Now is the time to stop, sit down on the grass, and 'listen' to the silence. It will be deafening. Many a magical moment of true peace and tranquillity I have enjoyed lying on the banks of Loch Garbad, split only by the splash of a Labrador Retriever diving into its ebony depths. Just relax, take all the time you need, and soak up the magic.

All that now remains is to retrace your steps back down to the Eas Mor car park. However, you really ought to take the detour to your left when you reach the signpost to the ecology library. This totally unique facility is well worth a visit for cultural and educational reasons, allowing you the opportunity to marvel at the impressive selection of wildlife publications which sit alongside a vast array of children's drawings, reflections and poems. One word of caution, though. Do put your dog on a lead at this point, because some serious cliffs lie in wait of unsuspecting wanderers.

Following the track steeply downhill will then lead to a series of terraced deep pools in the Allt Mor, all hewn out by the bare hands of Albert Holmes and his team, and perfect for letting your dog have a final swim to remove the muck before jumping back into your car, which itself can be reached by crossing the footbridge and strolling the last few yards through the woods.

Like so many walks on this island paradise, a magical stroll through the Hidden Valley and up to the Black Loch is an absolute must. Especially if you want to wallow in the sound of silence.

Aquaphobia, Ornithophobia and Smoked Mackerel

As wondrously serene and indescribably beautiful as Pladda surely is, my first visit there will definitely be my last. And believe me, there is a very good reason for this drastic decision, one to which I have alluded earlier in this book, viz., my own laughable fear of water in excess of ankle depth.

It was a Friday morning in the merry month of May, the day before my 'Big-Six-O' birthday bash which my wife had surreptitiously arranged to take place in our Kildonan cottage, complete with extended family, lifetime friends et al. It would turn out to be a fantastic weekend, and one which I will remember for all the best reasons, with the notable exception of that dreaded Friday, which I will remember for all the worst.

I really don't know whether to blame my son Derek, his wife Catriona or my good friend Ronnie Mann. Looking back at the whole experience with the benefit of objective hindsight, it was probably Derek's fault since it was his idea in the first place, but Catriona must shoulder some of the blame for egging him on. There again, the object of my discomfort was Ronnie's new 'rib' boat. So *tua culpa*, the lot of you.

I will admit that it did seem a good idea at the time. The sky was blue, the flat-calm of Kildonan Bay was even bluer, and the sun was melting the tarmac on Shore Road. It really was an absolute belter, a perfect day for sailing.

As I sat on the side of the rib waiting for Ronnie to kick-start the petrol engine and grasping at its edge with such force that I feared white knuckles might burst through ageing skin at any moment, I stared transfixed in terror at my pathetic little life-jacket, momentarily pondering the futility of its purpose, so totally consumed was I with one horrific vision. This was of an enormous, inquisitive basking shark inadvertently capsizing our boat out at sea and plunging me into the icy waves, the tiny jacket then doing its commendable best to keep me afloat while my arms flailed in panic like a Dutch windmill in a force-eight gale. It was less than an hour since I had ravenously devoured my toast-and-banana breakfast, and at that moment I knew it would only be a matter of time before I would see it again.

To my immense surprise and relief, I actually found the sail across the sea to be extremely exhilarating, our collective backsides bouncing in perfect sync with the ocean waves as the rib careered at seemingly enormous velocity towards Pladda. A few minutes later, we disembarked and began walking up the concrete jetty. It was then that my seriously ornithophobic daughter-in-law uttered her first terror-stricken words.

'Ian … birds! Hundreds of them!'

My own response was as customarily empathetic as usual.

'For heaven's sake, Catriona. Just what do you expect to find on a totally uninhabited island in the middle of the Firth of Clyde? Cuddly koala bears?'

To be fair, though, she was numerically correct. There were indeed hundreds of the feathered creatures, mainly seagulls, and all they did was sit there staring menacingly at us, no doubt poised to take off at any moment and descend on us from great height in a violent, merciless airborne attack designed to rip great chunks of flesh from bone.

'Did you ever watch that old Alfred Hitchcock film?' I asked Catriona, caringly.

'Don't, Ian,' she gasped breathlessly, clinging onto her husband's arm for dear life. 'Just don't.'

Thankfully, the aerial attack failed to materialise, and we all lived to tell the tale. As we wandered around the imposing lighthouse and its various outhouses, my thoughts turned to the plight of the old lightkeepers in days gone by, their emotions doubtlessly oscillating feverishly as the ferryman once more whisked them away from their beloved wives and weans for a whole fortnight of hard graft in near-isolation, and with the real potential for 'cabin fever' to enter the equation at any moment. There again, perhaps it might have been the sheer beauty of this tiny little isle which ultimately prevailed to keep them sane and content, with its glorious west-facing view of Low Kildonan village overlooked by the lush-green fields of High Kildonan up above, and its east-facing cavernous cliffs taking in the incredible panorama of the vast Ayrshire coastline. Who knows? I'm just glad that it was neither me nor mine who had to live such a lonely existence in performing a role so critically important to the safety and well-being of our ancient mariners. There but for the grace of God, as they say.

Back onto the rib, and back out to sea at near-supersonic speed, this time to the much deeper waters which lie off Pladda's east coast. Catriona's ordeal was over. Little did I know that mines was just beginning.

The very moment that Ronnie switched off the engine, the boat started bobbing. The more it bobbed, the more my head span. As the fishing rods and associated accoutrements got distributed all around, my toast-and-banana breakfast threatened to make its grisly reappearance. A few minutes passed, and then while Ronnie, Derek and Catriona started reeling in their copious catches of pollack and mackerel with unconcealed glee in anticipation of the evening's planned barbecue feast, I simultaneously began puking my guts up out the other side of the boat. For what seemed like an eternity, the boat bobbed and rocked like a rollercoaster out of control, the others fished as if they had been tasked to feed the entire village, and I vomited for Scotland. It was absolutely hellish.

Having received as much sympathy as I had shown Catriona during her earlier avian ordeal, it was a full two hours before the others decided enough was enough and that it was time to head back to shore. They immediately hit the pub for a few celebratory drinks. I lay on the couch in abject misery for the remainder of the afternoon.

Pladda is an utterly charming little island steeped in history, and I am so delighted to have set foot on its ruggedly beautiful expanses. However, the only means by which I could ever return would be upon consumption of excessive quantities of Arran Gin followed by a hefty intravenous injection of Propofol.

And as far as sailing for sailing's sake is concerned, wild horses would never get me back on a bloody rib.

A Tragic Tale
Unfortunately, Pladda has also witnessed its more serious moments, as former Arran coastguard guru, Davie McKinnon, can confirm.

'Aye, we've had quite a few incidents on Pladda, that's for sure. I'll give you just one example. One day we got a distress call from a fisherman who had noticed that another small fishing vessel appeared to have run aground on the concrete jetty on Pladda Isle. The boat looked as if it had gone adrift and hit the east side of the jetty, which was very unusual. It was plainly untethered and lying at a weird angle, and bobbing about in a very odd way.'

Davie immediately sped to Porta Buidhe (Yellow Port) at the western end of Kildonan, where one of *HMS Gannet's* enormous Sea King helicopters was waiting for him, its huge propeller blades roaring above his head as he sprinted towards the aircraft in the obligatory crouched position. Emergency service was one thing, careless decapitation quite another.

By the time the giant 'copter was half-way across Kildonan Bay, Davie's binoculars helped him to make out the silvery wake of the Arran lifeboat in the distance, as it screamed from its Lamlash base towards Pladda. Straight ahead, he noticed that another small fishing vessel had already reached the jetty, this he assumed belonging to the solitary fisherman who had made the distress call.

When the Sea King began its hovering descent onto the lower and flatter terrain of Pladda, Davie could see from the fisherman's body language that the mission was a lost cause. Rather than trying to board the drifting vessel, he was pacing up and down on the jetty beside his own, his chalk-white face sporting a look of terrible resignation.

The sight that greeted Davie McKinnon and the other emergency team members who had now joined him was one of sheer horror. The poor chap on the drifting vessel was dead. Lassoed to the winch, his prostrate blood-soaked body was wrapped all around it.

'He must have got stuck in the winch as it turned, and got pulled in, poor guy. He would have felt every single turn, every single cut. What a terrible way to go, absolutely awful.'

The team immediately carried out the obligatory search of the vessel. Down below in the hold they found two jackets, one of a young lad's size, and an opened packet of sweets. With no trace of anyone else either in the boat, in the sea or on the jetty, a frantic attempt was launched to ascertain the youngster's whereabouts, as Davie recalled.

'It turned out that the lad would have accompanied his dad on his fishing trips about nine times out of ten. Thankfully, that day had been the one-in-ten occasion that he had stayed at home. After all, there was absolutely nothing he could possibly have done to save him, and I shudder every time I think of the horrific scenes he would have had to witness.'

In the event, it was team leader Davie himself who had the unenviable task of cutting the thick wires, one by one, in order to 'unpeel' the deceased fisherman's bloodied body from the winch.

A truly gut-wrenching job, but just another day in the life of the teams of brave men who operate Arran's emergency services.

The Black Cave

The walk from Kildonan to the Black Cave, one of the island's most secluded, is nothing short of a heaven-sent opportunity to marvel at Arran's incredible variety of wildlife set against a truly spectacular seascape.

You can set off on your journey at any point along Shore Road from the elevated car park at Craigend farm to the western extremity of the village which is accessed by heading down the single track to the site of the former Cook's

Stores. From there, you can choose either to go through the gate into a farm field (keeping your dog on the lead when the local farmer's sheep or cattle are grazing) and along the winding path towards a second gate, or instead head down towards the sea and walk along the undulating shoreline until you emerge at this same gate. There you will come across a large information board, which will give you a potted history of the area and a vivid description of the wildlife, including a clear warning not to disturb the seals, which if the sea is calm you will be well-nigh certain to see frolicking in the waves or basking on the rocks.

A rough path continues parallel to the shore along Auchenhew Bay, which itself is divided into several smaller discrete bays, each with a locally-derived pet-name. Alternatively, you may prefer to walk along the beach itself, although you will have to negotiate your way over a few rocks, and depending on whether there have been any stormy conditions of late, possibly wade knee-high through some accumulations of seaweed as well. Either way, you are sure to find seagulls swooping through the breeze and oyster-catchers trotting along the sand, seals bobbing in the waves and gannets dive-bombing into the deep, and if you're very lucky, a family of otters scurrying along the rocks with the catch-of-the-day lodged firmly between the mother's razor-sharp teeth.

Kildonan is particularly famed for its large seal population, where on a clear and calm day it is possible to see anything up to one hundred of the beautiful creatures lying basking in the sunshine on the big black rocks of the bay. Sometimes during the summer months, dolphins can be spotted leaping and splashing around in this part of the mighty Atlantic Ocean which has been fortunate enough to find itself warmed by the Gulf Stream, while basking sharks and the occasional Minke whale are no strangers to Kildonan either.

Soon you will arrive at a larger rock formation guarding a small burn flowing downhill from Kildonan Waterfall, which itself can be quite spectacular after a few days of heavy rain. A concrete cattle-crossing will take you over the burn and into a flattish rock-strewn field, then back onto the shore and up to an old fence. Once across the fence, you will soon find yourself clambering over some progressively larger rocks as you make your way towards the foot of the cliffs at Bennan Head.

However, at this point, you would do well to heed the local advice, which is to proceed only if the tide is well out, lest you wish to find yourself cut off by the ocean from the big plate of fish and chips to which you may otherwise be looking forward on your return home. Another important point worth making here is that I have never taken my dogs past those sizeable boulders, for fear of them slipping, and God forbid, getting jammed between them.

Should the ocean conditions be favourable, though, and you decide to plod on, the Black Cave lies further around the corner past Bennan Head, and while it might not be quite as vast or impressive as King's Cave on the island's west coast, the eerie old cave is still well worth making the effort to visit. From the Black Cave, I have always then retraced my steps back along the shore to Kildonan, although I've occasionally taken the detour up the rough cattle-track which rises from the shoreline a few hundred yards past the fence on the Kildonan side. This track tends to get quite muddy at times, but leads up to a big field on the top of the cliff from which a crude path then takes you to the main circular road. From there, you can walk the mile or so to the right-turn leading to Kildonan, and head down Church Brae back into the village.

Another gloriously bracing walk on a God's own island.

The Far East

Giants' Graves ... or Burst Tyres?

The drive from Kildonan to Whiting Bay will take you less than fifteen minutes, and that even allows for the successful negotiation of one of the island's most notorious double bends, the like of which the Monaco Grand Prix circuit would be rightly proud. Indeed, meeting a service bus or an articulated lorry slap-bang on the geographically bewildering twin chicane above Dippen Point is an experience of which no self-respecting driver should ever be deprived. Personally, I have whizzed around those bends so often that I'm sure I could do it with my eyes shut. In fact, my wife is convinced that I often do. She cites multiple burst tyres in evidence.

Now, it is true that Arran's roads are a good bit narrower than most on the mainland. And it is also true that their general condition tends to have local tongues wagging in exasperation from time to time. However, those two excuses apart (and excellent excuses they are too), she does have a point about my driving adventures. It is therefore with considerable humility that I do concede that five burst tyres in the same number of years is not a particularly good record. I blame potholes and she blames vehicular velocity, so our interpretations of the root cause differ diametrically. And as I often point out to her in mitigation, my somewhat blemished track record is nothing compared to that of our well-known Kildonan neighbour, who once famously crashed his Land Rover into two different Stagecoach buses on the same day, his unforgettable explanation to the wife being, 'But one of them wasnae my fault', thereby volunteering the clearest possible confession that the other one most certainly was.

It was on this same section of Arran's coastal road, high on the cliffs at a location between Kildonan and Whiting Bay known locally as 'The Gerrey', that one quite amazing rescue operation took place a few years back, as former Arran Coastguard Station Master, Davie McKinnon, recalled.

'We got a call to say that a young calf had somehow managed to get itself stuck on a narrow ledge on the cliffs above the main road. The calf was only about four or five months old, and apparently it had wandered to the edge of the farm field above and slipped over the edge, where it was now standing rooted in a bit of a stew. It was in a pretty precarious situation, since there were sheer drops all around it. Because I'm a farmer myself, I got the job of going down to try to calm the calf down and get a harness fitted before it decided to take a dive over the edge.

'Once my team had lowered me down, I found myself facing the calf head-on, and it just stood there looking at me. However, it soon began to move backwards, one step at a time, until its hind legs were only a few feet away from the edge. I knew I had to get behind it, so I asked one of the team to get roped up quickly and come down to assist. As soon as he got lowered down onto the ledge at the calf's head-end, I began making my way very slowly around towards its tail-end. All seemed well until the poor beast suddenly began to get agitated, reversed another couple of steps and disappeared!

'We bolted to the edge of the cliff expecting a scene of total carnage. However, the young calf was lying on its back in a sort of V-shaped wedge of bushes, still alive but probably badly injured and seriously winded. So, we immediately got ourselves winched back up to the field and the team then hurried down to the foot of the cliff near the main road. No sooner had we got there than the calf suddenly sprang to its feet and bolted for freedom! After a bit of a search, the farmer eventually caught it and got the vet to check it over. Happily, it was fine and lived to tell the tale.'

Anyway, death-defying bovine adventures apart, now back to our own domestic squabbles, the net upshot of which is that whenever I feel the need to travel from our home in the village of Kildonan to our neighbouring Whiting Bay, I am invariably told to get my boots on and walk. And at five miles in distance and just under two hours in duration, a cracking walk it is too.

From the public car park at the old schoolhouse in Low Kildonan, a wooden signpost directs you to a rough track between a couple of houses, then uphill through a metal gate and onto a narrower path which takes you past Drimla farm. Simply continue up the farm road to its junction with the A841, then turn right and walk along the road for about half-a-mile until you reach another wooden signpost on the left-hand side, pointing you towards the heather-covered scrubland in the geberal direction of Whiting Bay. A narrow footpath then winds its way up the hill until it meets a wider forest road which you should then follow, always being alert that the occasional articulated lorry might suddenly appear out of the blue, no doubt laden with giant felled pines. Looking backwards from this point, the views over the bay towards Ailsa Craig and the Ayrshire coast are superb, Kildonan's very own Pladda lighthouse stealing the show as always.

Following the forest track uphill and slightly inland, the next couple of miles are nothing exceptional, save for the omnipresent opportunity to spot a red deer prancing with uncanny grace and agility from one side of the pine forest track to the other, a truly wonderful sight to behold. Far from being any sort of authority on wildlife, one thing I do know is how to spot a deer's proximity. Apparently, if you look closely at the smaller and younger pine trees – of 'Christmas tree' size, if you will – and notice any which are missing the very top shoot, this is the tell-tale sign of a resident deer, because that's the juicy part of the tree that they love to munch. I mean, with insight like this, who needs David Attenborough?

The forest track peaks and begins to snake downhill, gently at first but then quite steeply. Suddenly, the mighty ocean reveals itself once more from the heights, then the village of Whiting Bay comes into view, stretched out beneath your feet. The view from on high will delight you, the village in the foreground and the mystical Holy Island dominating the bay, with the outline of Arran's majestic Sleeping Warrior forming a spectacular distant backcloth. From this exalted vantage point, you might want to take a few minutes to absorb the panorama in front of you, an experience which will not immediately remind you of a dreich Monday morning at work.

The forest road continues downhill until you come to a fork, where a track dives backwards at an angle of about 45 degrees. This takes you to the 'Giants' Graves' and thereafter very steeply downhill into the village, while the wider forest road straight ahead leads to Glenashdale Falls and onwards towards Lamlash. If it's okay with you, we will take the former route for now.

The Giants' Graves are the famously historic remains of two Neolithic chambered tombs, and the site really is well worth a visit. Around 426 feet (130 metres) above sea-level, the two graves lie a few yards apart, formerly in a clearing in the heart of a dense pine forest, but ever since the trees were felled some twelve years back they can now clearly be seen in open space at the top of a hillock.

The cairn at the 'North Grave' lies on a north/south axis, and at six-yards-long by one-yard wide its shape is still very distinguishable today. Although the site has been looted of many of its artefacts over the centuries, a formal excavation in 1902 produced several articles of considerable archaeological significance, including pieces of pottery and ancient weapons such as arrowheads and knives constructed from flint.

The 'South Grave' cairn lies perpendicular to its northerly sibling, in other words east/west, and while it is roughly similar in width, it is just over half as long. The same early twentieth century excavation produced little more than boulders, stones and earth, but a further 'dig' in 1961 revealed fragments of burnt bone and rounded remains of pottery items.

This historical/archaeological account of the story of the Giants' Graves is perhaps slightly more believable than its rival in folklore, which centres around an ancient giant who once lived in Glenashdale, and who is reputed to have terrorised the local housewives. Apparently, the big oaf would pinch their hens' eggs each morning, and generally make their lives a misery. Then one day, totally scunnered by the absence of eggs on their breakfast tables, the menfolk of the locale decided to hatch (get it, hatch?) a cunning plan. So, they divided themselves into two teams and began running up and down the hillsides screaming oaths and insults at the big bully, causing him to give furiously manic chase, until he finally collapsed in a massive, perspiring, exhausted heap of flesh and bone, admittedly one considerably protein-enriched by egg albumen. And that was when the local men pounced and battered him to death, thereby restoring the delicate balance between supply and demand of eggs, and pushing up the value of both the Dow Jones and the FTSE 100 at a stroke. Sounds plausible enough to me.

So, whichever version you choose to believe (and do seek immediate medical assistance if it's the latter), a visit to the site of the Giants' Graves really is a fascinating experience. Standing on the summit of this strange little hillock overlooking the mighty ocean, one can only imagine the sheer gravitas with which the quaint little community must have viewed this 'sacred' place back in those primitive times.

Continuing downhill from the graves, you will soon reach the 'zig-zags', so called because of their multiple-Z-shaped appearance when viewed from the main road, and fashioned in recent years to replace the seemingly never-ending, gut-busting wooden steps which previously led up through the old forest. From the foot of the zig-zags, a right-turn will then take you along a track beside the Glenashdale Burn until you are reunited with the A841. A left-turn and a two-minute stroll along the pavement will then deliver your weary frame and parched lips right to the doorstep of the Eden Lodge, where you can wet your whistle on a pint of beer or a glass of vino in the recently reopened Shurig Bar, or if you feel peckish, enjoy a delightful meal in Felicity's Restaurant.

Once suitably fed and watered you then have a few options, for example to retrace your steps all the way back to your point of departure and repeat the whole gastronomic gig again in the excellent Kildonan Hotel, or jump on a bus to your next island destination. However, if forward planning is your bag and you've been really clever, you will already have arranged for someone to pick you up by car.

The choice, as they say, is yours.

'Viking Bay'

The area known as Whiting Bay, the name believed to have come from an ancient Norse derivation of 'Viking Bay' (for some reason, I had always assumed that it had something to do with the local fish population), is quite extensive geographically. It comprises a number of smaller settlements, including Sandbraes, King's Cross, Auchencairn, Knockankelly, South/Mid/North Kiskadale, Largiemhor, Largiemeanoch, Largiebeg and Auchencairn. Like many areas on Arran, Whiting Bay was undoubtedly inhabited in prehistoric times, as evidenced by various ancient monuments and artefacts, the most spectacular of which are the aforementioned Giants' Graves up on the heights from which you have just descended, although clear evidence of Viking occupation can also be seen in the form of the striking burial mound at King's Cross on the north side of the village, to which we will advance shortly.

Many generations of Whiting Bay inhabitants have witnessed the village's thoroughly chequered history from its primitive pre-historic era, through the relentless days of Nordic occupation, to the dramatic events of the fourteenth century when Robert the Bruce left his temporary King's Cross home to sail over to Ayrshire and onward to victory against the 'Sassenachs', and of course, continuing through to the present day. As with the belligerently proud smugglers all around the island, the ingeniously innovative villagers of Whiting Bay have had their moments too. Distilling hooch from illicit stills and night-time smuggling raids were once regular pastimes and proper little earners for the resourceful locals, as were the invention and recounting of terrifying supernatural tales of local demonic sightings to scare away any inquisitive exciseman who might otherwise have felt the need to be poking his big nose into their financial affairs.

However, like all of Arran's villages, it was always the mighty ocean that defined life in Whiting Bay. Up until the seventeenth century, contact with the Scottish mainland was fairly minimal, and it was only when the humble rowing boat became more readily available that those islanders courageous enough to tackle the perils of the unpredictable ocean waves were able to develop commercial links with the potentially lucrative ports on the Ayrshire coast. Then in the early eighteenth century, a 'packet service' was set up to carry islanders and mainlanders on their reciprocal sailings across the Firth of Clyde. Next came the smacks, mostly owned by local mariners, who would sail their assorted cargoes to the estuaries of the island's burns and wait until low tide to decant them into horse-drawn carts, for onward transportation to the sizeable array of small shops and businesses which punctuated not only Whiting Bay itself, but all the other island villages as well.

It wasn't until 1829 that the first 'steamer' service set sail from Glasgow's world-famous River Clyde, followed after the completion of the mainland railways in 1860 by another from the Ayrshire port of Ardrossan. Since the pier at Whiting Bay was still awaiting construction, the steamers' passengers had to be rowed ashore from tiny rowing boats to either the village's small jetty or the ferry landing at Kingscross. Eventually in 1901, Whiting Bay pier was completed, a relatively lengthy structure of its kind to access the deeper waters of the bay, although the landings at Kingscross continued for many years afterwards. Next came the tourist boom of the 1920s and 1930s, and the era of commercial competition between the Glasgow and South Western Railway and the Caledonian Steam Packet Company, during which Whiting Bay actually possessed its very own seafaring passenger vessel for a time. However, the heady days of steamboat domination eventually came to an end with the increasing use of motorised road transport on the island, which in 1964 heralded the death-knell for Whiting Bay pier.

Local stalwart Archie Nicol was born in 1934, the son of indigenous islander parents. He remembers the old days well, and is an ideal position to compare them with the new.

'My father was disabled, and I never knew him other than as an invalid. I started at Whiting Bay Primary School just as the Second World War was breaking out in 1939. Before long, we were joined by evacuee children from Glasgow, who were taken as a separate class into the church hall. I realised that those were very difficult times for the evacuees, but I had a good childhood. Whiting Bay was a busy, bustling village with shops galore. We had grocers, bakers, drapers, the Co-op which in those days was called the SCWS, a sweetie shop, newsagents, the pier buildings, tearooms and three separate garages selling fuel and carrying out mechanical repairs. And like every other village on Arran, we had a terrific bus service.'

Archie worked all his younger days as a farm labourer at Mayfield farm near Kildonan, until in 1989 he took the plunge and set up his own business building fences. He will always remember the strong community spirit and diligent work ethic which defined the village of Whiting Bay.

'Every man who wanted a job had a job. There were so many trades back then. Joiners, plumbers, electricians, driving buses, farm work ... you name it. The men worked hard and the women kept house, although some of them had paid jobs too. And quite often, the men would head straight for the pub for a well-earned pint after their shift ended at five-o'clock. There was only one boat each day, but none on a Sunday, because the sabbath day was always respected. The Village Hall was the hub of the community. There were film shows and whist drives every weekend. All the villagers went to the hall, and we all knew each other. The men would get their hair cut on a Saturday, then meet their wives and go to the pictures, although some of them just went to the pub!

'I remember that there was a 'pub race' in the village every year. The men had to down a pint at every pub in turn, and the women a half-pint. It started at the Eden Lodge and took in every single pub including the golf club, and it was very competitive. We also had various organisations and clubs, like drama and badminton. The main sport was football in those days, not rugby like it is today, and the rivalry between the villages was terrific, especially between Brodick with their blue Rangers' strips, and Lamlash in their black-and-white jerseys, when the sparks would really fly.

'The community spirit in Whiting Bay was outstanding. Nobody would ever want for anything. Even the local police officers were very much part of the community, not only here but in Brodick, Lamlash, Shiskine and Lochranza, all of which had police stations too. They would happily mix with the locals over a pint in the pub, and quite often turn a blind eye to wee things, but certainly not if you stepped badly out of line. The farmers used to walk their cattle down to the pier, and put them on the boat. I remember on one occasion, a pair of Whiting Bay worthies took their bull into the village, tied it to a house railing and went to the pub for a few pints, then got charged for being "drunk in charge of a bull!"

'Then, of course, the tourists started flocking to Arran in their droves, and the island got very busy. Local householders would move into their outhouses and farmers into their barns, just to free up accommodation for the holidaymakers. Almost everybody did it, and Whiting Bay had a huge number of boarding houses and letting properties, right up until the late 'sixties. I remember a lady from Glasgow called Annie Wiseman, who kept a ledger with all the details of letting properties and took 'a shilling in the pound', which she came around and collected at the end of the season.'

Although Archie has lived out in the countryside on the north side of Whiting Bay for many years now, he still holds a very fond affection for the village.

'Of course, life goes on and things change, but Whiting Bay is still a very nice little village. Yes, the pattern of living has changed, and many of the local islanders have been replaced by incomers who tend to keep themselves to themselves, but there is still a very good community spirit with lots of things going on. It's still a great wee place to live.'

A Whiting Bay man through-and-through, and very proud of it.

Kingscross Point

These days, there is no doubt that Whiting Bay is much more quintessentially residential in its infrastructure, although it still boasts some excellent commercial premises and a generous array of shops and stores. The village itself stretches over a mile in length, from the area of Cooper Angus holiday park on its south side to the Sandbraes equivalent on its north, although many of its 600-plus permanent residents live in the loftier properties on the adjacent hillside, beyond which lie the aesthetically-charming if physically-demanding steep fairways of Whiting Bay Golf Course.

Beyond the northern extremity of the village lies Kingscross Point, from which it is said that Robert the Bruce once set sail in the early fourteenth century in preparation for Scots' glory in the battle of Bannockburn. Of somewhat lesser historical significance, it also happens to be one of my own favourite spots on the whole island.

Simply turn right after the large playing field at the north end of the village, which also operates as a helipad site for medical emergencies, and drive on down a narrow track past the church, where a small parking space lies just above the sandy beach. From there, you can walk further down the same track and cross a bridge over the burn, then turn left and head up the hill. Once you have gone past the houses on your right, a narrow path veers up to your left between a couple of farm fields, at the top of which you will reach a tarmac road. Turn right, then follow the road all the way through the charming little hamlet of Kingscross to its far end, where a private road leads downhill to Point House. Parallel to this road, a narrow footpath will soon lead you brushing past some rather exotic bushes and trees, which depending on the time of year may also be bursting with blossom or berries. A couple of hundred yards down this steep and rocky path, the terrain levels out to reveal the spectacular sight of Holy Island sitting majestically over the ocean, at what will seem a mere stone's throw away.

From this wonderful vantage point, you will be able to enjoy the most amazing 180-degree panorama. To your left lies the huge expanse of Lamlash Bay, with the long jetty of St Molio's Fish Farm jutting out into the deeper waters, and the peaks of Clauchlands Hill and Dun Fionn providing a distant reference point. Straight ahead over the sea sits the mysterious and timeless dome-shaped Holy Island, about which more later. To your right, the bay then reluctantly gives way to the open seas of the Firth of Clyde, a couple of colourful marker-buoys bobbing about in the waves to warn off any vessels from straying over the shallower parts of the seabed.

Continuing your stroll through a copse of trees along the grassy banks of the Kingscross Point, you will soon discover a rather interestingly-landscaped and well-manicured open field, comprising large sections of rough lawn dotted with adjacent clumps of fern and shrubs. You will probably not be surprised to learn that this was once a small golf course, which explains the creatively-designed terrain. I know not where the tees and greens may formerly have been positioned, only that it must have been a very demanding course, with umpteen hazards lying in eager wait for stray golf balls, the weary golfers' fading spirits doubtlessly revived by the sheer beauty of their surroundings.

A well-worn path then takes you up a steep slope high above the ocean to one of Arran's most celebrated landmarks, an old Viking grave of a type which is said to be very rare in Great Britain. While the site itself has suffered considerable erosion and damage over the centuries, with a bit of imagination the burial mound is still vaguely recognisable for the function it once served. That was the cremation burial - in a longboat, would you believe - of one of the first Vikings to land on the shores of Kingscross. In more recent times, and in persuasive evidence, an archaeological dig uncovered such fascinating artefacts as burnt bone and charcoal, whalebone, iron rivets and even one bronze coin said to have been minted in York in the mid-ninth century. And as a fascinating juxtaposition in the timeline of history, close by this Viking burial ground lies an Iron Age fort, which just happens to be in direct line of sight across the bay to its sibling perched atop the aforementioned Dun Fionn.

Next, a short hike up the gentle slope of the old golf course will bring you to another rough footpath, leading you high above the shoreline through a series of gates and fields, and over a wooden stile and an adjacent electric fence of all things, which has itself provided a couple of memorable moments in the recent past.

The first occurred when my ever-mischievous golden Labrador, Saffy, somehow contrived to get herself chased around one of the adjoining fields by a couple of frolicking young horses, only to find her soaking-wet backside careering into the same electrified fence, at which point she let out a howl so blood-curdlingly hellish that the horses immediately turned on their heels and bolted for dear life. The second involved yours truly playing 'mister cool' one afternoon during a business call on my mobile, only for me to lean nonchalantly on the top fence-wire and yell out a deluge of terrible expletives which were sadly incapable of misinterpretation at the other end, while what was left of my hair was left standing on end like a French-combing session gone wrong.

The path then twists and turns through an area of tree-covered woodland, which in the springtime is positively laden with wild garlic, its unmistakably glorious aroma filling the air and tickling the nostrils. A short wooden walkway then leads towards another stile, and thence onto a beautiful sandy bay where man-and-dog can wash away the day's accumulated grime and sooth any associated electrical scorch-marks.

A final leisurely stroll along the beach will then take you back to the car park and a well-earned cup of your chosen potion.

Crime, What Crime?

At risk of tempting providence and being deported post-haste from these shores, I am about to make a rather bold statement. The island of Arran is almost crime-free. There, I've said it.

However, you will note that I snuck in the word 'almost'. And I chose that word very carefully, because believe it or not Arran has actually witnessed a few real crimes over the years. Please feel free to gasp.

I mean, what exactly is this island coming to? The next thing we know, we'll be locking our car doors, not to mention our house doors as well. And indeed, that sad day might not actually be too far away, especially if much-loved islander Lizzie McDonald (alas, not her real name) has anything to do with it. Do allow me to elucidate.

Now Lizzie is a wonderful lady, a veritable island gem. Hailing originally from Glasgow's big smoke, she moved to Arran almost thirty years ago, where she proceeded to raise her charming family. Lizzie now lives in the delightfully sprawling village of Whiting Bay on the island's east coast. She is well-known for her sterling work in more community events than you and I have had hot dinners. However, perhaps most poignantly of all, Lizzie is famed for her loveable naivety, an endearing quality which in abundant measure will go a very long way towards explaining the little tale with which I am about to regale you.

It all unfolded one rather breezy autumnal Sunday morning, when Lizzie was approached by an infamously resourceful Brodick worthy as she strode briskly along Shore Road in Whiting Bay, marvelling once more at the mighty ocean waves cascading over the sea wall and splashing onto the car windscreens of bewildered passing tourists who had never seen anything quite like it. Spotting a familiar face coming towards her, she wondered momentarily what the renowned Tam McGregor was doing down here in the south-end on a quiet peaceful Sunday. After all, half-a-dozen pints of lager in Brodick's Ormidale Hotel bar was much more Tam's Sabbath bag.

'Hiya, Lizzie!' the north-ender beamed endearingly through a brand-new set of false teeth which glistened so dazzlingly in the early morning sunshine that they could easily have crash-landed the overhead Ryanair flight that was about to make its final descent into Glasgow International Airport. 'Long time, no' see. How's it goin', hen?'

'Fine, Tam, fine,' replied Lizzie, in a tone which carried a deftly measured mix of social pleasantry and deep suspicion. 'So what brings you to Whiting Bay on a Sunday morning, then, Tam?'

'The bus!' Tam chortled, as if he had just delivered the world's most original wisecrack, before clocking Lizzie's singularly unimpressed glare and deciding to spill the dubious beans.

Apparently, the affable rogue, whose specialist skills resided in the noble arts of housebreaking and petty theft, had seen the light at last and had now gone 'legit'. Painter-and-decorator no less, and self-employed into the bargain. And now here he was plying his trade in Whiting Bay of all places. In characteristic naivety, Lizzie was taken in at once by Tam's heart-warming story, his credibility clearly corroborated by a pair of paint-splattered dungarees, if rendered slightly questionable by the glaring absence of any tools-of-the-trade whatsoever.

'So are you here for a painting job, then, Tam?'

'Aye, Lizzie. It's for an auld couple who live somewhere in the village. Their name's Ogilvy, but you widnae believe it, I've lost their phone number an' I've nae idea where they stay. Now that I'm a real businessman, I'll need tae gi'e masel' a bloody shake and hire a gorgeous secretary. Just like you, Lizzie! How are ye fixed for a job yoursel' these days, darlin'?'

'Ogilvy?' reflected Lizzie, stroking her chin and rubber-earring Tam's trademark sexist patter. 'Ogilvy? I'm afraid the name doesn't ring a bell, Tam.'

'Well, he's a fairly auld geezer, and he lives here in the village wae his wife. She's a wee bit younger than him. Sugar daddy, I'm thinkin'. He's also a keen collector o' antiques an' oil paintings an' things like that. Ring any bells noo, hen?'

'Oh, yes!' beamed the willing Lizzie. 'Eric, I think his first name is, and his lovely wife, Angela. It was the surname that threw me. They live at the far end of the village, just after the garage and down past the church. A really nice old couple.'

'Aye, that'll be them!' replied the self-professed poacher-turned gamekeeper, with a grin so menacing that it could have curdled freshly pasteurised milk, but which the ever-trusting Lizzie absorbed with consummate ease.

'An' you're bang on, Lizzie darlin', that's their names, Eric and Angela!' Tam continued. 'In fact, I think he ca's the auld burd Angie.'

Lizzie, by now completely sold on Tam's on-the-hoof patter, immediately began to point him in the direction of the elderly couple's abode, a fair distance away from where they presently stood blethering in the crisp sunshine. Lizzie McDonald was now on autopilot.

'Okay, Tam, here's what to do,' she counselled him. 'Turn around and walk straight through the village for about half a mile, until you pass the grocery store and garage on your left. Take the first right, then go past the Church on your left, and then …'

Suddenly, Lizzie stopped. A much better idea had just occurred to her.

'Oh, listen Tam, never mind all that! Have you got a piece of paper and a pen?'

The bold Tam McGregor immediately began rummaging around in the pockets of his manky dungarees, before pulling out a Ladbrokes' football coupon and a bookmakers' pen. A couple of minutes later, the notorious con-man had found himself the proud owner of a magnificent map of the village of Whiting Bay, beautifully hand-drawn onto the reverse side of his bookies' coupon. The map indicated, in the most impressive of detail, the route he should follow straight to the Ogilvy residence, the precise location of which Lizzie had most helpfully highlighted with the bright orange marker which she had found lurking in the pocket of her Regatta sports jacket.

'That's magic, Lizzie!' said the map's grateful new owner, as he bade her farewell and began striding away into the distance with considerably more purpose than paintbrushes.

216

'Wait a wee minute, Tam!' the aspiring cartographer shouted after him. 'I've just remembered. I think the Ogilvys spend the month of September in their holiday villa in Tenerife, so I'm not sure they'll be at home just now.'

'Aye, would that no' be just my bloody luck?' Tam replied, with a shrug of his muscular shoulders. 'Och, whit the hell? I'll chap on their door anyway, and if they're no' at hame I suppose I'll just have to get the next bus back tae Brodick.'

And off he went on a mission, arms pumping furiously.

Some four hours later and just as Lizzie was preparing Sunday's steak-pie dinner for the family, there was a loud knock on her front door. It smacked of authority. When she opened it, there stood the unmistakeably po-faced sergeant of the local constabulary. For once in his life, he actually appeared genuinely excited with his lot.

'Lizzie, I'm just checking in the neighbourhood to see if anyone has noticed anything suspicious this afternoon. I'm afraid there's been a serious crime in the village!'

Now, on the island of Arran, the term 'serious crime' has a somewhat different connotation from that which it might imply in, say, London's east-end or Liverpool's docklands. Thus, fearing that some poor old lady's hanging flower-basket had been nicked from straight above her front porch, Lizzie naturally sought elucidation on the precise nature of the offence.

'A housebreaking, Lizzie!' the steely-eyed bobby declared, clearly on the mission of a lifetime. 'A burglary, a real burglary! That's two in the last ten years, you know. Really makes you wonder what this island is coming to, doesn't it?'

'Oh my God!' Lizzie gasped. 'A burglary? And right here in Whiting Bay? And under our very noses? I'll never sleep tonight. Do you have any clues yet?'

'Nothing concrete so far, Lizzie,' came the sergeant's guarded reply. 'But we do know one thing for sure. The thief had an unwitting accomplice, almost certainly someone from the village.'

'And what makes you think that?' Lizzie enquired, deeply intrigued.

'Because some silly bugger drew him a map.'

Glenashdale Falls to Lamlash

The original track northwards from Whiting Bay to neighbouring Lamlash formerly ran along the 'high road' through the settlements of Auchencairn and Knockenkelly, nowadays a scenic waymarked walk which is very popular with tourists.

It wasn't until the mid-nineteenth century that the 'low road' was developed along the shoreline, surfaced in gravel at first but subsequently tarred early the following century, where it still serves the island today as an integral part of the circular shore road. The journey by car between the two east-coast villages takes just over ten minutes, but it's much more interesting to tackle the high-road on foot.

The starting point for your trek is at the entrance to a rough vehicular track, clearly waymarked to Glenashdale Falls (Eas a' Chrannaig), which sits opposite the bus bay in Whiting Bay, just south of the Ashdale Bridge. A short stroll of a few hundred yards takes you past a few houses on your left and along the tree-lined Glenashdale Burn, then through a wooden gate where a large signpost describes both the layout of the forest walks and the variety of indigenous wildlife, with particular emphasis on the beauty and vulnerability of Arran's red squirrel population. Here the track narrows, and another hundred yards along lies a spur to the left up the steep and oscillating zig-zags towards the Giants' Graves, which having already negotiated you should simply disregard and instead plough straight ahead in the direction of the falls.

The path remains level for a while, but then begins to climb fairly steeply, and you will soon find yourself crossing a wooden footbridge over a small stream high above the main burn, where on a calm day you might just be able to hear the distant and unmistakeable rumble of Glenashdale's 140-foot-high 'double waterfalls'. A taxing climb through the pine forest will eventually lead you up a set of wooden steps onto a sturdy viewing platform which juts out over the cliffs. And there straight in front, you will be able to grab your first spectacular sight of the 'lower falls', the burn water cascading from the big pool on high and crashing violently with a thunderous roar onto the rocks right beneath your feet, one of Arran's most photographed views. A further short climb will lead you to another viewing point, this right above the equally impressive 'higher falls', where if you lean slightly to your right over the protective fence, you will be able to see both falls at once. However, might I suggest that you don't lean too far over that same fence, lest your view of the falls should transpire to be all the more spectacular, if rather brief.

Continuing straight ahead and once more ignoring the sign to your left which also beckons you back towards the Giants' Graves, you will soon reach another wooden bridge, this over the Glenashdale Burn where a reasonably deep pool will provide a welcome drink and a decent swim for any dogs in your party. Considerable care should be taken not to let them wander, though, because the exposed head of the waterfall lies menacingly only a few yards downstream.

Following the well-defined path through the deep pine forest will soon lead you to a clearing, which is the site of another ancient Iron Age fort, then onwards to a sheltered viewing point, from which looking south in the distance, both the higher and lower Glenashdale Falls can again be seen in all their pomp.

As the footpath reaches the top of the forest, it meets a wider track running perpendicular to it, where a right-turn will lead you back down into Whiting Bay, and a left back up the slope in the direction of Lamlash. Following the latter route, a gentle climb of about three-hundred yards will take you onto the Forestry Commission road, where another right-turn will lead you past the steep slopes of Whiting Bay Golf Course and onwards past a quarry.

A further trek of about three miles will mesmerise you with some truly stunning views, both straight ahead towards the hills of Beinn Bhreac and A' Chruach, and over the bay to Holy Island. You will eventually reach another footpath down to your left just above the approaching woods near the south side of Lamlash, which will take you past a small pond to a 'fork'. Turn right and simply follow the well-worn path alongside the Monamore Burn until you reach a small car park. From there, you will be reunited with the forestry road which soon joins the single-track Ross Road, where a right-turn past the site of the old dyemill followed about half-a-mile further on by a left-turn will take you into the village of Lamlash. There, a good variety of watering holes and eateries sit patiently in wait to replenish your flagging reserves.

And after such an energetic trek, they'll be needing it.

It was some years back on this very route, accompanied by my dearly-departed Labradors, Tanna and Saffy, that I contrived to set out on my travels with two dogs only to return with three, and not for the first time I might add. I have never quite understood why things like this always seem to happen to me, but they do.

We had just completed the long return hike from Lamlash to Glenashdale Falls and back again, and we were heading downhill towards the forestry car park at the old dyemill, when my two Labs suddenly stopped in their tracks and stood there stalk-still, nostrils twitching and sniffing the air. Suddenly, out of the dense foliage appeared a big wiry-haired dog, looking lost and anxious. My own two immediately ran towards it, at which point the traumatised beast turned on its heels and bolted away again. After a series of rambling human-canine 'conversations', aided and abetted by the aroma of a handful of gravy-bite dog biscuits, the big stray eventually succumbed to temptation and came over to claim its share. Having by then established that the poor thing must have been wandering around on the hills totally bereft of human companionship, I immediately slipped one of my own dogs' leads over its neck, and the four of us made our way back down to the car. Tanna and Saffy jumped into the hatchback as usual, and I lifted our new-found companion onto the passenger seat beside me, then drove the half-mile or so to Lamlash police station.

As luck would have it, the place was empty, so I pressed the buzzer on the wall. After a moment or two, I was through to the duty officer in Kilmarnock police station of all places, to whom I explained my predicament. He informed me that the local bobbies must presently be 'out somewhere else' (a thought which strangely enough had already occurred to me). He then assured me that he would contact them at once and that I should stay put for the time being to await their imminent return.

Some twenty thumb-twiddling minutes later, a police car pulled into the driveway and two uniformed officers got out, sporting the obligatory solemn faces.

'Are you the guy with the two dogs?' the older one enquired, looking a tad irritated.

'Three dogs,' I replied cheerily.

'Show me!' he commanded, at which point I readily complied by opening the hatchback to reveal my own pair of muck-splattered Labs lying exhausted from their mountainous exertions.

'Where's the third one, then?' he snapped impatiently, so I took him around to the front passenger's door to reveal our latest acquisition, who by this time had scrambled across and was sitting on my own seat with his head resting nervously on the steering wheel, doubtlessly fearing imminent arrest.

'He's the driver,' I informed them.

'Oh!' said the same officer. 'So, there actually is a third dog, then?'

'What do you mean?' I replied, feigning deep emotional injury. 'Did you not believe me?'

It was the younger one who spoke this time.

'Sir, we were in Whiting Bay with the speed camera when we got the call, so we just thought that someone was taking the piss as usual. It happens all the time.'

Anyway, as they say, all's well that ends well. Not only did the police officers finally accept my temporary tally of three dogs, and then by employing the process of subtraction conclude that one of them, viz the driver, was indeed surplus to my own canine requirements, but the senior officer even managed to identify the dog itself. Apparently, it belonged to a regular holidaymaker from the London area and it had developed an amazing knack of getting itself lost in the hills on a fairly frequent basis. In the event, the two officers returned the dog to its rightful owner together with my telephone number in case she felt the need to call and thank me, but she managed to resist the temptation, so there we go.

Speaking of speed cameras, here's another little tale for posterity. This one concerns the plight of the mainland-based 'traffic police' who every now and again feel the need to invade our rural communities and impose their unwelcome presence on the unsuspecting locals. This particular episode is rumoured to have occurred here on Arran, but while I'm not entirely convinced, the thought really appeals to me and I sincerely hope that it did.

One day a few years back, it is said that the white-helmeted brigade decided to set up a speed-trap in the village of Whiting Bay. Armed with the latest electronic hand-held apparatus, costing a tidy five-grand apiece, they spent the first part of the morning aiming their brand-new, state-of-the-art radar devices at passing vehicles, initially catching a few speeding motorists, but later drawing a complete blank once the island's jungle drums had started beating. Then, just as a well-known local builder's antiquated white Ford Transit van crawled into the village at near-walking pace, one of the traffic cops began staring in disbelief at his radar screen. The read-out was informing him that the old clapped-out van had been travelling at an astonishing 558 miles-per-hour. Not only that, but the device then completely seized up and could not be reset. The two officers immediately reported this strange development to their superiors based in Glasgow's Pitt Street headquarters, who told them to stand down and return to the mainland, while they began their investigations into this most bizarre phenomenon.

It later transpired that when pointing his radar device in the general direction of the lumbering Ford Transit, the officer had inadvertently latched onto a NATO Tornado jet which had been taking part in a low-flying military exercise over the Firth of Clyde. Further investigation also revealed that the two traffic cops had just had an extremely lucky escape, because the aircraft's on-board computer had not only detected and jammed the 'enemy' radar equipment, but it had also automatically armed a live air-to-ground missile to neutralise the 'hostile threat'. Fortunately, the French pilot managed to clock the status of his missile system and was able to put it back on manual before the missile launched automatically.

My own local source of the story, who chuckled heartily throughout its telling, did go on to point out that the incident could have had a much more serious footnote.

'Aye, can you just imagine?' he smiled. 'Yet another huge pothole on Arran's roads!'

The Lord of the Glen

It was a lovely summer's morning back in the late 'seventies, in the days when Nan still had her frizzy little Carole King hairdo and me my shoulder-length George Harrison mop. We really thought we were the business, the bee's knees, the coolest dudes on the planet. Alas, my grandchildren have since seen the photographs.

I was in one of my infamous grumpy moods, having been dragged along to a remote wooden tearoom situated in the splendid isolation of the Arran countryside, to partake of one of the local proprietor's much-acclaimed fruit scones, when any self-respecting twenty-something golfing aspirant ought to have been ripping huge divots out of the fairways as usual. The tearoom was located at Glenscorrodale farm, high in the hills of the Ross Road, the single-track cross-country route which leads the occasional adventurous motorist from Lamlash on Arran's east coast to Sliddery on its west.

'Oh Jillian!' Nan exclaimed gleefully to our two-year-old daughter. 'Listen! Listen to who's singing! It's Pinky & Perky!'

Now for those of you who, like myself, now find your once-dark flowing locks falling out in great silver clumps, you may remember that Pinky & Perky were a pair of famous contemporary 'puppet pigs' who commanded a wide television audience of mesmerised children with their trademark (and exceedingly annoying) high-pitched singing voices. Imagine my amusement at Nan's expense, then, when the young lady in charge of the tearoom walked over to the tiny record-player in the corner, and with a warm smile switched the turntable speed down from 78 rpm to 33, to reveal the real artists. Unfortunately, they were the Bee Gees, and I hated the bloody Bee Gees. To me, their screeching wails sounded like a kitchen waste disposal unit in urgent need of repair.

'On second thoughts, could you just put Pinky & Perky back on again?' I said to her.

She laughed heartily and came over to introduce herself. Her name was Elizabeth McConnell, and as we later learned, she was revered the whole island over as home-baker supreme. She then introduced the eager teenage lad who was now wiping our table and placing assorted crockery in front of us.

'And this is my son, Jack.'

Little did we know that this same young lad was standing on the threshold of the most meteoric career in public service. In only a few years' time, Jack McConnell would commence that career as a Mathematics teacher, before becoming immersed in the cut-throat world of politics, from which he would quickly rise to national and international prominence. At first serving as a councillor in Stirling District Council whilst still extolling the joys of quadratic equations and differential calculus to teenage pupils, he would be elected as Council Leader in 1990. Next, he would occupy the heady post of General Secretary of the Scottish Labour Party for six more years before being appointed Minister for Finance in the late Donald Dewar's newly-devolved Scottish Parliament. Then at the turn of the millennium, McConnell would accept the poisoned chalice that was Minister for Education, Europe & External Relations, which was when his professional path and mine would first cross, this at the official opening of the new St Stephen's Primary School in Clydebank. The following year, his appointment would be to the 'big job', First Minister of Scotland no less, a role he would perform with great distinction for six years more. These days he now wallows, somewhat self-deprecatingly it must be said, in the grand title of 'Lord McConnell of Glenscorrodale'.

Not bad for a humble farmer's boy from the hinterland of Arran, don't you agree?

I met Lord McConnell recently in Felicity's at Eden Lodge, a delightful bar/restaurant on the south side of Whiting Bay's sweeping coastline.

'The last time I met you, I addressed you as "First Minister", I said, in deferential receipt of his strong handshake. 'And the time before that, it was "Minister". So what do I call you this time?'

'Jack will do fine!' he replied with a smile which oozed warmth and friendship. 'We're on Arran.'

Having known and admired Jack McConnell as a prominent politician over several years in my former professional life, I had painstakingly researched his highly impressive CV and prepared a long list of searching questions. I needn't have bothered.

'Just tell me what you want to know,' he began.

'I want to know how a sheep-farmer's son from Arran ended up as First Minister of Scotland and then in the House of Lords.'

It was the only question I would need to ask that morning, as I listened to Jack McConnell's own personal account of his fascinating journey through life.

Jack was born the son of Ayrshire sheep-farmer, Willie McConnell, who very sadly passed away in the spring of 2018. When young Jack was only two years old, the family upped sticks and sailed over the Firth of Clyde to set up home on the Island of Arran. Home was to be the rented Glenscorrodale farm, perched beside the aforementioned Ross Road, a rather dilapidated hill farm which was in need of a great deal of repair. Willie immediately set about renovating the property, and got himself a loan sufficient to allow him to purchase some 500 hill-sheep. No stranger to hard graft for many years by then, Willie soon realised that the proceeds from the farm alone would fall considerably short of allowing him to feed wife Elizabeth and their family of four young children. For Willie McConnell, life would always be about juggling several jobs at the one time, just to keep the farm going and the wolf from the door.

'It was very hard going for my dad,' Jack reflected ruefully. 'The income from the farm simply wasn't enough to sustain the family, so he would go out and pick up other jobs here and there, mainly labouring. I remember the tension and apprehension when he went to market each year. Quite literally, the price of a lamb at the sales would determine what kind of winter we would have. Two pounds either way on the price of each lamb would make a big difference to our annual income, the difference between a good winter and a bad one.'

I asked him if the hardship associated with his early childhood had in any way contributed to his future involvement in politics.

'When I look back on it, yes. I would be very young when the concept of inequality first hit me, probably about seven or eight. It all just seemed so unfair to me. My own father was working his fingers to the bone, while others had it all handed to them on a plate. It just didn't seem right.'

Young Jack McConnell might not have realised it at the time, but he was already developing an acute sense of social justice. However, he was also beginning to realise that if he wanted to improve his own prospects in life and contribute in some meaningful way to bettering things for others, he would have to grab the bull by the horns.

'My whole attitude changed one winter's day, when I saw my dad out on the hills, planting trees. I was still in primary school at the time, probably about eight years old, and the sight of him toiling away in the pouring rain had the most profound effect on me. My first reaction was to feel really sorry for him. My second was to say to myself, "I'm going to get out of here!" And I knew that the only way I could do that was to work hard at school, and get myself some really good academic qualifications. To be honest, I hadn't been particularly well behaved at school, but I now realised that it was time to roll up my sleeves and get stuck in.'

Tellingly, one of Jack's former teachers told him recently that she remembered a couple of things from his primary school days which she now recognised, in hindsight, had probably earmarked him for the type of career he was later to pursue.

'She told me that I always had "an opinion"!' Jack laughed. 'That no matter what topic the class was discussing, I was never slow to come forward with my own opinion, which is certainly something you need to do when you're a politician. She also said that I told her I wanted to be a "sums teacher" when I left school, so I guess I had a pretty clear idea of where I wanted to go in life.'

The turning point in the McConnell family's fortunes came one day in the summer of 1969.

'We were sitting outside the farm at our garden table having a bite to eat in the sunshine,' Jack recalled. 'A car stopped, then a lady got out of the passenger's seat and asked my mum if there was any chance of a cup of tea. The next thing we knew, this family of complete strangers were sitting beside us drinking tea and tucking into my mum's homemade scones and shortbread biscuits. And that was when my mum clocked her big opportunity. Sell tea and home baking in the garden to passing motorists!'

By the following summer, Willie and Elizabeth McConnell had taken the idea to the next level, and got the whole family duly signed up. Willie would develop the facilities and get on with the arduous task of working the farm, Elizabeth would capitalise on her famed home baking and presentation skills, and Jack and his cousins would serve the teas and snacks. However, they realised that one big challenge needed to be addressed, and that was this. Sitting at a garden table in the summer sunshine was all fine and dandy, but what about the vagaries of our climate? In other words, the infamous Scottish rain? So Willie set about building a small wooden hut, capable of housing a modest four tables to accommodate the peckish passers-by whenever the wet stuff decided to batter down on the island's bewildered holidaymakers.

'The tearoom took off really quickly,' Jack recalled, 'and before long it had become obvious that we were going to need a lot more space, so my dad bought a wooden hut that had been situated on the seafront at Brodick. We immediately tripled our capacity to twelve tables, and before long we were serving not just teas and snacks, but proper meals too. Our reputation spread, and soon we were getting busloads of tourists stopping, which when you consider the isolated location of Glenscorrodale was quite something. We didn't have a drinks licence, but our guests could bring bottles of wine and spirits with them, and I would happily stay up late waiting for them to leave while doing my homework!

'My mum got a number of awards for her food. In fact, in the 'seventies, she received the ultimate accolade by being listed in the Egon Ronay good food guide, and more than once as well. The award was for "gourmet meals on a family budget". So, what had started out as a quaint little idea had now blossomed into a really successful family business. We were all very proud of it.'

The McConnell family's life was all about the island itself, and trips to the mainland were normally to visit relatives. Indeed, by the time he had left primary school, young Jack had never even been on a mainland bus or train. Not that he was in any way insular in his outlook on life, though. In fact, quite the opposite.

'When I was only fourteen, I got a chance to take part in a foreign exchange visit to Paris. I jumped at the chance. So, there I was, this wee lad from the wilds of rural Arran who had never even been on a train before, sitting all by himself on an aeroplane flying to the city of Paris. It was very exciting, but a bit daunting too. I remember the feeling of apprehension when the plane landed at the airport and I realised that I would have to try to locate a French family whom I had never met before and with whom I'd be living for three weeks. And I'll never forget the great sense of relief I felt when I saw a family standing at the top of the steps holding a photograph, clearly waiting on someone they were expecting but didn't know. They were sporting big warm smiles, and I knew it was all going to work out fine. I had a fabulous time in Paris, and the whole experience really helped me to grow as a person.'

That little sojourn to Paris turned out to be a real character-builder for the fledgling Jack McConnell. At only fourteen years of age and the first time away from his family, Jack had found himself living with a foreign family in one of the biggest cities in the world, armed only with the mere handful of French phrases that he had picked up at school. It was a very steep learning curve, that's for sure, and one Jack would have to continue to climb very quickly in the ferocious life of politics which lurked just around the corner.

About the same time that his mother was picking up her prestigious Egon Ronay awards, the ever-inquisitive Jack was developing an acute awareness of the prominent political and social issues pervading mid-'seventies Scottish culture.

'The whole concept of inequality was a big deal for me. For example, I just couldn't understand why my dad who worked so hard on the farm had to rent it, while others owned their own homes and businesses. And my thoughts had nothing to do with party politics at the time, because I'm fairly sure that being farmers, most of our family and friends would be Tory voters anyway, so socialist politics weren't even on my radar back then. It was simply that my dad seemed to work harder than most, but for much less reward, and the inequality of it all really bothered me.'

It was during the winter of 1975 that one particular television programme transpired to have a huge influence on Jack. BBC's 'Play for Today', *Just Another Saturday*, was written by John McKenzie and starred Scottish comedian/actor Billy Connolly among others. It was about a young Orange Lodge band-leader who was looking forward to marching his band through the streets of Glasgow on the big annual Orange Walk, only to become deeply disillusioned by the drunkenness and violence that ensued as the parade reached one of the city's Catholic areas.

'I was already becoming very aware of the prejudice and hatred in our society. That programme really helped me think about the big issues facing us at the time, and made me determined to do my own bit towards bringing about a more tolerant society.'

Jack's late teenage years were spent between his academic pursuits in Stirling University, where he studied mathematics, and the long summers on Arran, where he worked as a barman in Whiting Bay's Shurig Bar while continuing to help his parents out on the farm and in the tearoom at Glenscorrodale. Happily, as a result of the latter's success and the family's determined work ethic, Willie and Elizabeth McConnell then bought the Rock Hotel in Blackwaterfoot, selling up a few years later to try their luck with Nags Bar and Bistro in Whiting Bay, which with its famed discos and live bands was a real honeypot for the rebel-rousing youth of the post-Woodstock era.

'There was something of a hippy culture on Arran in these days,' Jack reflected. 'In the summertime, they would come over in their droves and pitch their tents. The pubs would be absolutely mobbed, with rock bands and discos galore. Sometimes, the bars would get so busy that they had to shut the doors for safety reasons. There was a very distinctive holiday feel to Arran, and the whole place was bouncing.'

Like so many others who feature in this book, Jack readily concedes that the modern-day Arran has changed enormously over the years.

'Tourism has always been Arran's lifeblood, and the island is still heavily dependent on tourists today. However, the pattern and experience have changed dramatically. For example, there are far fewer public bars and B & Bs nowadays, but the tourist season is much longer and the quality is much higher. The big game-changer was the success that the late Iain Johnston achieved with the Auchrannie Hotel, which drove the businesses on Arran to deliver a much higher quality experience over a much longer holiday season. With many other businesses like Arran Provisions, Arran Aromatics, the cheese factory, the distillery and A Taste Of Arran upping their game too, the island suddenly became very "sexy". Hotels like the Auchrannie, the Kinloch, the Kildonan, the Glenisle, the Douglas, and so many others have now taken the Arran experience to a whole new level. Arran is an island very much on the up, and it deserves to be, because the islanders are a resilient lot.'

Thus ended my fascinating chat with Lord McConnell of Glenscorrodale, who absolutely insisted on being called Jack, a humble farmer's boy from half-way up the Ross Road who had climbed to the very top of the political tree. On that spring morning, we chatted about everything from Jack's journey through childhood to adulthood, to the factors which affected his thinking and choices in life, to his reflective perspective on Arran itself, the island he cherishes so dearly. However, there was one area from which he so deftly steered me away each time I tried to lure him. The world of politics, which has dominated his entire adult life.

As he sipped the very last drop from his second cup of cappuccino, I gave it one last valiant go.

'So Jack, who have been the biggest influences in your life? Your role models, I mean?'

'My dad.'

'And in your political life?'

'My dad. I think we'll leave it at that.'

I had just endeavoured to push Jack McConnell out of his comfort zone. Alas, Lord McConnell of Glenscorrodale was having none of it.

The Village of Lamlash

Anyway, now back to the car and to Arran's circular A841 road. And, of course, minus your Sat Nav, which as you will recall is still 'sleeping with the fishes' in the depths of the Kilbrannan Sound.

Heading north from Whiting Bay, the road heads a few hundred yards inland and high above a rather unusually rugged stretch of the island's otherwise sandy eastern coastline, to a point unsurprisingly called The Heights. Then on a twisting, multi-chicaned journey back down towards sea level, a truly spectacular view comes into view, in the shape of the delightfully sprawling village of Lamlash, as it stretches its full length along the magnificent bay which itself rests peacefully in the shelter of the imposing Holy Island. Many centuries ago, Lamlash was known by its Gaelic name of Loch an Eilean, which translates to 'loch of the island', referring to the glorious crescent-shaped Lamlash Bay.

On the left-hand side of the road opposite the police station sits the modern-day Arran High School, which serves the island's secondary-aged pupils, many of whom are bussed from its various outlying 'airts and pairts' to access their schooling. However, and as previously rehearsed through the words of Liz Dale, life wasn't always that simple for Arran's teenagers.

Indeed, away back in the late 'thirties, the timing of the construction of the original Arran secondary school could hardly have been worse for the island's teenagers. Completed and ready for occupation in 1939 just as the Second World War beckoned, it was immediately requisitioned by the Royal Navy before a single Arran pupil had set foot in the place, to be reconfigured as a barracks and canteen for Navy personnel. It was only after the cessation of hostilities in 1946 that the building was returned to public use to operate as the sole 'junior secondary school' for Arran, providing first-to-third year education only, with the more academically able chosen few temporarily leaving the island to continue their studies.

Eventually, in 1974, after many years of vigorous campaigning by determined local activists, this vital educational facility was upgraded to the six-year comprehensive Arran High School, at long last catering for all the island's secondary-aged pupils and signalling a very welcome end to the heart-breaking practice of banishing children overseas for months on end to receive their schooling, some of them as young as eleven years of age. In 1982, the village's younger children were transferred to the brand-new, five-classroom Lamlash Primary School, constructed adjacent to the upgraded Arran High School, which itself was then further extended and modernised in 1985 to provide additional classroom, recreational and ancillary accommodation.

Opposite the village's medical centre, fire station and tennis courts sits a walled and wooded area of land where once stood a large resplendent building known as the White House, which after the Great War of 1914-18 was the official residence of Mary, Duchess of Hamilton. The famous old house was later commandeered as the headquarters of the 11th Scottish Commandos during the Second World War.

One of the saddest days in Arran's long and distinguished history was 25 April 1829, a day which witnessed the port of Lamlash serving as the departure point for almost a hundred distraught islanders who had been ousted from their humble farming livelihoods during the 'island clearances', in pursuit of a new life in Megantic County, near the Canadian city of Quebec. That awful day is now commemorated by a rock formation in the centre of the village, erected in 1977 by the descendants of those who were forced to make that horrendously dispiriting journey in search of a land of milk and honey which tragically proved to be the complete antithesis of their promised good fortune.

Until its demolition, the late lamented Lamlash Pier had undergone significant changes, starting out as a rather crude stone-built structure in the early nineteenth century and being replaced by a much more modern customised affair in the late 1880s, which would serve the village and its neighbouring rural communities until its demise, along with that of its similarly-fated neighbour in Whiting Bay, in the early 1960s.

Oddly enough, it was Lamlash Pier which provided my very own introduction to the island of Arran away back in 1953, when I was a mere toddler. I have three significant memories about that particular holiday. In order of rapidly-escalating unpleasantness, those are as follows.

Firstly, my Uncle Angus chucking a bag of sherbet-lemon sweeties to me from the deck of the ferry, only for the damned things to fall about half-an-inch short of the pier and plunge into the ocean waves like a dagger through my heart. Secondly, slipping on a rain-soaked doormat outside Kineil, our Lamlash boarding house, then having my broken arm encased in 'stookie' at the local cottage hospital. And finally, sitting terrified in a dentist's chair and having a huge mask shoved over my innocent little face, the purpose of which apparently was to administer the gaseous anaesthetic required to render me unconscious while my tooth got yanked out, but the real reason for which I was certain at the time was unimaginably much more sinister.

All in all - and the stunning beauty of Lamlash village notwithstanding - my very first visit to Arran left a great deal to be desired. It was a bloody nightmare from start to finish. In fact, when I think about it, it's a wonder I ever came back.

Holy Island

Holy Island, or Eilean Molaise as it was once called in homage to St Molaise, the Irish hermit monk who preached on Arran away back in the seventh century, retains its quaint mystique to this day.

For some strange reason, the tiny isle visually defines much of Arran's eastern coastline. Approaching Whiting Bay from the south, it suddenly appears out of nowhere with its lofty and craggy peaks, presenting as a strange and mysterious entity stretching from the bay towards the skyline. From Kingscross Point a bit further north, Holy Island's towering majesty seems to boss the whole vista, and its eerie proximity to the point makes you feel that you could chuck a stone across the sea onto its pebbled shores. From the village of Lamlash itself, the little isle sits contentedly as a glorious centrepiece to the bay. Then for the more adventurous who have tackled the magnificent walk up Clauchlands Hill to the peak at the ancient fort of Dun Fionn, Holy Island rests regally beneath your feet, as the calm waters of Lamlash Bay lap gently onto the shores underneath its steep slopes. Even from as far up the east coast as the village of Corrie, the distinctive teapot-shaped outline of this sinister but incredibly beautiful little isle somehow commands the beholder's attention like a brilliant flare in a night-time sky. Once seen, the vision that is Holy Island will always be etched indelibly in your mind's eye, as many a peasant farmer and intrepid traveller alike would happily have testified over the centuries.

The tiny isle is itself steeped in history and positively laden with historical treasures. It is officially designated as a 'Sacred Site' and has a long spiritual heritage which dates as far back as the sixth century and the ancient kingdom of Dal Riada. Numerous ancient relics can still be found in the immediate vicinity of the distinctive Saint's Cave, adjacent to which stand both the 'Pulpit Rock' (otherwise known as the 'Judgement Stone') and the Saint's Well, which even today is reputed to have great healing powers, although present-day EU regulations forbid its crystal-clear waters being used for drinking purposes. *Quelle surprise*, as our continental chums might say.

However mysterious, remote and historically embellished it might be, Holy Island is still readily accessible to the public and can be reached by a small ferry which local mariner, Jim Blakey, operates on a regular basis from Lamlash Pier. It is well worth a visit, albeit one which has its limitations in respect of the ongoing work of the island's Buddhist meditation centre. It was in 1992 that the Ropka Trust became official custodians of the island, their 'mothership' being based at the Samye Ling Monastery and Tibetan Buddhist Centre located near Eskdalemuir in Dumfriesshire, under the leadership of Lama Yeshe Losal Rinpoche, Executive Director of the Holy Island Project.

At the northern end of Holy Island sits the Centre for World Peace and Health, which hosts a retreat facility and various meditation courses for those who wish to cleanse their cluttered souls (and many choose to do so, including a number of very famous A-list celebrities). At its southern end, the former lighthouse cottages now serve as a cloistered Tibetan Buddhist retreat for women. Interestingly enough, Arran's only other Buddhist retreat is now located at the old Glenscorrodale farm on the Ross Road, which was of course the childhood home of Jack McConnell, the former First Minister of Scotland.

Holy Island itself may well be only one of a number of so-called 'holy islands' scattered all around the British coastline, but it is a very special one indeed. Two miles (three kilometres) in length by about one mile (one kilometre) wide, its highest point is the peak of Mullach Mor, the ascent of which many a rambler has mastered in fair weather or foul.

On a personal note, the very first time I visited Holy Island was one gorgeous summer's afternoon back in the early 'eighties, when I escorted my then eight-year-old daughter and four-year-old son on the tiny motorised boat which sailed several times each day from Lamlash Pier. That day, and against my better judgement, I had little choice but to leave Nan with her two wooden walking sticks and our manic mutt, Cindy, sitting on a travelling rug on the village's beachside lawn. I remember several things about that little sojourn, most of them exceptionally pleasant, but alas, not all.

The sailing itself was exhilarating, especially for the kids who sang like linnets and dangled their tiny mitts in the ocean waves, as their landlubber chaperone spent the entire crossing grateful that he had sent them to swimming lessons from an early age, and safe in the knowledge that they might therefore be able to come to his aid should the boat suddenly sink without warning. I wouldn't go as far as to say that my aquatic courage knows no bounds, but believe me, it's right up there with my technological incompetence.

The three of us spent the most wonderful afternoon on Holy Island. We walked along the shore and up the gentle slopes through the heather, marvelling at the amazing variety of wildlife trotting around on the land and swooping from the skies above. One of my most vivid memories was of standing near a raised ledge, mesmerised by the glorious spectacle of Arran as viewed from this mysterious little island, the whole two-mile length of Lamlash village stretched out before our very eyes, its brilliant-white buildings glistening in the sunshine and their front-facing windows reflecting the sun's rays like newly-polished mirrors.

And the sound of silence. A deep and deafening silence. Save, that was, for the faint swish of waves lapping gently on the shore, the unmistakeable squawk-squawk-squawking of the seagulls overhead and the omnipresent stereophonic, 'Daddy, can I get another packet of Tootie Fruities?' from a couple of weans who were beginning to push their luck just a bit too far. And then there was the dog barking. And barking and barking. In fact, when I think about it, it couldn't possibly have been silence at all, more like a shift in a heavy ammunitions factory.

I tried not to worry too much about the barking, since we were all having such great fun, but I knew fine well who the dog was, because I recognised the 'voice'. It was Cindy, of course it was. And Cindy only ever barked continuously under one particular set of prevailing circumstances, viz, the sight of her lord-and-master walking away and leaving her behind, which I had done an hour or so earlier. As Nan would later inform me in a fit of arm-flailing *pique*, Cindy had yapped incessantly for the entire afternoon, sending fellow picnickers bolting in the direction of the village's shops and pubs for peace and quiet, and prompting one demented tourist to yell at her in sheer exasperation, 'Would you shut that f-----g thing up!', to which she herself had similarly snapped, 'That's not a thing, that's my dog and her name's Cindy, so go and get a life!'

Anyway, do yourself a massive favour, book a sailing over to the incomparable Holy Island and you will not be disappointed. A large part of the island operates as a nature reserve, being populated by wild Eriskay ponies, Saanen goats and Soay sheep. A programme to replant native trees is well underway, with around 35,000 having taken root since the project began in 1992. The very rare Rock Whitebeam tree grows on the island, itself a critically important link in the evolution of the Arran Whitebeam species, three varieties of which are indigenous and unique to the island of Arran. To protect the environment, solar panels have been constructed to pre-heat water and a 'reed bed' sewage system installed, with plans afoot to utilise wind energy as a significant source of electrical power.

Alighting from the fifteen-minute sailing from Lamlash, you will be greeted by a colourful assortment of Tibetan flags and mound-shaped Buddhist structures called 'stupas', and quite possibly by one of the community volunteers as well, who will proceed to explain some basic island 'do's and don'ts'. Those include refrainment from smoking, drinking alcohol, lighting fires and camping, a ban on bringing dogs and bicycles to the island, and an earnest plea to visitors not to access its east side in order to protect the delicate balance of nature and wildlife.

A left-turn from the jetty will take you through a gap in the stone-built wall, and uphill through a field where a waymarked signpost directs you towards the summit of Mullach Mor, which if you have already succeeded in mastering the mighty Goat Fell, you will be relieved to learn stands at just over half its height. Traversing a wooden stile, a relaxing and scenic stroll through the native trees and ferns will soon lead you to another, beyond which lie the island's heather-strewn slopes, which provide home to the aforementioned ponies, goats, sheep and other assorted indigenous creatures which no doubt scurry around in the welcome camouflage of the undergrowth.

The path up the slopes of Mullach Mor is fairly rough compared to many of Arran's other waymarked walks, and increasingly rocky as you continue your ascent, but it will be well worth the effort to keep plodding on. It then drops into a small hollow, which heralds the beginning of a final strenuous clamber up to the summit, where on a clear day the 360-degree panorama will take your breath away.

Looking east, the western seaboard of southern Scotland stretches out before you in all its glory. Panning to the north, the bluish peaks of the distant Campsie Hills and the geometrically near-symmetrical Ben Lomond can just be made out, whilst straight ahead lies the entire coastline of the county of Ayrshire, and further south, the Galloway hills with the rounded summit of the Merrick standing aloof. Then, due south, the faint outline of the County Antrim cliffs in Northern Ireland may just be visible, even if the more distant Rathlin Island and the Isle of Man may not, but at least you'll be safe in the knowledge that you've been looking in the right direction. Turning due west, the Arran 'mainland' dominates the show, with the majestic peaks of the Sleeping Warrior rising to the north-end of the island, while the lush green fields and sandy bays define the more temperate south-end.

One little word of warning here, though. Having reached the peak of the imposing Mullach Mor, it would not be a particularly good idea to then career back down the slopes in a spirit of reckless abandon, for fear of plunging off the adjacent cliffs which lurk menacingly on either side of your descent, doubtless to render your skeletal frame, your camera and its rich photographic footage reduced to smithereens on the rocks below. Instead, just take your time, stick to the path and stay clear of the roped-off areas, and you might live to tell the tale. As indeed might your camera.

A bit further down your descent, Pillar Rock lighthouse can be seen to the left, famous as the very first square version of the 'Stevenson lighthouses'. Continuing downhill in a south-westerly direction, you will soon come across 'Wee Donald', another Stevenson lighthouse, this one facing over towards Kingscross Point on the north side of Arran's Whiting Bay. At this juncture, please respect the privacy of the small community of nuns who occupy the surrounding buildings on their intensive 'retreats', some of which can last up to four years at a time.

A coastal path then leads you past a succession of rocks adorned by 'paintings' which depict The Buddha and other Tibetan Buddhist icons, after which you will reach the Holy Well, on the far side of which a series of steps will take you up to the old cave said to have been inhabited by St Molaise, its walls and roof decorated by ancient scribblings and drawings, reputed to be of Viking heritage.

Finally, another short stroll along the coastline will bring you back to the jetty with its accompanying boathouse, where you can rest your weary legs until Jim arrives in his trusty little ferry to take you back across Lamlash Bay to your point of departure.

Or, if you like, from total peace and tranquillity to the relative hustle-and-bustle of seaside village life.

Lamlash Bay and the Ravages of War

You may remember the 'Battle of Largs' from your history lessons at school. There again, you may not.

Indeed, you may even have attended the Ayrshire seaside town's annual Viking Festival, staged in commemoration of the Scandinavian influence on that charming little part of our country, and of course in celebration of the Scots' successful repulsion of their Norse foes. However, what is somewhat less well-known about the famous old battle of 2 October 1263 was the central role played by the island of Arran.

First, a wee bit of background. The history books show that Viking invasions of Scotland began as far back as the eighth century, leading to Scandinavian settlements being established all along the country's western seaboard. From the beginning of the ninth through to the mid-thirteenth century, the Orkney Isles, the Hebrides, most of Galloway, and all of Scotland's west coast including the Mull of Kintyre, Bute, the Cumbraes and the island of Arran itself were under Viking control, the overlord of whom would always be the reigning King of Norway, whoever that happened to be at the time.

While the Vikings were world-renowned for their magnificent longboats, mastery of the high seas and fearlessness in battle, they were also infamous for their merciless plundering-and-pillaging raids of peace-loving lands. Their ruthless reputation wasn't always totally merited, though, since they were also skilled trading merchants, and instead of banishing the local communities they had vanquished, they often settled down among them, where they established themselves as the ruling class and let the natives live in relative peace.

By the middle of the thirteenth century, Arran was still under strong Viking control. The sparse records of the times indicate that the island's then two-thousand-plus indigenous population had been left to its own devices, rather than suffer the indignity of being hounded out, and there are no accounts of massacres, mistreatment or even plundering of any kind. What is known is that the island's already sparse food supplies and other essential goods, produced by the toil and sweat of its farmers and tradespeople, were readily grabbed by their Scandinavian masters, who by then had succeeded in increasing the island's overall population by some forty percent.

What none of the islanders knew, though, was that the largest Viking fleet in history was about to assemble in Lamlash Bay, in the aftermath of the Battle of Largs, a key turning point in Norwegian King Hakon Hakonsson's doomed crusade to demonstrate his power and establish vice-like control over Scottish waters and land. And so, as the downtrodden Vikings licked their wounds in despair, the island of Arran was about to be stripped bare of many of its life-sustaining resources, in order that Hakon could equip his mighty fleet on its sorry retreat home via the Hebrides. How the islanders must have trembled in foreboding when his huge armada of galleys began pulling into Lamlash Bay on that drizzly October morning.

There are various, often conflicting accounts of the Battle of Largs. By then and after almost five centuries of Norwegian control, Alexander III, King of Scots, was in no mood to see his beloved country continue to be oppressed. His late father, Alexander II, had famously and courageously succeeded in establishing 'royal authority' in most strategic areas of the Scottish mainland and had begun the laborious and perilous process of extending such into the northern Highlands, Argyll and Galloway. Now the daring young King Alexander was damned sure he was going to reclaim the western seaboard into the Scottish realm as well. After a series of increasingly heated exchanges between the two heads of state and their diplomatic minions, the talks eventually broke down. Sparks were about to fly.

In the late summer of 1263, Alexander launched an attack on the Norse-held island of Skye. The power-mad Hakon retaliated by sending his fleet – the largest ever to have set sail from Norway – to re-establish control of the island and push down into the Firth of Clyde. With his vast fleet anchored in the choppy waters between the Cumbraes and the mainland port of Largs, he then unleashed his bloodthirsty Viking warriors on an area known at the time as Lennox, which comprised the settlements around Loch Lomond, where they plundered and ravaged everything in sight, gaining control of the entire Clyde basin.

However, what the invading hordes didn't know was that the infamous Scottish weather was about to enter the fray. On the evening of 30 September, a dreadful storm blew up and several Norse longships ran aground on the Ayrshire coast near the location of the modern-day town of Largs. Within a couple of days, 2 October to be precise, Alexander had marched his main Scottish cavalry and infantry to the scene, to find the beleaguered Vikings trying to salvage what was left of their damaged vessels.

With the bulk of the Norwegian forces on the beach and a smaller contingent gathered on an adjacent hillock, the Scots saw their opportunity to split their foes in two, only for the Norsemen on the heights to scramble back down to lend support to their comrades on the beach. However, rather than reacting with enthusiasm at the sight of reinforcements joining the battle, those on the shore interpreted the move as a rapid retreat from the marauding Scots' army and began fleeing in panic back to their ships at sea, but not before much blood-and-guts was spilled at the water's edge. There then followed an all-day-long battle for capture of the hillock and the beach, with the Norwegians eventually seizing back control of both, by which time the Scots had withdrawn in the belief that they had inflicted quite sufficient damage. The Norwegians were then able to collect their dead, board their longships and put to sea.

And thus the demoralised Norse fleet set sail for the port of Lamlash on Arran's east coast, where they then began to relieve the local islanders of their hard-earned foodstuffs, earthenware and other essential commodities, before heading north to the island of Orkney to lick their wounds over the coming harsh winter months.

With much of his larger fleet still intact, Haakon had intended to return the following spring and continue the fight for supremacy of Scotland's western waters. However, during the bleak days of winter, he took seriously ill and died. His successor, King Magnus Hakonsson, having much less of a taste for battle, then duly signed the 'Treaty of Perth' some three years later, leasing Scotland's western seaboard back to the Scots themselves, for a fee which the latter honoured for a spell before deciding to tell the Norwegians to go and get lost.

In the intervening years from the thirteenth century through to the present day, many a heated argument has taken place between those eager historians who view the Battle of Largs as an important victory for the Scots over their Norse foes, and those who argue that it was actually pretty indecisive in the great scheme of things. However, one thing about which they all agree was the central role played by Lamlash Bay in the lead-up to, and aftermath of the battle. It wasn't the village's first encounter with the hostilities of war, and it certainly wouldn't be its last.

In more modern times, the bay has often been utilised by various British governments as a strategically important naval rendezvous location. For example, just before the outbreak of World War I in 1914, the British fleet was despatched to Lamlash Bay as a major show of strength directed at Ulster, which was threatening to oppose Prime Minister Herbert Asquith's Liberal government in its granting of home rule to Ireland, the northern coastline of which (now Northern Ireland) is close enough to be seen from the southern tip of Arran. In the event, a British civil war was scuppered only by the onset of the 'Great War', the immediacy and scale of which dwarfed those of the Irish stand-off. Then throughout the 1914-18 war itself, Lamlash Bay was deployed almost continuously as a strategic rendezvous hub, with many islanders actively involved in counter-espionage activities and emergency operations.

Thereafter, from the outbreak of World War II in 1939 through to its conclusion in 1945, Lamlash Bay was again earmarked as a central strategic base for many of Britain's vast battleships, including the ill-fated HMS Hood, known and revered nationally as the 'Mighty Hood' until its sinking by German shells in May 1941 put paid to its widely-perceived invincibility and shattered the nation's already sagging morale. Another awesome vessel to suffer a similarly disastrous fate was the aircraft carrier, HMS Dasher, which set sail from the shadow of Holy Island one Saturday morning in March 1943, only to be sunk off the Ayrshire coast by two enormous explosions, resulting in the loss of nearly 400 souls, and triggering a deafening silence from the military authorities as to the cause of its sinking, known not to be from German shells.

Lamlash Bay may well have played centre-stage to more than its fair share of warlords and warmongers down through the centuries, but it still remains one of the most stunningly beautiful maritime havens in Scotland.

And changing the mood somewhat, it has also played host to the Arran Fishing Festival, and the infamous 'Irish Boys' of that ilk.

The Arran Fishing Festival

Another tale from the unwritten memoirs of the Arran Coastguard Team.

This one concerns the notorious antics of the 'Irish boys', the ranks of hardy fishermen from the Emerald Isle who used to venture every year across the Irish Sea to Scotland's west coast, ostensibly to compete in the once-famed Arran Fishing Festival. However, the truth is that the event simply presented the lads with a wonderful excuse to flee their respective colleens for a whole weekend, in order to drink themselves to oblivion.

How times change. Several years back, literally hundreds of fishermen would sail their assorted vessels across the sea to Arran, in order to participate in its highly competitive annual fishing festival. In those days, the island's coastal waters were positively laden with cod, haddock, hake, dab, plaice, turbot and other such highly sought-after species of indigenous fish. Sadly, those same waters have now seen their white fish population dwindle almost to the point of extinction, with only the likes of prawns, langoustines and scallops somehow managing to survive in significant numbers. Indeed, so concerning to the islanders was the near wipe-out of white fish that the Community of Arran Seabed Trust was set up, resulting in Lamlash Bay being declared a 'no-take zone' in 2008, and a consequential total ban on fishing ordered.

Folklore has it that the Arran Coastguard Team received an emergency call-out one balmy summer's evening during the famed fishing festival, just as the sun was setting over Lamlash Bay. The team was briefed that there had been some kind of incident on board an Irish-registered fishing boat, and that several people were badly injured, some of them quite possibly in need of urgent medical assistance.

And so, the coastguard and lifeboat squads, accompanied by the local police constable, immediately set sail for the coordinates they had been given. By the time both vessels had zipped their way over the gentle waves towards the stricken fishing boat, their respective crews could clearly see that something was seriously amiss, in that not one single fisherman was standing ready to greet them, which was very strange indeed. Instead, around half-a-dozen bodies could be seen strewn all over the deck, some writhing around in considerable discomfort and others completely prostrate, most of them covered in blood and snotters.

The emergency crewmen clambered onto the fishing boat as fast as their limbs could carry them, where they found a total of seven Irishmen in various states of consciousness ranging from almost to not at all. Moreover, the boat smelled like a distillery. As the designated first-aiders attended to the injured sailors, the others carried out a quick search of the vessel, only to find something most unusual for a fishing boat in a fishing competition.

No fish. Not a single one.

However, their search soon revealed something else entirely. Whatever the boat's hold may have lacked in piscatorial reward, it had more than made up for in alcoholic treasure. Fifteen dozen cans of Guinness, ten bottles of Irish whiskey, six of vodka and six more of gin. And that was what was still remaining. Clearly, the rest of the liquid provisions – and they must have been substantial - had already been guzzled by those now sprawling around the deck. Suddenly, the verbal silence was shattered.

'Me teeth!' one of the Irish lads began slurring through bubbles of crimson spittle. 'Me feckin' teeth! Oi'll kill 'im, dat Liam! Oi'll feckin' kill 'im!'

Those few select utterances were enough for the police officer to begin his debriefing of the most sober, or more accurately the least inebriated crew member. His questions soon established the most important fact of all, namely that the original crew was indeed seven in number, and quite astonishingly, that nobody had fallen overboard. The rest would wait, including the intriguing dental conundrum.

The 'Irish boys' were then bundled unceremoniously into the lifeboat and whisked off in the general direction of the police cells that awaited them in the village of Lamlash, where they would all sleep it off until the next morning, when no doubt the full story would emerge. It did, and it was this.

In line with tradition, the 'Irish boys' had started diving into their voluminous carry-out the very moment they set sail from their native County Wicklow, and their eager consumption of alcohol had continued apace all the way across the Irish Sea. By the time they had arrived at their chosen maritime location in Lamlash Bay, each and every one of them was as drunk as the proverbial skunk. In fact, it was a miracle that they had managed to find their way there at all.

As late afternoon became early evening, one of them – a burly fifty-something brute of a guy who called himself Conor – decided that he really ought to bring a degree of respectability to the whole exercise, and began casting a bated fishing line overboard in a laughable attempt to engage with Arran's aquatic population. No sooner had he done so and drunkenly announced his laudable intention to his fellow crew members, than his false teeth slithered out of his gob and plummeted into the depths of the bay.

Everybody, including the enterprising Conor himself, immediately collapsed into fits of howling laughter. Another few cans of Guinness and umpteen more shots of their respective tipples apiece, and the hilarity escalated, by which time Conor's best mate, the bushy-red-bearded Liam, had hatched a cunning plan.

Removing his own false teeth under cover of semi-darkness and communal inebriation, Liam proceeded to assemble his fishing gear, then wrapped the set of wallies around the end of his line, before casting it into the water. After a few minutes, Liam made an excited announcement to whomsoever was still sober enough to listen.

'Oi've got one lads! Oi've got one! An' it's a feckin' whopper!'

As he proceeded to go through the charade of pretending to struggle with the weight of his dubious monster-from-the-deep, a couple of his mates, including the bold Conor himself, staggered to their feet while the rest just continued cavorting around on deck, happily swigging away from their bottles of hooch. Eventually, Liam reeled in his 'catch', at which point Conor could scarcely believe his eyes.

'It's me teeth!' he roared. 'It's me false teeth! Liam, old sham, you've caught me teeth!'

Ripping the offending articles off Liam's line with a smile as wide as the Irish Sea itself, Conor gave the false teeth a quick wipe on the sleeve of his woollen jumper and shoved them into his mouth. The smile immediately turned into a scowl.

'Them ain't moi teeth!' he rasped, and instantly heaved the things overboard into the ocean. Liam looked on in disbelieving horror.

'Conor … you … you … you big gobshoit! Them was moi teeth! Them was me own teeth!'

Clenching his massive fist, Liam caught his friend-of-a-lifetime right on the chin with a delightful uppercut, whereupon the big man hit the deck like a felled oak. Conor's brother-in-law, Oisin, immediately shot to his feet and walloped Liam flush on the nose. Within a matter of seconds, all hands on deck were randomly swinging away at each other in inebriated fury, reminiscent of a glorious western saloon bar punch-up in an old John Wayne film. In the event, all seven drunken rogues somehow succeeded in punching each others' lights out, and not a single man was left standing.

For the Arran polis, the mystery was solved. After a good hearty Scottish breakfast, the 'Irish boys' were ferried back out to their anchored fishing boat in Lamlash Bay, from whence they rather sheepishly set sail back homewards towards County Wicklow.

And needless to say, without the coveted Arran Fishing Festival trophy.

And Back to Base

Alas, we now come to the very last leg of our travels around the enchanted little island of Arran.

A drive over the hill-road from Lamlash to Brodick will take you less than ten minutes. Pleasant enough that this vehicular sojourn will undoubtedly prove to be as you dart around the multiple chicane bends adjacent to the village's well-manicured golf course before making your steep descent parallel to Fairy Glen and onward to your destination, there is, however, a much more interesting way to negotiate the final stage of your circumnavigatory adventures.

Yes, you've guessed it, deployment of good old Shanks' Pony once more, and returning to another delightful section of Arran's trademark Coastal Way. However, and very importantly, this is a walk which you only ought to negotiate at low tide. Also, and at risk of incurring your wrath by asking you to retrace a few earlier steps, let me say in mitigation that those same steps will be few in number and well worth retracing.

Heading north from Lamlash village centre past two well-known local hostelries, the Pier Head Tavern on your left and the Drift Inn on your right, the main drag prepares to sweep left up the hill, while a lesser road dives at right-angles along the contours of the rocky but beautifully scenic Clauchlands Shore. Following this shore route, you will pass the local council offices and a long row of stunning residential properties facing Lamlash Bay, with its ever-present armada of yachts in the foreground and the dramatic outline of Holy Island bringing up the rear. After the last house in the row, you will recognise the track to your left leading up to the cottages at Prospect Hill, down which you may recall tramping in exhaustion from your earlier exertions over the heights of Clauchlands Hill and Dun Fionn.

This time, though, just ignore that track and continue along the tarmacked shore road past the Outdoor Learning Centre, thereby negotiating a modest half-mile of the aforementioned step-retracing process, with which I'm sure you will manage to cope as you marvel once more at seafaring vessels and seals galore bobbing in the bay and great flocks of seabirds swooping overhead.

Once you reach the car park at Clauchlands Point, a gate opens onto a rough track which meanders alongside the pebbled shore. A gentle stroll along this track soon leads to Clauchlands Point, where a wooden seat invites you to rest your weary backside for a couple of minutes before deciding on your next trajectory. From the point, two tracks veer left and right, the former rising steeply towards Dun Fionn, which having negotiated before you should therefore disregard on this occasion, and the latter hugging the coastline, which you should take. The only exception to this strategy would be at high tide, when the Dun Fionn route should tempt you away from the soggy and potentially treacherous underfoot conditions as you later approach the area of Corriegills.

Following the shoreline, the path continues until the unmistakeable outline of the mighty Goat Fell comes into view, signalling that the final part of your island circumnavigation will shortly be coming to an end. It is perhaps worth pointing out at this juncture that the coastal path does deteriorate somewhat in quality as you approach the rural houses near Corriegills Point, alternating as it does between uneven and marshy, although still eminently passable as long as your feet are clad in a pair of decent walking boots. Proceeding to the right along the crude path, you should then take a sharpish left-turn up past a couple of buildings.

The track continues uphill, then veers left towards a waymarked signpost which directs you through a small wooded area and onwards to a succession of wooden stiles and open fields where another sign at the final stile points downhill and then left towards an obvious clearing in the hedgerow. From there, a right-turn will lead you down to yet another stile, this taking you onto Strathwhillan Road, where a left-turn will point you back towards the main drag of the A841.

Turning right again, a very steep descent will lead you straight to Brodick's mammoth new ferry terminal, but not before you have passed Strathwhillan House, nowadays a grand self-catering property which will forever be etched on my memory as the scene of a truly unforgettable 1960s television adaptation of one of author Neil Munro's brilliant Para Handy tales.

With the inimitable skipper's much-adored puffer, The Vital Spark, moored at the old Brodick pier, the tale depicted Sunny Jim, the ship's ever-cheery mate, pushing the injured Dan MacPhail, its miserably-dour engineer, on a crude four-wheeled wooden barrow-like contraption up the punishingly-steep brae towards the island's cottage hospital, which in this episode was 'played' by none other than Strathwhillan House itself. The crescendo of their utterly hopeless efforts came when Sunny Jim, trying valiantly but failing miserably to find a fencepost or something similar onto which to lasso the rope and hold the barrow in place while he opened the hospital gate, instead handed it to MacPhail himself with the immortal words, 'here, haud it yersel', Dan,' at which point the pair of them began careering back down the cavernous brae at tremendous velocity and crashed back onto the pier, plunging straight into the sea and taking the local minister with them.

Anyway, with a bit of luck you should encounter no such supersonic vehicular contraptions on the final instalment of your journey back downhill towards Brodick Ferry Terminal. However, when you walk onto the pier just as the good old 'Caley Isles' begins rolling in towards the brand-new concrete linkspan, what you will see are the joyous faces of the various maws, paws and bairns waving excitedly from the top deck of the giant boat. After all, they're about to set foot on God's own island. Sadly, though, you are about to leave.

And so, while you stare glumly towards the big ferry as it prepares to whisk you away from the enchanted island of Arran, just take one final look up towards the summit of the imperious Goat Fell mountain, and its subliminal message to you will be unmistakeably clear.

'Haste ye back.'